THE

PRESIDENT

IN THE

LEGISLATIVE

ARENA

AMERICAN POLITICS

AND POLITICAL ECONOMY SERIES

Edited by Benjamin I. Page

THE
PRESIDENT
IN THE
LEGISLATIVE
ARENA

JON R. BOND AND
RICHARD FLEISHER

THE UNIVERSITY OF CHICAGO PRESS
Chicago and London

The University of Chicago Press, Chicago 60637
The University of Chicago Press, Ltd., London

99 98 97 96 95 94 93 92 91   5 4 3 2

LIBRARY OF CONGRESS CATALOGING-IN-PUBLICATION DATA

Bond, Jon R.
  The president in the legislative arena / Jon R. Bond and Richard Fleisher.
    p.   cm.—(American politics and political economy series)
  ISBN 0-226-06409-3 (cloth); ISBN 0-226-06410-7 (paper)
  1. Presidents—United States.   2. Executive power—United States.
3. United States. Congress. I. Fleisher, Richard.   II. Title.   III. Series.
JK585.B52   1990
353.03'13—dc20
                                                        89-48004
                                                        CIP

∞ The paper used in this publication meets the minimum requirements of the
American National Standard for Information Sciences—Permanence of Paper for
Printed Library Materials, ANSI Z39.48-1984.

To Lynn Elizabeth and
to Lisa, Steven, and Eric

Contents

PREFACE

In this book we analyze presidential success in Congress and the conditions that contribute to success. Our emphasis on success is a departure from the concern with presidential influence that has tended to dominate previous studies of presidential-congressional relations. While scholarly concern with presidential influence is appropriate and has contributed to a better understanding of presidential-congressional relations, it sketches an incomplete picture. We believe that a shift in focus to the broader concept of presidential success is justified.

Presidential success can arise from a number of causal processes of which presidential influence is only one—and not even the most likely one. Many students of presidential-congressional relations argue that success resulting from forces which the president cannot control are theoretically unimportant. We disagree. From the perspective of democratic theory (focusing on questions of responsiveness, representation, and accountability) in the American system of separation of powers, it is vitally important to understand the conditions under which the president's positions prevail regardless of whether success results from his skilled leadership and influence or from forces beyond his control. Because the public holds the president primarily accountable for national conditions while separation of powers denies him the authority to act unilaterally, the question of success is broader and more important than the issue of influence.

This book uses roll call votes as the unit of analysis. Analyzing roll call votes permits us to address the important question of the conditions under which the president's position wins or loses in the House and the Senate. In addition, we have recorded how many votes the president received from members of each of four party factions (liberal Democrats, conservative Democrats, liberal Republicans, and conservative Republicans) on each roll call. Thus, like studies that utilize presidential support scores, ours also can analyze the behavior of different collections of individuals and how the various factions respond to the independent variables of interest.

We identify four linkage agents that might explain variation in presidential success with Congress—political parties, political ideology, public approval, and leadership skill. These linkage agents fall into two broad categories— presidency-centered explanations (public approval and leadership skill) and Congress-centered explanations (party and ideology). These linkage agents operate within constraints imposed by the institutional context of Congress (specifically activities of congressional leaders and committees). We analyze each of these influences and find that, although none are exceptionally strong, the presidency-centered explanations (public approval and skill) explain the least.

In the final chapter we return to a discussion of the issues that the framers of the Constitution struggled with two hundred years ago—how to construct a democratic government that is accountable and representative. We discuss the implications of the president's being a relatively weak legislative actor from the perspective of democratic theory. We conclude by observing that there is a trade-off between accountability and representation of diverse interests in a highly pluralistic society. The present arrangement between the branches makes it extremely difficult for the president to fulfill promises made during the election period. Yet the public tends to hold the president accountable if he fails to deliver. Any attempt to strengthen presidential power, however, is likely to lessen the representation of many minority interests in a fragmented society.

This study of presidential-congressional relations is the culmination of a research interest that started in 1975 when the two authors were graduate students at the University of Illinois. Since that time the two of us have analyzed the interactions of presidents and Congresses while four different presidents have occupied the White House, four different members have served as Speaker of the House, and five different senators have served as majority leader. Another way to look at the length of time that has passed while we have worked on this project is to consider that, although we are now in the age of PCs and BITNET, we started analyzing data for this project using computer cards and sending drafts on yellow pads through the U.S. mail.

In any project that has been on going for a long period of time, the authors accumulate a great number of debts to many friends, colleagues, and critics who have commented on various portions of the manuscript. This project is certainly no exception. We considered trying to present the list in some rational order. The enormity of the task combined with our less than perfect recall caused us to abandon that idea. In no particular order, the following individuals provided encouragement, guidance, advice, and criticism that kept us on track, saved countless errors, and made the finished product better than it would have been without their help: John Tryneski, Ben Page, Joe Cooper, David Brady, Mo Fiorina, Dick Fenno, Chuck Jones, Gary Jacobson, Tom Mann, Sam Kernell, John Chubb, Joe White, Sukie Hammond, Ron Peters, Gary Copeland, Dave Morgan, Mike Levy, Stan Bach, Bert Rockman, Roger Davidson, Lee Sigelman, Barry Rundquist, Cary Covington, Lester Seligman, Glenn Parker, Jack Johannes, Jeff Cohen, Cathy Rudder, Anne Hopkins, Keith Hamm, Bob Harmel, George Edwards, Bob Bernstein, Frank Baumgartner, Gretchen Casper, Bryan Jones, Arnie Vedlitz, Charlie Johnson, Harvey Tucker, Paul Kantor, David Lawrence, Russell Renka, Steve Shull, Jim Garand, Mark Petracca, Jeff Fishel, Morris Ogul, Mark Peterson, Jim McCormick, and Terry Sullivan. We also owe a special debt to Marcia Bastian, who converted our ASCII files into hard copy and produced the tables. In addition, we wish to acknowledge and thank the Department of Political Science and the College of Liberal Arts at Texas A&M University, and the Department of Political Science and the Graduate School of Arts and Sciences at Fordham University for supplying the authors with release time and graduate assistants. In addition, Jon Bond is grateful to the Brookings Institution for providing office space and an intellectually exciting environment during his year in Washington.

Parts of chapter 6 appeared in our article "Are There Two Presidencies? Yes, but Only for Republicans," *Journal of Politics* 50 (August 1988), published by the University of Texas Press. They are reprinted with permission.

Chapter 1

Introduction

> I have watched the Congress from either the inside or the outside, man and boy, for more than forty years, and I've never seen a Congress that didn't eventually take the measure of the President it was dealing with.
>
> Lyndon Johnson

From the moment a president takes office, he is looking to the next election, if not for himself, at least for his party. But the president's success, on which he and his party will be judged, is a hostage of the last election.

Lyndon Johnson's landslide victory in the 1964 election set the stage for the most successful presidential performance in the legislative arena since Franklin Roosevelt's first one hundred days in 1933. Although President Johnson viewed his victory as a popular mandate for his Great Society program, his political experience made him conscious that Congress stood between him and success. The quotation above demonstrates Johnson's keen awareness of the inevitable congressional obstacles.

The Problem of
Governmental Responsiveness

Policymaking in a democracy is supposed to be responsive to popular preferences. Elections are the primary mechanism for holding policymakers accountable if they are not responsive. In the United States, the linkage between popular preferences and governmental responses is confounded by the constitutional separation of powers. As Richard Neustadt (1960, 33) has aptly observed, the Constitution created a "government of separated institutions *sharing* powers." In the American system, policymaking requires cooperation among politicians serving within the constraints of different institutions and responding to conflicting sets of popular preferences.

Candidates for both the presidency and Congress make promises about the future direction of public policy. But it is the president the public holds accountable. Polls taken before Presidents Carter and Reagan took office showed that the public expected the president to provide prosperity, peace, and security (Edwards 1983, 189). Consequently, the public punishes the president more than members of Congress if expectations are not met. Voters turned the incumbent president or his party out of power in five of the ten presidential elections between 1952 and 1988. In contrast, voters in congressional elections over the same period returned an average of more than 90 percent of House incumbents and 75 percent of Senate incumbents.

Although the public expects the president to provide leadership to solve the nation's problems and holds him accountable for failures, the Constitution denies him the authority to act unilaterally. Instead, the president typically must get congressional approval if he is to achieve his policy goals and respond to popular expectations. Because members of Congress must respond to different sets of popular preferences than the president, they will inevitably have a different perspective on how best to solve the nation's problems. These differing institutional perspectives ensure that the president will eventually face rebuff by Congress, a fact of political life that every new president quickly learns if he didn't know it already.

Presidential-congressional relations therefore pose a fundamental linkage issue: What are the conditions and agents that might bridge the inevitable conflict between the president and Congress and permit the formation of policy in response to popular preferences? This book seeks to answer the question with an analysis of presidential success in Congress over the period from 1953 through 1984.

Because of the president's unique relationship with the public, presidential success in Congress is a key to understanding and evaluating the linkage between the public and government. Focusing the analysis on presidential success is an attempt to build upon and go beyond previous research on presidential-congressional relations.

In his now classic analysis *Presidential Power* (1960), Richard Neustadt defined the problem of presidential-congressional relations in terms of presidential influence: "what a President can do . . . as one man among many, to carry his own choices through that maze of personalities and institutions called the government of the United States" (i). Following Neustadt's focus, most students of presidential-congressional relations are interested in success only because it is associated with influence. Although presidential influence may increase success, the presidents' policy preferences may prevail for reasons that have nothing to do with influence. For example, a high "success" rate may result if the president and Congress have highly similar policy preferences. In such a situation, regardless of whether the resident is weak or powerful, his preferences will succeed because they correspond to what most members of Congress want to do anyway. Many students of presidential-congressional relations, therefore, have been searching for data and research designs to analyze the extent to which the president can *influence* Congress to do what it otherwise would not have done. Successes resulting from causes not under the president's control are viewed as uninteresting and unimportant.

Although the study of presidential power is appropriate and has contributed to a better understanding of presidential-congressional relations, it sketches an incomplete picture. Moreover, the quest to pin down presidential influence has been elusive. A recent innovative attempt is Kiewiet and Mc-Cubbins's (1988) analysis of the appropriations process. They theorize that the president exerts more influence over congressional appropriations if he prefers to spend less than Congress because his power to veto appropriations that exceed his preferences gives him a strategic advantage. They determine whether the president is in a strategically favorable or unfavorable situation by comparing his request with what is actually appropriated. The analysis reveals that, ceteris paribus, when the president asks for less than Congress appropriates, Congress appropriates almost exactly with he requests ($b = 1.01$); when the president asks for more than Congress appropriates, Congress appropriates less than half of his request ($b = 0.46$). They interpret these results as strong support for their theory and attribute the difference between the coefficients to presidential influence.

Although Kiewiet and McCubbins's theory makes sense, the empirical analysis is problematical. First, the empirical measures are somewhat circular: the key independent variable (the president's strategic position) is measured relative to the dependent variable (whether the president's request is less than or greater than what Congress appropriates). Second, because they do not have an estimate of congressional preferences independent of the president's request, they do not know whether the actual appropriation levels reflect true congressional preferences or presidential influence. Although we do not know the precise mix, the appropriations in both strategic situations probably reflect some combination of congressional preferences and presidential influence. But there is no evidence presented to support the conclusion that the difference they find is due entirely to presidential influence.

Other interesting and innovative analyses use vote counts maintained by the Office of Congressional Relations during the Kennedy/Johnson administration. These studies focus on votes most important to the president. They attempt to observe presidential influence by analyzing relationships between various presidential activities and congressional support (Covington 1987a, 1987b, 1988) or by looking at changes in support over time as an issue moves through the legislative process (Sullivan 1988). But even these careful analyses of a unique data set are not definitive tests of presidential influence, because they cannot eliminate alternative explanations. They cannot determine what Congress would have done in the absence of presidential lobbying, and they cannot determine whether the outcome resulted from the president's influence or from forces internal to Congress (e.g., activities of the party leadership and whip organization in Congress). Thus, despite some clever attempts, the analysis of presidential influence remains inconclusive.

We believe that the emphasis on presidential influence is too narrow. The problem of governmental responsiveness in a system of separate institutions sharing power makes it important to analyze the conditions that might lead to presidential success, regardless of whether success results from the president's influence or from forces beyond his control. Because the public holds the president primarily accountable for national conditions, the question of whether the outcomes of the legislative process are consistent with presidential preferences takes on a great deal of importance for understanding and evaluating the linkages between the public and government. Thus the question of presidential success is broader and, we would argue, more important than the question of influence.

Our concern with governmental responsiveness represents a continuation of the fundamental problem facing the framers of the Constitution two hundred years ago in Philadelphia. While the framers sought to strengthen popular government, the issue that occupied most of their attention was how to limit government from responding to the passions of a tyrannical majority.

SEPARATION OF POWERS

A fundamental characteristic of the American political system that differentiates it from most other democratic nations is the separation of powers between the executive and the legislature. Unlike parliamentary governments in which executive and legislative powers are merged, the government created by the United States Constitution has two separate arenas of policymaking, housed at opposite ends of Pennsylvania Avenue.[1]

The Fundamental Political Maxim

In the intense political debate surrounding the drafting and ratification of the Constitution, all sides seemed to agree on one fundamental political maxim: good government requires the separation of legislative, executive, and judicial powers. During the debate at the Constitutional Convention in 1787, the delegates often invoked this principle. George Mason (delegate from Virginia),

---

1. The judiciary, of course, is also a separate policymaking arena. Although we recognize the importance of the judiciary as a policymaking institution, this study focuses on executive-legislative relations.

for example, cautioned against "making the Executive the mere creature of the Legislature as a violation of the fundamental principle of good Government." [2] Rufus King (delegate from Massachusetts) agreed, urging "the House to recur to the primitive axiom that the three great departments of Governments should be separate and independent." [3] During the ratification debate, Madison answered the charge that the proposed Constitution violated "the political maxim that the legislative, executive, and judiciary departments ought to be separate and distinct." He accepted the premise on which the charge is based, arguing that the charge is not supported:

> No political truth is certainly of greater intrinsic value or is stamped with the authority of more enlightened patrons of liberty than that on which the objection is founded. The accumulation of all powers, legislative, executive, and judiciary, in the same hands, whether of one, a few, or many, and whether hereditary, self-appointed, or elective, may justly be pronounced the very definition of tyranny. Were the federal Constitution, therefore, really chargeable with this accumulation of power, or with a mixture of powers, having a dangerous tendency to such an accumulation, no further arguments would be necessary to inspire a universal reprobation of the system. I persuade myself, however, that it will be apparent to everyone that the charge cannot be supported (Madison 1961a, 301).

Separate but Interdependent Powers

The framers had a clear view of the difference between the legislative and executive powers that they sought to separate. Hamilton (1961b, 450) made the distinction as follows: "The essence of the legislative authority is to enact laws, or, in other words, to prescribe rules for the regulation of the society; while the execution of the laws and the employment of the common strength, either for this purpose or for the common defense, seem to comprise all the functions of the executive magistrate." If the separation of powers is to achieve its goal of limiting abuses of governmental power, however, then powers need not be "wholly unconnected with each other." Instead, the framers believed that because power is of an encroaching nature, "unless these departments be so far connected and blended as to give to each a constitutional control over the others, the degree of separation which the maxim requires, as essential to a free government, can never in practice be duly maintained" (Madison 1961b, 308). Therefore the Constitution made the separate branches interdependent through a series of checks.

The goal of this arrangement was to prevent tyranny by making it more

2. From Madison's notes, 2 June 1787 (Benton 1986a, 423).
3. From Madison's notes, 20 July 1787 (Benton 1986a, 427).

difficult for government to act. The checks are automatic, operating against good laws as well as bad. But the framers considered the inefficiency worth the price: "The injury which may possibly be done by defeating a few good laws will be amply compensated by the advantage of preventing a number of bad ones" (Hamilton 1961a, 444).

THE LEGISLATIVE PRESIDENCY

The Constitutional Bases of the Legislative Presidency

The Constitution gives the president limited legislative responsibilities. The most important are (1) the executive veto subject to override by two-thirds of both chambers (article I, section 7) and (2) the duty to give Congress information on the state of the Union and to "recommend to their Consideration such Measures as he shall judge necessary and expedient" (article II, section 3).[4]

The debate at the Constitutional Convention suggests that the framers considered the veto an important and dangerous power (see Benton 1986a, 791–828), and the executive veto continues to provide the president with significant leverage in the legislative process today. It was included primarily to enable to the president to protect executive powers and prerogatives from the "propensity of the legislative department to intrude upon the rights, and absorb the powers, of the other departments." Without the veto, Hamilton argued, the president "would be absolutely unable to defend himself against the depredations of the [legislature]," and "the legislative and executive powers might speedily come to be blended in the same hands" (Hamilton 1961a, 442).

Although the duty to recommend legislation to Congress has become one of the president's most significant tools of legislative leadership, this provision does not appear to have been the subject of extensive concern at the convention. The Report of the Committee of Detail at the Constitutional Convention had originally proposed the following wording: the president "shall, from time to time, give information to the Legislature, of the state of the Union: he may recommend to their consideration such measures as he shall judge necessary, and expedient." Gouverneur Morris (delegate from Pennsylvania) moved to strike "he may" and insert "and" after legislature "in order to make it the *duty* of the President to recommend, and thence prevent umbrage or

---

4. Article II, section 3 also gives the president power to call one or both houses of Congress into session and adjourn them if they cannot reach agreement on a time. The president has occasionally called Congress into "special session," but the power to adjourn has never been used (Corwin 1973, 147). Article I, section 3 gives the vice-president the office of president of the Senate with a vote to break ties. While this power is occasionally important, the vice-president is generally viewed with suspicion and does not regularly preside over the Senate (Peabody 1981, 55).

cavil at his doing it."[5] Morris's motion was accepted without any record of debate or a vote of the convention.

Neither was the president's duty to recommend legislation a point of contention during the ratification debate. While several Federalist papers deal at length with controversies about establishing a single executive, the method of electing the president, the length of the president's term, and most of the president's powers (the veto, appointments, negotiating treaties), there is only passing reference to the power to recommend legislation. Hamilton (1961c, 463) says only that "no objection has been made to this class of authorities; nor could they possibly admit of any."

This system of separate institutions sharing powers has remained intact for nearly two hundred years. However, while the president's constitutional powers have changed little, the growth of governmental activity has magnified the power and importance of the executive in the American system of separate but interdependent institutions.[6]

In earlier times, presidents could debate the proper limits of the powers of the presidency. Some adopted President James Buchanan's limited view that the president has only those powers specifically granted in the Constitution. Others adopted President Theodore Roosevelt's activist view that the president is a "steward of the people" with the duty to do anything the nation needs or demands that is not forbidden by the Constitution or law (Corwin 1973, 111–12). Presidents since FDR and the New Deal, however, no longer engage in this debate. Changes in the scope of government and the problems it seeks to solve have forced modern presidents to be active legislative leaders. As Stephen Wayne (1978, 2) notes, "the president has always had a legislative role, but there has not always been a legislative presidency."

The Legislative Imperative

Thus the modern president has no choice but to enter the legislative arena. When the president enters the legislative arena, the separation of executive and legislative elections ensures that he will remain an outsider. And the Constitution provides him with meager resources to use to gain acceptance of his policy preferences in Congress.

5. From Madison's notes, 24 August 1787 (Benton 1986b, 1254, emphasis in original).

6. The debate over establishing a meeting time for Congress suggests that the framers would be surprised at the growth of governmental activity. The Constitution mandates Congress to meet at least once a year (article I, section 4). In his notes on the convention, Madison reports that Rufus King (delegate from Massachusetts) "could not think there would be a necessity for a meeting every year. . . . The most numerous objects of legislation belong to the States. Those of the National Legislature were but few." Nathaniel Gorham (also from Massachusetts), however, thought that Congress should meet at least once every year as a check on the executive (Benton 1986a, 187).

What the president needs most from members of Congress is their votes. Political scientist Anthony King (1983, 247) has summarized the president's dependence on congressional votes as follows:

> All you [the president] really need from Congress is votes, but you need those votes very badly. Moreover, under the American system, you need votes all the time and all kinds of votes: votes for and against bills, votes for and against amendments, votes to appropriate funds, votes not to appropriate funds, votes to increase the budget, votes to cut the budget, votes to enable you to reorganize the executive branch, votes to strengthen you (or not to weaken you) in your dealings with administrative agencies, votes to sustain your vetoes, votes to override legislative vetoes, votes in the Senate to ratify the treaties you have negotiated and to confirm the nominations you have made, votes (every century or so) in opposition to efforts to impeach you. You need votes to enable you to build up a record, to win reelection, to win—who knows?—a place in history.

Votes, therefore, are the basic commodity of presidential-congressional relations. And every president must confront what may be termed the legislative imperative: The American system dictates that the president must seek votes from Congress, yet there is no guarantee he will succeed. The only guarantee is that the same system which requires action and leadership from the president also creates conflicting political and institutional pressures which limit his success.

The Ebb and Flow of Presidential-Congressional Relations

Measuring presidential success in securing votes from Congress is admittedly difficult. The concept of "success" inevitably involves a subjective evaluation of the content, complexity, and importance of the votes on which the president wins and loses. Any quantitative summary of presidential success, therefore, is subject to criticism. We will discuss the issue of measuring success in greater detail in chapter 3, but to get a general indication of the ebb and flow of relations between the president and Congress, we will look at a defensible and commonly used measure—Congressional Quarterly's calculation of presidential victories on all votes on which the president takes a clear-cut position. Although this measure does not reveal how much of the president's program passes, it does provide a general overview. Figure 1.1 plots the percentages from 1953 to 1984.

Two conclusions emerge from an examination of this figure. First, over the past three decades, Congress usually supported the president's publicly expressed positions on issues that came to the floors of the House and Senate. Only Ford experienced low percentages throughout his time in office, but the unusual circumstances by which he came to power caused him to be viewed as

Figure 1.1 Presidential Victories on Roll Call Votes in Congress

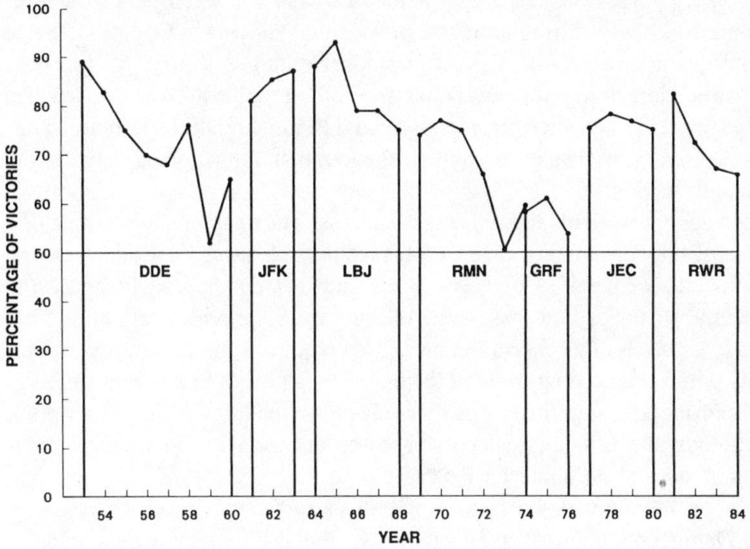

Source: *Congressional Quarterly Almanac.*

"a temporary, 'substitute' president" (Kellerman 1984, x). By parliamentary standards, however, presidential success on floor votes is low. Unlike legislatures in modern European parliamentary systems, the United States Congress remains a separate, autonomous institution with the will and power to go its own way.

Second, there is substantial variation in success across presidents and over time within administrations. The ebb and flow of presidential success on the floor of Congress is a critical component of presidential-congressional relations. While success on floor votes is only one of several important decision points in the process, explaining variation in presidential success at this point in the process is necessary for an understanding of the linkage between these two policymaking institutions. Hence the research question guiding this study is: Under what conditions do presidents succeed on floor votes in Congress?

THE REMAINDER OF THE BOOK

In the chapters that follow, we attempt to answer this question. In chapter 2 we begin with a critical review of four linkage agents (i.e., political parties, political ideology, the president's popularity with the public, and the president's leadership skill) that previous research has identified as sources of presidential success in Congress. This review of the strengths and limitations of the theory and evidence in previous research provides the basis for developing a theoretical framework that we use to analyze presidential success in Congress. Since the study examines presidential-congressional relations from 1953 to 1984, we must be alert to any temporal changes in the relationships. Furthermore, because the study analyzes presidential-congressional relations in both chambers of Congress, we can assess any differences that might appear between the House and the Senate.

In chapter 3 we look at presidential success. The chapter starts with a discussion of the different measures of presidential success, evaluating the strengths and weaknesses of each. We argue that our approach, analyzing presidential victories and losses on roll call votes, provides an appropriate measure of success that meets the necessary requirements of validity and reliability while overcoming some of the major problems of box scores and individual presidential support scores. The chapter concludes with a description of the trends in presidential success based on our measure, including a comparison of success on important votes.

Chapter 4 examines the impact of four party factions in Congress (i.e., liberal Democrats, conservative Democrats, liberal Republicans, and conservative Republicans) on presidential-congressional relations. We look at the size of the party factions across presidents and analyze the behavior of the factions in support of and in opposition to the president. We conclude with an analysis of the effects of unified support and opposition and a discussion of trade-offs.

Chapter 5 analyzes the role of party and committee leaders. We look at how often the various leaders support the president and at the effects of different combinations of leader support on the unity of the various party factions.

Chapter 6 considers the "two presidencies" thesis. We analyze whether the president is more successful on foreign policy votes than on domestic votes and, if so, which factions provide the additional support.

In chapter 7 we explore the impact of presidential popularity on support and on the behavior of the different groups. We present the results of two types of analysis designed to test the effects of popularity. The first test conceptualizes popularity as an interval level variable in which we examine the effects of the level of presidential popularity on wins and losses and on support from members of Congress. The second test analyzes the effects of presidential popularity conceptualized as a broad context in which small changes in the level of popularity are not nearly as important as moving from being popular to being unpopular.

Chapter 8 analyzes the effects of the president's leadership skill on presidential-congressional relations. The skills theory represents a major alternative explanation to our emphasis on political and institutional variables in Congress. In this chapter we present a more systematic empirical test of the impact of skills than has been employed to date.

In the concluding chapter we discuss the implications of our theory and findings for understanding presidential-congressional relations. We return to an issue raised earlier in this introduction—namely, the problem of forging cooperation in a system with built-in conflict. Exploring presidential-congressional relations in these terms allows us to assess the quality of the link provided by the various linkage agents in American politics.

CHAPTER **2**

SOURCES OF LINKAGE:
LITERATURE AND THEORY

The constitutional separation of powers guarantees that the president will be frustrated by Congress. Frustration with Congress is not limited to modern presidents, but rather emerged early in the nation's history. James Madison, "Father of the Constitution," experienced the results of his handiwork. During the launching of the frigate *Adams* in 1813, an opposition member of Congress who was standing next to President Madison commented sarcastically, "What a pity, sir, that the vessel of state won't glide as smoothly in her course as this vessel does." "It would, sir," Madison retorted, "if the crew would do their duty as well" (quoted in Adler 1966, 24). And Abraham Lincoln, one of the nation's most admired presidents, liked to jest, "I have been told I was on the road to hell, but I had no idea it was just a mile down the road with a Dome on it" (quoted in Udall 1988, 3). Despite the inevitable conflict, however, there are periods of cooperation. Some presidents experience greater success than others, and even the least successful president wins some of the time. What are the possible sources of linkage that might explain variation in presidential success in Congress?

Richard Neustadt proposes one set of answers in *Presidential Power* (1960). In focusing on what the president can personally do to overcome the inevitable conflict, Neustadt provides a presidency-centered explanation of linkage between the executive and the legislature. He observes that the American system precludes the president from using the power of command, especially in dealing with Congress. Lyndon Johnson could have been referring to Congress when he said, "A long time ago I learned that telling a man to go to hell and making him go are two different propositions" (quoted in Udall 1988, 239). According to Neustadt, if the president is to succeed in bridging the gap between the institutions, he must be a supreme politician and rely on his powers of persuasion, bargaining, and compromise. The explanation of variation in presidential success, therefore, focuses on what the president does and how well he does it.

There are, however, alternatives to a presidency-centered explanation of institutional linkage. A major alternative is a Congress-centered explanation. The United States Congress is an institution composed of strong-willed politicians who have goals and policy preferences of their own. The electoral system forces them to be more responsive to parochial, local interests than to the national concerns of the president. The Constitution grants Congress institutional autonomy from the executive, and the institution is structured to help its members achieve their goals. Consequently, presidential success is determined in large measure by the results of the last election. If the last election brings individuals to Congress whose local interests and preferences coincide with the president's, then he will enjoy greater success. If, on the other hand, most members of Congress have preferences different from the president's, then he will suffer more defeats, and no amount of bargaining and persuasion can do much to improve his success.

The tension between Congress-centered and presidency-centered explanations is apparent in the literature. Previous research on presidential-congressional relations has identified four linkage agents that might mitigate the inevitable conflict between the president and Congress and serve as sources of support for the president's policy preferences. These are (1) political parties, (2) political ideology, (3) the president's popularity with the public, and (4) the president's leadership skill.

Note that party and ideology are properties that members bring with them to the institution of Congress. Because the president has little control over the partisan and ideological mix in Congress, these agents may be viewed as Congress-centered explanations of linkage. Presidential popularity and leadership skill, on the other hand, focus on perceptions and activities of the president. Because perceptions of the president's popularity and leadership are determined by what he does (or fails to do), these agents may be viewed as presidency-centered explanations of linkage. In this chapter, we review the theory of how each of these linkage agents might link the president and Congress and the empirical evidence supporting or refuting each theory. This discussion provides the basis for the theoretical framework and thesis of this book.

POLITICAL PARTIES

Political scientists have long noted that political parties are important linkage agents in democratic systems. To understand how political parties facilitate linkage, it is useful to distinguish between party in the electorate and party in government.[1] The party in the electorate serves to link voters to candidates.

---

1. Students of political parties often make this distinction. See, for example, Key (1964) and Souraf (1983).

The linkage between voters and candidates resulting from activities of the party in the electorate, in turn, forms a basis for linking partisan officeholders in the presidency and Congress.

Party Linkage in the Electorate

Party identification is a major determinant of vote choice in both presidential and congressional elections. Although analyses of recent elections suggest that the impact of party identification has declined, party continues to be a significant determinant of voting behavior (Campbell et al. 1960; DeClercq, Hurley, and Luttbeg, 1975; Mann and Wolfinger 1980).

A major reason why parties serve to link voters and candidates is that party labels and activity reduce voters' information costs. The process of recruiting and nominating candidates for myriad offices reduces and simplifies the choices available to voters. Although some voters may not be enthusiastic about the candidates who emerge from this winnowing process, most citizens do not have the time or motivation to acquire the level of information necessary to make rational choices among a larger number of candidates separated by finer issue differences. By reducing the choices to one nominee from each party, the competing parties can use their limited campaign resources to focus public attention on broader differences in perspective and direction. And because each candidate's party is printed on the ballot, large numbers of voters, most of whom have preexisting partisan attachments, have the minimum level of information necessary to cast a meaningful vote.

Party Linkage in Government

Partisan forces also serve to link the president and members of Congress. Previous research on presidential-congressional relations reveals that members of the president's party in Congress are more likely to support his policy positions than are members of the opposition (Edwards 1984, 180–84). Paul Light's interviews with members of previous presidential administrations confirm the importance of party as a source of support. According to a member of President Johnson's liaison staff, "You can cajole Congress and try to buy the votes, but if you don't have your party on board there isn't much hope." Similarly, a Carter aide noted, "We can always find support in Congress, even when we are under fire in the polls. The Congress is still a party institution, and we can count on a few votes by bringing out the party standard" (quoted in Light 1983, 27).

Partisan support is important to explaining the policy success of both majority and minority presidents. Having members of their own party in Congress provides all presidents with a base upon which to build majority coalitions in support of their policy preferences. Majority presidents have an advantage because their partisans are more numerous and they control the committee structure and leadership. But minority presidents frequently achieve victories on the floor in part because they do not have to build a majority from nothing.

Members of the president's party are predisposed to support his policy preferences for several reasons. First, because members of the same political party must satisfy similar electoral coalitions, they share many of the same goals and have a wide range of policy preferences in common. For many members of the president's party, constituency interests and presidential support are not in conflict. Although the strength of presidential coattails may have decreased in recent years (Ferejohn and Calvert 1984), V. O. Key's (1964, 658) observation remains valid: "When a president goes into office a substantial number of legislators of his party stand committed to the broad policy orientation of the president."

Second, members of the president's party who seek reelection must run on his record as well as their own. Consequently, members of the president's party have an incentive to help him succeed as a leader. John Kingdon (1981, 180) found that Republican representatives "often referred to their stake in the administration's success" as a reason for supporting President Nixon's policy positions. Research on congressional elections reveals that this concern on the part of members of the president's party is justified. Edward Tufte (1975, 824) presents evidence that "the vote cast in midterm congressional elections is a referendum on the performance of the president and his administration's management of the economy." Gary Jacobson and Samuel Kernell (1983, 19) argue that this so-called referendum is not a direct voter evaluation of presidential performance. Rather, voter decisions in congressional elections are more a function of evaluations of the candidates running in the state or district. Presidential performance, however, is an important indirect influence because it affects the decisions of potential candidates and contributors. Thus "the relative quality of a party's candidates and the vitality of their campaigns—the things which have the strongest impact on individual voters—are . . . a direct function of" national events and conditions, including presidential performance.

Third, members of the same party share a psychological attachment to a common political symbol; they are, in a sense, members of the same political family. George Edwards (1984, 184–85) notes that "members of the president's party typically have personal loyalties or emotional commitments to their party and their party leader, which the president can often translate into votes when necessary." American political parties, of course, are diverse and decentralized, so disagreements between the president and members of his party are inevitable. But the conflict within the president's party is not as intense as the conflict with the opposition. As Neustadt (1960, 187) says: "Bargaining 'within the family' has a rather different quality than bargaining with members of the rival clan."

Finally, the president has political resources such as patronage, influence over the distribution of "porkbarrel" programs, and control over campaign resources that he may use to reward loyal party members and to punish those who oppose him. This incentive is probably not as important as the others discussed above. Presidential actions to punish unsupportive representatives are not likely to succeed against incumbents who occupy safe seats, an electoral status which applies to most members of the House and many in the Senate.[2] And even the least loyal member of the president's party is likely to be more supportive than a replacement from the opposition. For these reasons, presidents hesitate to punish members of their own party. Randall Ripley (1969, 126), for example, reports that President Eisenhower was reluctant to publicly criticize Republicans who opposed him because he thought "it would do more harm than good." The Republican party's "eleventh commandment"—to avoid criticizing fellow Republicans—invoked recently by President Reagan is another example.

Although presidential efforts to punish unsupportive members of Congress are rare and of limited success, there are some examples. The most extensive effort was Franklin Roosevelt's attempt to purge conservative Democrats from the party in the 1938 primaries (Milkis 1984). John Ferejohn (1974, 72) found evidence that President Johnson personally reviewed the Army Corps of Engineers' budget and made certain that members of Congress "who opposed him on issues he felt were important did not get new starts in the budget." One of the issues important to Johnson was the Vietnam War. At a White House reception, Senator Frank Church (D–Idaho) found out that opposing the president's policy in Vietnam could be costly. Johnson asked Church where he got his ideas on Vietnam. "From Walter Lippmann," Church replied. Johnson snapped, "Next time you need a dam in Idaho, you just go talk to Walter Lippmann" (quoted in Udall 1988, 239). And David Mayhew (1974, 43) reports an example of President Nixon's using campaign resources to help defeat a senator of his party who did not support him.

Using these political resources to aid supporters is more likely. Edwards (1984, 191–92) reports that presidents provide myriad favors for members of Congress. The nature of these favors ranges from flattery and social contact with the president to help with constituent problems and campaign aid. And presidential favors and attention go disproportionately to members of the president's party (Covington 1987b).[3] Because most members of Congress

2. Incumbency advantage in congressional elections is well documented. See Jacobson (1987, 26–29) and Hinckley (1981, 37–40).

3. One type of favor, dinner invitations to the White House, goes to strong supporters regardless of party. But the largest proportion of invitations goes to supporters of the president's party. See Covington (1988).

can get reelected without the president's help, the effects of this activity are limited. But doing favors for members of Congress at least creates a store-house of goodwill that might increase support on some key issues, and a few members might be influenced by these activities. Thus political parties serve to link members of Congress with one another and to the president.

Limitations of the Party Link

While parties perform a significant linkage function in the United States, in comparison to political parties in most other Western democracies, American parties are quite weak and undisciplined. Even in the heyday of congressional party voting during the late nineteenth and early twentieth centuries, party loyalty among members of Congress barely reached the levels found in most responsible party systems (Brady and Althoff 1974). The reforms of the pe-riod 1909–11 and the rise of the seniority system reduced party leaders' abil-ity to command support form the membership (Cooper and Brady 1981; Polsby, Gallaher, and Rundquist 1969). And there is evidence of further de-cline of parties in recent years.

Among the electorate, a growing number of voters are calling themselves independents and a shrinking number are calling themselves "strong" par-tisans (Nie, Verba, and Petrocik 1979, 48–49; Hill and Luttbeg 1983, chap. 2; Crotty 1984, 28–29). In both presidential and congressional elections, party identifiers are increasingly likely to defect from their party's candidate (Nie, Verba, and Petrocik 1979, 50–55; Jacobson 1987, 109). Candidates for Congress have become less dependent on party for campaign organization and finance. And once a representative is in office, the advantages of incumbency tend to insulate him or her from national tides and to decrease the effective-ness of presidential coattails (Fiorina 1984; Ferejohn and Calvert 1984).

The weakening of parties as a linkage agent in the electorate profoundly affects their ability to serve as a linkage agent in government. Although party voting in Congress is a function of both the partisanship of the electorate and the powers and skill of party leaders, Melissa Collie and David Brady (1985, 283) present evidence that a partisan electorate is the more salient force. Their analysis suggests that despite weak congressional leadership, with a partisan electorate, members of Congress will vote with the president and with their party because "their electoral fate is linked to their president's and party's fate." Similarly, Morris Fiorina (1984) argues that the insulation of congres-sional incumbents from national tides and presidential coattails has resulted in a Congress that is less responsive to party leadership, less subject to presi-dential leadership, and less accountable for the failure to govern. And Thomas Cronin (1982, 295) notes that changes in the electorate that enhance incum-bents' reelection chances reduce the connection between the president and his partisans in Congress because they are "less dependent on the White House and less fearful of any penalty for ignoring presidential party appeals."

Over the past three decades, there has been a decline in "party unity" roll calls in Congress—i.e., votes on which a majority of one party vote in opposition to a majority of the other party.[4] William Crotty (1984, 253) summarizes the trend: "Party votes fell from 46 percent in the 1960s to 43 percent in the 1960s to 39 percent in the 1970s."[5] Democrats, of course, have long had difficulty maintaining unity because southern Democrats are consistently less likely to support the party leadership. But it appears that northern Democrats also have become less predictable. Barbara Sinclair's (1981, 207) analysis of roll call votes in the House during the Carter and Reagan presidencies reveals that "northern Democrats could no longer be relied upon to provide a solid bloc of support. Junior members, especially those elected from previously Republican districts, defected from the party position fairly frequently."

For the president and his party's congressional leaders, these trends mean that the task of building winning coalitions on the House and Senate floors has become more uncertain and difficult. Although a president whose party controls Congress continues to have an advantage, the benefits associated with party control are limited. Furthermore, the increase in split ticket voting has increased the likelihood that a president will face a Congress controlled by the opposition (Fiorina 1984; Jacobson 1987, 150–51; Asher 1980, 78). The declining impact of party in Congress led a frustrated Joseph Califano (an advisor to Presidents Johnson and Carter) to conclude that "the political party is at best of marginal relevance to the performance of the Oval Office" (Califano 1975, 146). Califano, of course, overstates the point. Nonetheless, his understandable frustration with American political parties suggests that presidents who seek to provide policy leadership in a system of separated powers and weak parties must find other ways to link their preferences with those of members of Congress.

POLITICAL IDEOLOGY

Political ideology is a second linkage agent that might serve as a basis of presidential support in Congress. Whereas the link between the president and Congress provided by political parties results largely from electoral forces, the link provided by ideology derives more from shared values. Because ideology is a major influence on roll call votes in Congress, the president can

4. This definition is one used by Congressional Quarterly, Inc., in its voting studies reported in the *Congressional Quarterly Almanac* (annually 1953–84) each year. Other definitions of "party votes" reveal the same pattern.

5. Note, however, that party unity increased during the Reagan presidency.

attract support from members of both parties who have ideologies similar to his and thus share his policy preferences.

Party and ideology, of course, are related, and for most members of Congress they are reinforcing. But each party encompasses individuals with widely differing policy preferences which may be arrayed along a liberal-conservative continuum. Ideological diversity within the parties means that some members of each party will be cross-pressured by an ideology that is outside their party's mainstream. The weak party system allows individual members great latitude to cross party lines and vote in response to their own ideological or policy preferences. Hence on most conflictual issues the president can attract support from some cross-pressured members of the opposition, but he will lose some cross-pressured members of his party.

Ideology and Congressional Behavior

The influence of ideology on roll call votes in Congress is well established. Kingdon (1981, 268) found that for many members of Congress, ideology is an important voting cue that structures their decisions: "At least for a congressman who is at either end of a given spectrum, ideology is a means to array the amendments and the proponents on a continuum, enabling him to vote for the one nearest him." While ideology is less useful for moderates than it is for ideologues on the left or right, its influence "is nearly always present" (Kingdon 1981, 271). Similarly, Jerrold Schneider (1979, 30) presents evidence that "ideology plays a preponderant role in congressmen's voting decisions." And contrary to those who argue that congressional coalitions are highly fluid from one policy area to another (Clausen 1973; Matthews and Stimson 1975; Kessel 1984, chap. 7), Schneider finds "very high ideological consistency among all policy dimensions." He concludes:

> In substantive terms, the findings establish unidimensionality; that is
> being strongly, moderately, or not at all liberal in one policy dimension
> corresponds very highly with being liberal or conservative to the same
> degree in all of the other dimensions, allowing ideological terms . . . to
> be used validly to denote distinct ranges of senators and congressmen
> on a single liberal-conservative, or left-right, spectrum or dimension
> (Schneider 1979, 195).[6]

Ideology influences roll call decision making for several reasons. First, the recruitment process—nomination and election—brings individuals to Congress who have well-formed and strongly held attitudes on major policy issues. The attitudes of these representatives are relatively stable over time,

---

6. For further evidence of unidimensional ideological influence on roll call voting, see Poole (1981) and Schneider (1984).

and once they are in office, their behavior reflects their personal values. Kingdon (1981, 269–70) quotes a congressional staffer who made the point as follows: "There's a lot less soul-searching and introspection than you might
think. Very little midnight oil is burned. Most members come here with well-
formed predispositions. They're very opinionated and their minds are made
up beforehand. There's very little you can do to change their minds."

Second, an incumbent's position along a liberal-conservative continuum
may affect his/her reelection prospects. Richard Fenno (1978, 144) found that
members of Congress believe that their voting records are important for reelection. The conventional wisdom is, "If you get too far from your district,
you'll lose it." Getting too far from the district is more a function of general
voting patterns than of a single vote. Two-thirds of the representatives in
Fenno's study believed that a single discrepant vote could not defeat them, but
that "voter disapproval of their 'total,' 'overall' policy performance could."
And overall performance is indicated by the incumbent's ideological voting
pattern. One congressman in his study noted: "People have a sense of a per-
son's voting record—that I am a progressive Democrat. I am one of eight who
got 100 percent from the environmental groups. I was one of 20 who got 100
percent from the ADA. People see these articles in the paper and they leave an
impression."

Quantitative research tends to support the conventional wisdom about the
importance of voting records for reelection. Two recent studies of House elections found that incumbents with ideologically discrepant voting records relative to their districts were more likely to attract well-financed, experienced
challengers (Bond, Covington, and Fleisher 1985) and were more likely to be
defeated (Johannes and McAdams 1981). And a study of the Senate by Martin
Thomas (1985, 96) reveals that senators seeking reelection tend to shift the
"ideological tenor of their roll call voting" in the direction of their constituency and likely opponents. Retiring senators, on the other hand, tended to
shift in the opposite direction.

These studies reveal that ideology and constituency are not separate influences on congressional behavior. Instead, a representative's personal ideology
is constrained by constituency interest. Although some representatives (especially senators with longer terms) may feel the need to make a marginal adjustment in their voting behavior as an election draws near, these shifts are not
from one end of the spectrum to the other. Such drastic shifts are usually not
necessary. Members of Congress are part of the politically active elite in their
home states and districts. The recruitment process makes it unlikely that these
successful politicians will have views far out of their constituency's mainstream. As Sinclair points out, most members' views on most issues are similar to those of their constituencies—or at least their reelection constituencies.

Consequently, votes based on personal ideology are usually votes supporting constituency preferences (Sinclair 1981, 218).[7]

Finally, ideology emerges as an important determinant of roll call voting because of patterns of interaction and cue-taking in Congress. Members of Congress often must express a public position on roll calls about which they either have very little information or have a plethora of undistilled, conflicting information that is virtually useless. To make politically "correct" decisions in the limited time available, they turn to each other for information and advice. Kingdon's (1981, 75–82) research reveals that the most important criterion used in selecting cue-givers is policy and ideological agreement. Selective perception causes these politicians to view the reinforcing information as persuasive and "to dismiss the rest as coming from the wrong crowd or as not convincing" (Kingdon 1981, 270–71). Thus the tendency to seek information from colleagues who have similar political values interacts with selective perception to explain the formation of ideological and partisan voting blocs on floor votes.

A president's policy positions tend to reflect his party's ideological mainstream. Because ideology influences decision making in Congress, it serves as a linkage agent between the president and Congress. Previous research demonstrates that ideological forces exert a significant influence on presidential-congressional relations.

For example, Lewis Froman (1963, 91) reports that conservative southern Democrats provided President Kennedy with almost 27 percent less support on domestic issues than did northern Democrats. On the other hand, Louis Koenig (1981, 167) notes that "a *de facto* liberal coalition of Northern and Western Democrats and 'Liberal Republicans' provided the Kennedy administration with most of its successes." In his study of congressional decision making during the Nixon administration, Kingdon (1981, 186) found that many southern Democrats crossed party lines to support President Nixon because of "simple attitudinal agreement." He quotes (270) a Republican congressman whose ideology reinforced his predisposition to support the President's position opposing the Elementary and Secondary Education Act: "First, I'm a conservative by inclination, and I don't believe in massive federal aid to schools. So, I was predisposed against Perkins and the committee. Second, I'm a Republican, and I'll support the administration when I can. In this case, happily enough, the two coincided, so I didn't have any problem."

---

7. Also see Poole and Rosenthal (1984). They find that senators from the same state and same party have very similar ideological voting patterns, whereas senators from the same state but from different parties are highly dissimilar. This finding suggests that representatives from different parties represent different reelection constituencies (or "support coalitions," as Poole and Rosenthal call them).

In a previous study of presidential-congressional relations from Eisenhower to Ford, we found that ideological conflict between the president and members of Congress was associated with lower support. In general, as ideological differences increase, the president tends to lose support from members of both parties at about the same rate, although support from the opposition is lower at all levels of ideological conflict (Bond and Fleisher 1980, 75).

Thus ideological forces in Congress often cause the formation of bipartisan coalitions to support or oppose the president's policy preferences. These ideological forces help explain why majority presidents have only a limited advantage over minority presidents in building majority support for their positions in Congress. Majority presidents inevitably experience defections of partisans who have ideologies in conflict with theirs. Minority presidents, on the other hand, can frequently build working majorities composed of their partisan base and like-minded members of the opposition.

Limitations of the Ideological Link

While political values shared between the president and members of Congress provide an important linkage source, the effects of ideology are limited for several reasons. First, most members of Congress are pragmatic politicians who do not have views and preferences at the extremes of a liberal-conservative continuum. Because the typical American voter is not strongly ideological, most representatives' electoral self-interest is probably best served by avoiding ideological extremes. As noted above, ideology is a less important voting cue for moderates than it is for ideological extremists (Kingdon 1981, 268).

Second, many votes that may be important to the president do not involve ideological issues. Distributive or "porkbarrel" programs, for example, typically do not produce ideological divisions. Even conservatives who want to cut domestic spending and liberals who want to reduce defense spending work to protect domestic and defense programs in their districts. Presidents who attempt to tamper with these programs are likely to find few friends in Congress, as President Carter discovered when he opposed several water projects in 1977, and as President Reagan discovered when he vetoed the highway bill in 1987.

Finally, ideological voting blocs are relatively informal coalitions composed of individuals who have similar values. The "conservative coalition" of Republicans and southern Democrats, for example, appears on certain votes and sometimes has a significant influence on the outcome of floor votes (Shelley 1983; Brady and Bullock 1980; Manley 1973). But this coalition of conservatives has no formal organization with elected leaders to serve as a communication and information center. Although there are several ideologically based caucuses in Congress, these organizations are less institutional-ized than are parties, and their leaders do not command the same status and respect as do party leaders. Without an integrated institutional structure and respected leadership, ideological coalition formation remains relatively ad hoc.

Thus, as is the case with political parties, ideology serves as a source of linkage, but its effects are limited. These forces are relatively constant be-tween elections, yet presidential success varies between elections as well as across presidents. These considerations have led students of presidential-congressional relations to look for other potential sources of linkage. The two remaining linkage agents, the president's popularity with the public and the skill with which the president deals with Congress, form the basis of a presidency-centered explanation of presidential-congressional relations.

PRESIDENTIAL POPULARITY

Because party and ideology are stable, their effect on congressional decisions to support the president is relatively fixed between elections. Presidential popularity, in contrast, is highly fluid. No president since Franklin Roosevelt has been able to avoid wide variation in public support over the course of his term (Mueller 1970; Lowi 1985, 14). Because members of Congress are elected representatives who are supposed to be responsive to popular prefer-ences, the president's popularity might influence congressional decisions to support or oppose his policy preferences on floor votes, the point in the legis-lative process most open to public scrutiny.

Presidential Popularity and Congressional Behavior
The belief that presidential popularity affects support in Congress is widely accepted among Washington insiders. President Johnson, for example, recog-nized the importance of popular support. Shortly after his landslide victory in the 1964 election, he told one of his aides, "I keep hitting hard because I know that this honeymoon won't last. Every day I lose a little more political capital" (quoted in Valenti 1975, 144). More recently, a Carter aide echoed the sentiment: "No president whose popularity is as low as this president's has much clout on the Hill" (quoted in Edwards 1980, 87).

The president's popularity may influence congressional decisions to sup-port his preferences for two reasons. First, the desire for reelection might lead members to adjust their support for the president in response to his popu-larity—i.e., members of Congress support the president when it is in their self-interest to do so. Neustadt (1960, 46) argues that "the essence of a Presi-dent's persuasive task with congressmen . . . *is to induce them to believe that what he wants of them is what their own appraisal of their own responsibili-ties requires them to do in their interest, not his*" (emphasis in original). The president's "public prestige" affects those subjective calculations of self-interest because

> most members of the Washington community depend upon outsiders to
> support them. . . . Dependent men must take account of popular reac-
> tions to *their* actions. What their publics may think of them becomes a
> factor, therefore, in deciding how to deal with the desires of a Presi-
> dent. His prestige enters into that decision; their publics are part of his
> (Neustadt 1960, 86, emphasis in original).

Similarly, Edwards (1980, 88) makes the point as follows: "Members of Congress may choose to be close to or independent from the president, depending on his popularity, to increase their chances of reelection."

Second, role theory provides a plausible explanation of why a president's popularity might influence support for his preferences in Congress (Edwards 1980, 88). Many members of Congress believe that their role as a representative is to reflect constituency opinion. For example, Roger Davidson (1969, 118–19) found that about one-third of the House members in his study agreed that "a representative ought to work for what his constituents want even though this may not always agree with his personal views." Representatives who hold this role orientation should increase or decrease their support for the president in response to changes in his standing with the public. Thus electoral self-interest and role perception provide a theoretical basis for expecting that a president's popularity will affect support for his policy preferences in Congress.

Evidence of the Influence of Presidential Popularity

Edwards (1980) was the first to test this theory systematically with quantitative data. In a study of presidential-congressional relations for the period 1953 through 1976 (Eisenhower through Ford), Edwards found high correlations between presidential popularity and congressional support. His most important finding was that members of Congress are less responsive to the president's *overall* popularity and more responsive to his popularity among subgroups in the public that are part of their own electoral coalitions—i.e., Democrats in Congress respond to the president's popularity among Democratic voters, and Republicans respond to his popularity among Republican voters (Edwards 1980, 92–93). Based on this analysis, Edwards concludes that a president "should be concerned with his prestige among members of both parties, because all members of Congress respond to his prestige, particularly his popularity among their electoral supporters" (109).

Rivers and Rose (1985) argue that Edwards's analysis understates the extent to which presidential success in Congress depends on the president's popularity with the public. Their analysis suggests that there is a simultaneous relationship between presidential program formulation and success in Congress—i.e., success at one point in time tends to be associated with increased requests in subsequent years, which then leads to lower approval rates. Because of this simultaneity, bivariate correlations between presidential popularity and success in Congress, as in Edwards's (1980) analysis, will understate the true relationship. Controlling for simultaneity, Rivers and Rose (1985, 193–95) find that a 1 percent increase in public approval of the president leads to about a 1 percent increase in congressional approval of presidential requests. They conclude that public opinion is a more important source of presidential success than indicated by previous studies.

Charles Ostrom and Dennis Simon (1985) also found a significant relationship between presidential popularity and presidential success for the period 1953 through 1980. They analyzed the cumulative rate of roll call victories from the beginning of a given Congress to the current month as a function of the president's popularity in the current month, party control of Congress, and how active the president was in proposing legislation. The results of this analysis suggest that, controlling for partisan control of Congress and presidential legislative activity, "the cumulative rate of roll call victories will decline by three points for every ten point drop in approval" (Ostrom and Simon 1985, 349).

Thus there is systematic empirical evidence to support the theory that variation in the president's popularity with the public influences congressional support for his policy preferences. A closer examination of the theory and evidence, however, suggests that the effects of presidential popularity are marginal at best.

Limitations of the Popularity Explanation
The empirical evidence presented by researchers seeking to demonstrate a strong relationship between public approval of the president and support in Congress is mixed. Even those studies that purport to find a strong relationship have problems that raise doubts about the evidence.

Although Edwards (1980) reports some high correlations, as Rivers and Rose (1985, 184) observe, his results are "decidedly mixed." Edwards found some negative partial correlations, yet he tends to ignore the inconsistent findings and to emphasize the strong positive relationships for his conclusion about the importance of presidential popularity.

Rivers and Rose (1985), however, also fail to provide convincing evidence that public approval is a more important source of presidential success than indicated by Edwards (1980). They use highly sophisticated methods in an attempt to show that simpler methods fail to reveal the true (strong) relationship. A reexamination of Rivers and Rose's results (1985, 192), however, reveals that they clearly overstate the importance of public opinion. They note that Edwards did not report significance tests or standard errors. As result, we cannot judge the reliability of Edwards's parameter estimates. They correct this deficiency and use the lack of statistical significance to conclude that some variables in their model are not important. Yet they argue that the president's Gallup approval rating has a "substantial effect" on success in Congress (193), even though the coefficient for popularity is not statistically significant. A significance level of .05, of course, is an arbitrary line. But Rivers and Rose argue that significance tests are appropriate criteria to determine the reliability of parameter estimates, then fail to apply consistently the criteria they establish to interpret their results.

The evidence from the Ostrom and Simon (1985) analysis is also ambiguous. Their study also seeks to analyze the simultaneous relationships between public approval and presidential legislative success. They use Gallup polls to estimate public approval each month from January 1953 to December 1980. The measure of presidential legislative success, however, is the "cumulative proportion of domestic policy votes . . . in which the position advocated by the president was victorious" (340). The summation of presidential success is restarted at the beginning of each new Congress (341). In the model of public approval, including the president's cumulative legislative success as an explanatory variable makes theoretical sense. It seems reasonable to suppose that public approval of the president in a given month might be influenced by his legislative successes in previous months. But analyzing the cumulative legislative success rate as a function of the current month's public approval makes little theoretical sense. It is hard to imagine how the level of public approval in December could affect the cumulative rate of successes over the previous eleven months, because most of the victories occurred before the observation of popularity. Consequently, it is unclear what Ostrom and Simon's analysis tells us about the effects of public approval on presidential success.

We see therefore that there are problems with the evidence from these studies purporting to show that public approval has a strong effect on presidential success in Congress. Furthermore, other studies present evidence that the effect of presidential popularity is marginal at best. Paul Light's analysis of congressional action on presidential proposals from Kennedy to Carter finds that popularity has a significant effect on congressional action, but the strength of the relationship is much weaker than that reported by Edwards (1980). The correlations between presidential popularity and congressional action on presidential programs are .28 for spending programs, .27 for large programs, and .19 for new programs (Light 1981–82, 73).

Similarly, our study of presidential support from members of the House between 1959 and 1974 (Eisenhower to Ford) reveals limited and indirect effects for public opinion. We found that, controlling for ideological conflict between the president and a member of Congress, overall presidential popularity is related to support, but partisan forces condition the relationship. Presidential popularity is directly related to support from members of the president's party and inversely related to support from members of the opposition—that is, popular presidents tend to receive more support from members of their party but less support from members of the opposition (Bond and Fleisher 1980, 75).

Another study updated the analysis through 1983, using the same basic model to analyze an improved measure of presidential support scores (Bond, Fleisher, and Northrup 1988). Consistent with the earlier findings, this updated analysis suggests that presidential popularity has a statistically significant effect on individual levels of support, but the substantive effects are marginal. Although the relationship for opposition members was not negative as in the earlier study, the relationship was much weaker (and in some cases not significant) for opposition members.

Two considerations explain why presidential popularity might have little effect—or even negative effects—on the opposition. First, popular and unpopular presidents may behave differently in their dealings with Congress. Feeling that they have the support of the people, popular presidents may be less compromising. An unwillingness to compromise on partisan presidential proposals is likely to lead to increased partisan voting in Congress and, hence, more support from the president's party and less support from the opposition.

Second is the question of credit. Nelson Polsby (1986, 207) observes: "[M]uch of the sharpest kind of partisan conflict on Capitol Hill revolves . . . around the question of credit. Members of the party in opposition to the President must ask themselves whether they can afford to support programs that may help to perpetuate the administration in office." Few voters have information about levels of presidential support in Congress. As noted above, the primary determinants of the outcomes of congressional elections are the relative quality of the candidates and the vigor of their campaigns (Jacobson and Kernell 1983). Members of the president's party tend to get credit for his policies even if they do not support them; members of the opposition are not likely to receive credit even if they do. Consequently, members of the opposition are likely to follow their basic partisan predisposition and oppose the positions of popular presidents because they have little to gain from their support and much to lose if the president succeeds.

We will use the estimates from the 1980 study to estimate the substantive effects of public approval. The regression model estimates (Bond and Fleisher 1980, 75) indicate that, ceteris paribus, if a president's popularity declines by the relatively large amount of 25 percent, presidential support scores of members of the president's party will decrease by an average of 6.75 percent and those of the opposition will increase by an average of 4 percent. These figures are relatively small, and except when the expected vote is very close, the effect on the probability of victory is likely to be marginal. Moreover, a change in popularity of 25 percent over the course of a four-year term is common, but changes from month to month are seldom greater than 5 percent. Thus while popularity with the public might influence congressional support indirectly over the course of the term by increasing party unity, it cannot overcome the basic partisan and ideological predispositions of members of Congress.

In another study of presidential-congressional relations, analyzing votes rather than individuals, we found further evidence that public approval has only marginal effects on presidential success. Our analysis of conflictual presidential roll calls from Eisenhower through Carter reveals that the president does not win more votes, nor does he receive higher levels of support, when he is popular than when he is unpopular. Similarly, presidential success on roll calls is not affected by the change in popularity over the previous six months. And contrary to the major finding of Edwards's research, partisan groups in Congress are no more responsive to the president's popularity among their party identifiers in the public than they are to his overall popularity.[8] The pattern of weak (and sometimes negative) relationships is not substantially different in the House and Senate, for domestic or foreign policy issues, for key votes or nonkey votes, or for different presidents (Bond and Fleisher 1984).

The mixed evidence in the literature suggests that considerable confusion prevails concerning the nature of the relationship between presidential popularity and support for the president's policy preferences in Congress. This confusion can be traced to two related problems. One problem is methodological; the other is theoretical.

Methodologically, the study of the effects of popularity on congressional behavior has utilized different units of analysis (individuals, months, years, programs, votes), different measures of support, different time frames, and different statistical procedures. These methodological differences could affect the results and interpretations of the findings. We need to spend much more effort sorting out issues of research design and method. Decisions about methods should be guided by theory.

In addition, there are theoretical problems. Some of the confusion results from lack of clarity about what the theory linking popularity and presidential support actually predicts. Edwards's (1980) argument and analysis suggest

---

8. Edwards's (1980) finding that partisan public approval is strongly correlated with partisan support in Congress is largely spurious. We will discuss this issue in greater detail in chapter 7.

that presidential popularity exerts strong, direct effects on congressional decision making. Despite Rivers and Rose's (1985) criticisms of his interpretation,
Edwards reports some very strong relationships between partisan public approval and partisan support in Congress which seem to support his conclusions about the importance of presidential popularity. But virtually every
study of congressional behavior suggest that such external forces as public
opinion will have marginal effects at best. Moreover, in his discussion of
"presidential prestige" as a source of presidential power, Neustadt (1960, 87)
emphasizes that it "is a factor operating mostly in the background as a conditioner, not the determinant, of what Washingtonians will do about a President's request." [9]

Thus studies of congressional behavior and Neustadt's theory lead one to
expect that presidential popularity will have only a marginal impact on voting
decisions of representatives in Congress. Liberal Democrats, for example, did
not become solid supporters of President Reagan even at the zenith of his
popularity. The expectation of marginal effects is not to deny that for some
individuals on some votes, the president's popularity with the public is a crucial—perhaps even deciding—consideration. But the available evidence does
suggest that, in general, presidential popularity is not likely to alter greatly the
decisions of individuals already in Congress. Instead, its effects are likely to
be indirect, operating through the electoral process to alter the distribution of
partisan and ideological forces in Congress through changes in membership.

PRESIDENTIAL LEADERSHIP SKILL

The study of presidential-congressional relations has been greatly influenced
by Richard Neustadt's classic *Presidential Power* (1960). Neustadt focused on
"personal power and politics." He was interested in "what a President can do
to make his own will felt within his own Administration; what he can do, as
one man among many, to carry his own choices through that maze of personalities and institutions called the government of the United States" (i).

According to Neustadt, one of the most important sources of influence in
Congress is the president's "professional reputation" as skilled or unskilled
(chap. 4). Of all the forces that might link the president and Congress, the
president's reputation as a leader is the one over which he has the most control.
The president's reputation as a leader is defined largely by the perceptions of
Washingtonians, but the president has the capacity to mold perceptions: "Everything he personally says and does (or fails to say, omits to do), becomes
significant in everyone's appraisals" (80).

9. In a recent analysis, Edwards (1989, chap. 6) has modified his earlier position and now
agrees that the effects of public approval are marginal.

Although every act contributes to the president's reputation, it is unlikely that any single act will completely set or alter it. Instead, a professional reputation results from "the residual impressions of tenacity and skill accumulating in the minds of Washingtonians-at-large" (63). But first impressions are especially important:

> Ideally, any President who valued personal power would start his term
> with vivid demonstrations of tenacity and skill in every sphere, thereby
> establishing a reputation sure to stand the shocks of daily disarray until
> he was prepared to demonstrate again. This is no more than Franklin
> Roosevelt did in his first term. It is the ideal formula for others
> (63–64).

Elements of Skill

Students of presidential-congressional relations agree on the essential elements of leadership skill. Although leadership skill cannot be reduced to a check list or a set of "commandments" that if followed will ensure success with Congress, scholars have identified several activities, tactics, and resources that seem to be associated with perceptions of skilled presidential leadership. The items on the list are of two general types: (1) interpersonal skills and (2) structuring skills.

Interpersonal Skills Interpersonal skills involve the president or his representatives in face-to-face contact with members of Congress. The activities involved are well known and do not require extensive elaboration.

First, the president must have an intimate knowledge of Congress and its members; he must "know the deck." To gain this knowledge, the president must spend time with members of Congress to learn their likes and dislikes, their needs and goals, and where the levers of power lie (Edwards 1980, 117–18; Christenson 1982, 255–56).

Second, the president should consult with members of Congress, especially congressional leaders, and give them advance notice before initiating major policy proposals. Consultation gives the president a feel for how his proposal will be received and an opportunity to implicate members in formation of the policy. Advance notice gives his supporters a chance to review the proposal and to accommodate themselves to it (Edwards 1980, 119–20; Christenson 1982, 257–58; Jones 1983, 110).

Third, the president must follow through and use the resources at his disposal to persuade members to support his policy, or at least not to oppose it. President Johnson was fond of saying, "There is only one way for a President to deal with Congress, and that is continuously, incessantly, and without interruption" (quoted in Kearns 1976, 226). In his continuous dealings with Congress, the president should use his intimate knowledge of Congress to anticipate reactions and to preempt problems before they become unmanageable (Edwards 1980, 120).

At the heart of the concept of follow-through are bargaining and the use of the various carrots and sticks available to enhance the president's bargaining position. The president may trade favors, supply members with services and personal amenities, and use personal appeals; he may enlist the aid of cabinet members, other members of Congress, or influential individuals in a member's constituency. If softer methods of persuasion fail, he may engage in arm-twisting by making implicit or explicit threats (Edwards 1980, 120, 128–73; Christenson 1982, 262–63; Jones 1983, 109). If these activities cannot convert potential opponents or undecided members into supporters, the president may be able to convince them to "take a walk" and not vote against him (Covington 1985).

A final interpersonal skill is the ability to compromise. Because members of Congress have power independent of the president, he often must meet them part way in return for their support. But he must know when to compromise. If he gives in too soon, it may be seen as a sign of weakness, and he will lose more than necessary. If he waits too long, he may be viewed as stubborn, and resistance in Congress will harden (Edwards 1980, 166; Christenson 1982, 266; Jones 1983, 110).

Structuring Skills   Structuring skills also contribute to a president's professional reputation. Although structuring skills may involve the president in direct personal contact with members of Congress, that is not their primary focus. Instead, the emphasis in the notion of structuring skills is the president's success in manipulating the environment in which followers operate or in taking advantage of any favorable conditions that might exist in the political environment. Previous research has identified several activities associated with structuring skills.

Perhaps the most important structuring resource available to the president is his power to set Congress's agenda. The president should carefully choose the issues to place on the agenda and present them to Congress so as to "structure" the situation to his advantage. Complex issues involve more than two sides. In fact, there are likely to be as many perspectives and opinions as there are members of Congress. The president, therefore, must frame the issue so as to limit the choices open to members of Congress (Malbin 1983, 216).

President Reagan, for example, seems to have benefited from this type of skill. During his first year in office, he structured the process by focusing on the budget and taxes—issues on which most Republicans and conservative southern Democrats tend to agree. And he used the congressional budget reconciliation process to enhance his chances of success. The new budget process allowed Reagan to achieve most of his policy goals by concentrating on only a handful of votes early in the session rather than having to mobilize majorities on many votes across the entire session.

President Carter, on the other hand, did not use his agenda-setting powers to his advantage. Instead of focusing his early legislative agenda on a few important issues on which his fellow partisans could agree, he bombarded Congress with a vast array of complex, controversial legislation that divided his party. He lost some important votes early in the year, and his first victory on a key vote (defense spending) resulted from strong Republican support offsetting opposition from a majority of Democrats (Fleisher and Bond 1985, 754–56).

A second structuring skill closely related to agenda control is setting priorities. The president needs to determine which issues are most important to him, submit proposals to Congress in a measured way, and concentrate his efforts on them in order of priority. Setting priorities yields a double advantage: not only does it result in a more efficient use of the president's time, it increases the chances that Congress will focus attention on the issues about which the president cares the most. Congress can deal with only a limited number of complex issues at any time. A president who is not sensitive to "the pace and workload of Congress" runs the risk of overloading the system (Jones 1983, 109; Ornstein 1983, 206).

Asking for more than even a cooperative Congress can give may result in failure of key parts of the president's program. The proposals fail not because Congress rejects them, but because they languish in the labyrinth of conflicting congressional priorities, crowded committee agendas, and complex rules. President Johnson was especially aware of this possibility. Edwards (1980, 119) reports that Johnson sent bills to Congress "one by one rather than in a clump," and "he sent them when the agendas of the receiving committees were clear so that they could be considered right away."

In addition to substantive importance, there is also a strategic consideration in setting priorities. The president should consider the order in which proposals will be submitted to Congress. He should try to avoid sending highly controversial and divisive issues early in his term "so that failure . . . at the outset of his administration (or even passage, under circumstances that sow undue rancor and bitterness) will not jeopardize the fate of subsequent bills" (Christenson 1982, 257).

A final structuring skill is a good sense of timing. Congress is more receptive to presidential leadership at some times than at others. The president needs to read the mood of Congress and adjust his activities accordingly. Because Congress is generally more disposed to cooperate during the president's first year in office, the president can often benefit by acting fast, as Johnson and Reagan aptly demonstrated (Jones 1983, 108–9; Edwards 1980, 119; Light 1983, viii–ix, 218–19). In addition, unexpected events may provide the president with opportunities for success. For example, after the assassination of President Kennedy, "a contrite and guilt-ridden Congress was ready to give Johnson the unfulfilled portions of Kennedy's program," and the OPEC boycott made Congress receptive to comprehensive energy legislation (Christenson 1982, 256).

Thus leadership skill involves interpersonal interactions between the president and members of Congress and structuring activities. Although the various elements of skill are conceptually distinct, they interact and become inseparably intertwined in the world of Washington politics. While recognizing the interrelatedness of the elements, it is nonetheless appropriate to ask which type of skill—interpersonal or structuring—is more important to the president's professional reputation.

Most discussions of presidential leadership skill seem to emphasize interpersonal skills—bargaining, arm-twisting, doing favors, etc. One analyst explicitly argues that interpersonal skills are most important: "What seems to count most is the ability to engage in skilled interpersonal activity" (Kellerman 1984, 15). Reflection on how the different types of skill operate, however, suggests that structuring skills are likely to have a more enduring effect and therefore have a greater potential to influence success in Congress.

Neustadt (1980, 63) notes that the president "need not be concerned with every flaw in his performance day by day." If the president leaves a key supporter off a guest list or if he misreads a situation and botches negotiations on a bill, the damage is likely to be limited and short term. Better performance on future interactions can make up for earlier mistakes, although a persistent pattern would inflict more lasting damage on his reputation.

Mistakes on structuring activities, on the other hand, are likely to have broader and more enduring effects. A poorly planned agenda or a failure to set priorities threatens success on many issues and continues to limit the president's influence long after the initial mistake was made. And a timing mistake often cannot be undone. Thus, although skill at interpersonal interaction is necessary, if leadership skills affect overall success, structuring skills are likely to matter more.

Evidence of the Importance of Skills

What evidence is there to support the theory that the president's leadership skill has an important influence on his success in Congress? Before considering the empirical evidence, we need to discuss how the theory defines "important influence on success," because the definition of this concept determines the type of evidence necessary to support or reject the theory.

One might suppose that the definition is obvious and straightforward: success is defined in terms of winning and losing; skills are important if we observe that, under given political conditions, skilled presidents win more often than do unskilled presidents. But proponents of the skills theory have a more subtle and limited definition which rejects the view that skills increase the president's overall rate of victories.

Neustadt clearly views the president's reputation as skilled or unskilled as a contextual influence. He argues, "Reputation, of itself, does not persuade, but it can make persuasion easier, or harder, or impossible" (Neustadt 1960, 63).

Similarly, in the most comprehensive and systematic analysis of presidential leadership since Neustadt, Barbara Kellerman (1984, 52) argues that a skilled president will be better able to get his way when he wants it, but the effects will not be evident on aggregate wins and losses. Her analysis of leadership skills does not claim or seek to prove that the president's activities are "decisive in any particular situation, or vis-à-vis any particular member or faction of the political elite." She seeks to "show only that influence is an important element of the political process, and that it appears to determine political outcomes some of the time."

The empirical evidence required to test the skills theory is limited to a small number of cases. Kellerman (1984, 50) argues that to understand presidential leadership it is

> more revealing to study the president's attempts at influence on a few
> issues of major importance to him than to measure his success in the
> aggregate. . . . [O]nly a relatively few measures involve the president's
> personal leadership to a significant degree. There are relatively few po-
> litical battles dear to each president; it is, therefore, those few that
> provide a reasonable test of the president's political skills.

This view explicitly rejects quantitative analysis of the effects of skills. Kellerman (1984, 49) argues "strongly that . . . quantitative indicators . . . preclude [one] from unearthing the rich detail that is often the real story of White House–Congressional interactions." The bulk of the empirical evidence testing the skills theory, therefore, consists of case studies.[10]

Cases are selected on the basis of their significance to the president. The goal is to use evidence from a particular case to develop broader, more general

---

10. The major exception is Edwards (1980, chap. 7). Edwards analyzes support for presidents from northern Democrats, southern Democrats, and Republicans. He finds no evidence that presidents with reputations as highly skilled do systematically better with any group in Congress. Based on this evidence he concludes that skills are not a major determinant of presidential influence with members of Congress. He reaches the same conclusion in an updated analysis which refines his measures of influence and includes data from the Reagan administration (Edwards 1986a, 1989).

conclusions. Malbin (1983, 213) argues, for example, that because the National Energy Plan was "the highest domestic priority of President Carter's first year in office," it is "a good window through which to view the Carter administration's later problems. What happened to that package should tell us something *more general* about the character of legislative-executive relations" (emphasis added). Let's look at the evidence from some of the cases used to analyze presidential leadership skills. The most often studied issues in recent years have been Carter's National Energy Plan and Reagan's budget cuts. These cases present a striking contrast in styles and results.

Carter's energy proposal is generally viewed as a defeat for the president, and the cause of the defeat is seen to be Carter's distaste for politicking and lack of follow-through. Although he eventually learned the importance of politics and improved his performance after the package got bogged down in the Senate, the activity was too late to salvage his reputation. Despite the fact that most of the major provisions of the president's proposal were passed, the process left a bad taste in the mouths of many participants (Kellerman 1984, chap. 10; Malbin 1983).

Reagan, in contrast, did everything right to secure approval of his budget cuts in 1981. The major battleground, of course, was the House, where the Democrats were in the majority. Yet Reagan's skilled lobbying, personal appeals, trading favors, and compromise kept Republicans unified and wooed enough "boll weevil" Democrats to build a majority in support of the cuts (Kellerman 1984, chap. 11; Ornstein 1983, 206).

Other cases fit together with these examples like pieces of a jigsaw puzzle to construct a picture of presidential-congressional relations with skills as the focal point.

- President Kennedy failed to win approval of federal aid to education, the proposal he said was most important to his program, because he made only weak attempts to reward support and punish nonsupport (Kellerman 1984, chap. 6).
- President Johnson, in contrast, won approval of the Economic Opportunity Act, the major component of his War on Poverty, because he worked hard and effectively used the available resources. Although political conditions were favorable, Johnson's skill is viewed as the cause of his legislative success: "What is important is that we understand that without Johnson's fierce determination, legislation such as the EOA would never have seen the light of day" (Kellerman 1984, chap. 7, quotation at 123).
- President Nixon repeatedly referred to welfare reform as "his highest domestic priority." Yet his Family Assistance Plan failed because of meager and sporadic support, failure to capitalize on opportunities, and "inept" leadership (Kellerman 1984, chap. 8, quote at 126).

- President Ford, in contrast, was successful on his proposed tax cut
  in 1975 because of his skillful use of a variety of political tactics
  (Kellerman, 1984, chap. 9).

But like the picture on a jigsaw puzzle, the image produced by these cases is
full of cracks.

Limitations of the Skills Explanation

Variation in leadership skills across presidents is inadequate to explain the ebb
and flow of presidential success for several reasons. First, if all the theory
seeks to do is show that skills determine outcomes on a small number of issues
some of the time, then how can we answer the question, "So what?" No one
doubts that skills are crucial on some issues. But if there is no relationship in
general, it is wrong to place skills at the heart of the analysis when they operate only at the periphery.

Second, the empirical evidence offered in support of the skills theory is
based on a small number of cases selected because they were major presidential proposals on which presidential interest and activity were high. Such cases,
however, are neither typical nor representative of presidential-congressional
relations. King (1983, 265) notes that "occasions of prolonged, intimate
presidential-congressional conversation should not be regarded as typical. The
presidency and Congress are indeed separate institutions, politically as well as
physically." Furthermore, basing the analysis exclusively on such cases assumes that the only relevant empirical test is on issues initiated by the president. But other important issues arise in Congress that the president must
respond to and try to influence. Hence evidence from presidential initiatives
provides an incomplete test. Because the test is incomplete and the cases are
not typical, the conclusions should not be generalized.

Third, the selection of cases may be biased; cases may be chosen because
they are consistent with the conventional view of a president's skills or because they demonstrate that skills are important. For example, Kellerman
chose Kennedy's aid to education proposal for analysis because of its stated
importance to the president. According to the evidence she presents, the proposal failed because Kennedy was unskilled at persuasion. But she notes that
Kennedy had several successes: a minimum wage bill, aid to depressed areas,
and a housing bill (Kellerman 1984, 87). We wonder if analyzing one of these
successes would lead to a different conclusion about Kennedy's skills and their
effects in Congress.

Similarly, the most often studied issue of Carter's administration is his
National Energy Plan. Different analysts come to the same conclusion: the
proposal failed because of Carter's inept leadership. Why not another case,
the ratification of the Panama Canal treaties, for example? This issue was cer-

tainly one of the major priorities of the Carter administration, and the president "carefully planned political operations" and engaged in the usual politicking to win the necessary two-thirds vote on the Senate floor (Christenson 1982, 263).

Finally, the case of Nixon's Family Assistance Plan was supposedly chosen because it was a high presidential priority. But then we discover that despite the rhetoric, Nixon's support for the bill was sporadic and at times ambivalent and unconcerned (Kellerman 1984, 126). We are left wondering if this case was selected because it "fits" with the conventional view of Nixon as unskilled. Why not another case on which he was active?

Given the complexities and idiosyncrasies of politics, it is unlikely that every case will be consistent with any theory or explanation. Yet case studies of presidential skills provide no cases that run counter to the theory. Social scientists will always worry about bias when all cases of failure are associated with poor skills and all cases of success are associated with high skills.

A final problem with the skills theory involves interpreting the evidence. One interpretation problem is in determining whether a case was a success or failure. Although whether the president won or lost is usually clear, sometimes there is room for doubt, even on highly visible, important issues. The case of Carter's energy proposal comes to mind again. As noted previously, the studies of this case consistently view it as a defeat for the president. Yet most of the major provisions were passed. And after passing most of Carter's National Energy Plan, Congress also gave him a synthetic fuels program and coupled a windfall profits tax to oil price deregulation. As a result, President Carter claimed energy policy as one of his administration's most important achievements, apparently with some justification. The policies seemed to have had the desired effects. By the end of Carter's term, domestic drilling was up and consumption was down (Malbin 1983, 237).

Another interpretation problem concerns the evidence necessary to reject the theory. Even if we accept the interpretation of a case as a success or failure, the interpretation of competing evidence in several case studies leads us to ask what we would have to observe to reject skills as an explanation. For example, President Ford's winning the tax cut in 1975 is presented as support for the skills theory. But this request was an admission that his earlier tax surcharge was a mistake, and his performance on the tax cut issue is described as "uneven" (Kellerman 1984, chap. 9). If uneven performance on a proposal to correct a mistake is evidence in support of the skills theory, then what does nonsupportive evidence look like?

Similarly, Johnson's success on the EOA and Reagan's success on the budget cuts are interpreted as resulting from uncommonly skilled leadership. In both cases, however, contextual variables provided the president with a tremendous advantage. In Johnson's case, his landslide election in 1964 brought many liberal Democrats to Congress. Even presidential advisors credit the election results for his successes:

> When Johnson lost 48 Democratic House seats in the 1966 election, he found himself, despite his alleged wizardry, in the same condition of stalemate that had thwarted Kennedy and, indeed, every Democratic President since 1938. Had the sequence been different, had Johnson been elected to the Presidency in 1960 with Kennedy as his Vice President, and had Johnson then offered the 87th Congress the same program actually offered by Kennedy, the probability is that he would have had no more success than Kennedy—perhaps even less because he appealed less effectively to public opinion. And, if Johnson had died in 1963 and Kennedy had beaten Goldwater by a large margin in 1964, then Kennedy would have had those extra votes in the House of Representatives, and the pundits of the press would have contrasted his cool management of Congress with the frenetic and bumbling efforts of his predecessor. In the end, arithmetic is decisive (Schlesinger 1978, 742).

In Reagan's case, the 1980 election had left the Democratic party in disarray. The Republicans regained the presidency and won control of the Senate. Although Democrats still controlled the House of Representatives, their majority was slim and contained more than three dozen conservative Democrats who were in basic agreement with Reagan's economic philosophy. According to Richard Cheney (R–Wyoming), chairman of the House Republican Policy Committee, Reagan's success in 1981 was not due primarily to his personal dealings with members of Congress but was the result of the 1980 landslide election, public support, the assassination attempt, and the fact that he proposed policies in which Republicans believed (personal interview reported in Edwards 1986a, 8).

In both the Johnson and the Reagan cases, these contextual advantages are noted, but their impact on the successful outcome is downplayed and the president's skilled performance is emphasized. In the analysis of the Reagan budget cuts, for example, Kellerman (1984, 245) says: "If it can be argued that for various reasons the Democrats had a predisposition to go along with the Reagan budget, that does not mean that the president was anything other than highly effective." Perhaps he was. But the important issue is whether his politicking, effective as it was, changed the outcome.

King (1983, 258–65) suggests it did not. He compares Reagan's budget victory and his victory on the sale of AWACS (Airborne Warning and Control System) to Saudi Arabia. Both cases were characterized by high presidential activity, and the AWACS victory was viewed in the press as a repeat performance of the budget battle. A headline in *Time* magazine read, "AWACS: He Does It Again!" King argues that this perception of a repeat performance by the president was understandable but wrong. While Reagan's politicking on the AWACS vote probably changed a defeat into a 52–48 victory, his success on the budget vote was due mainly to favorable political conditions rather than to his skilled persuasion.

Studies of unskilled presidents also downplay the impact of contextual variables. The analysis of Kennedy's aid to education proposal notes several obstacles, including the narrow election victory, a generally cautious Congress, a reduced number of Democrats in the House, and the debacle of the Bay of Pigs invasion. But these conditions are interpreted as excuses: "To acknowledge that circumstances sapped Kennedy's energies and capacities away from the education bill is not to say that they explain or excuse its failure to pass" (Kellerman 1984, 87).

In addition, the improved energy situation during the Carter administration is credited to outside events. After noting Carter's successes on energy policy, Malbin (1983, 237) concludes, "Still, the extent to which the administration can claim credit for all these accomplishments is limited." The improvements were more a result of "developments abroad than of events in the United States."

Thus it seems that if the president is perceived as skilled, he gets credit for a success, and favorable contextual forces beyond his control are downplayed. But if the president is perceived as unskilled, then a failure is his fault despite any unfavorable conditions, and any successes are the result of variables he could not control.

The difficulty in interpreting the evidence from these cases stems in part from the lack of a common baseline from which to compare. Case studies compare presidents without explicitly controlling for the balance of political forces facing each one. As a result, we cannot determine whether the outcome of the case was due to the president's skill or to the political conditions in which the president operated. Evaluating the success of one president against another without controlling for different political conditions is like trying to determine the winner of a race that did not have a common starting line for all runners.

Thus the evidence that variation in presidential leadership skill systematically affects legislative success is limited and ambiguous. The skills explanation, nonetheless, occupies a central, if not dominant, position in the literature. The lack of systematic evidence, however, should raise doubts. We must recognize that presidential activities, no matter how skillfully executed, cannot fundamentally alter the policy preferences of members of Congress. Anthony King (1983, 254) argues that

> it would be quite wrong to conclude that a president's warmth, charm, and knowledge of congressmen's susceptibilities can ever be crucial ex-

> cept at the margin (however important that margin may be to any
> particular president). Harry Truman could not have got national health
> insurance through the Eightieth Congress had he been Lyndon Johnson,
> John Kennedy, Franklin Roosevelt, Machiavelli, and Odysseus all rolled
> into one.

Presidential leadership skill operates at the margin because "members of Congress have their own political needs and priorities, which the president, whoever he is, is mostly powerless to affect" (King 1983, 265).

In summary, the literature identifies political parties, political ideology, popularity with the public, and presidential leadership skill as linkage agents that can serve as sources of presidential support in Congress. Each source is characterized by inherent limitations, and there is no guarantee that the president will be able to exploit the potential advantages to secure the votes he needs. Knowledge of the effects and limitations of the systematic forces that influence congressional behavior provides a foundation for a theory to explain the linkage between the president and Congress. Following is a theoretical framework built upon this knowledge.

THEORETICAL FRAMEWORK

Thus far we have discussed the four linkage agents separately. In this section, we present a theory of how the various linkage agents interact to influence presidential-congressional relations. Although none of the potential sources of presidential support in Congress guarantee success, some provide a stronger link than others. Each linkage agent, therefore, does not contribute equally to our ability to explain the ebb and flow of presidential success in Congress.

Thesis

The prevailing perspective in much of the literature emphasizes presidential variables—the president's leadership skill and popularity with the public—as the key to understanding presidential-congressional relations. Because American political parties are weak and undisciplined, presidential success in Congress is mainly a function of presidential politicking (Neustadt 1960; Kellerman 1984) and ability to rally public support (Neustadt 1960; Edwards 1980, 1983; Lowi 1985; Kernell 1986).

Our reading of the literature leads to a different conclusion. While none of the linkage agents are exceptionally strong, the literature nonetheless provides clear and unambiguous evidence that party and ideology affect congressional behavior in systematic and predictable ways. The evidence that presidential variables (i.e., skill and popularity) affect congressional behavior, however, is mixed and inconclusive. Hence our theory of presidential-congressional relations departs from the prevailing emphasis on presidential variables and focuses on congressional variables.

The general thesis of this study is that congressional support for the president is mainly a function of members' partisan and ideological predispositions operating within constraints imposed by the institutional structure of Congress.[11] Between elections, the basic parameters of presidential-congressional relations set by these political and institutional forces in Congress are relatively fixed. Although presidential variables such as the president's leadership skill and his popularity with the public may influence success at the margins, there is little that the president can do to move members of Congress very far from their basic political predispositions. Over the longer term, however, perceptions of the presidents' leadership skill and his popularity with the public may influence presidential-congressional relations indirectly by altering the political composition of Congress through the electoral process.[12]

Assumptions

This thesis is based on several assumptions. First are assumptions about the motivations of presidents and members of Congress. On any given issue in Congress, the president decides to support, oppose, or express no public position. When the president makes this decision, he is motivated by one or more of the following considerations: (1) his own sincere preferences about the issue; (2) strategic position taking for electoral benefit; or (3) strategic posturing to endorse what Congress will do anyway in an effort to improve his personal standing. Although all three considerations influence presidential positions, the list above is in descending order from most common to least common— i.e., most presidential positions are sincere expressions of preferences; occasionally the president takes a position contrary to his true preference to avoid saddling members of his party with an unpopular position in an upcoming election; very few positions are cases in which the president takes a stand contrary to his personal preference to improve his success rate with Congress.[13]

President Reagan's position on the Trade Bill and the provision requiring 60 days' notice of plant closings that passed the 100th Congress in 1988 illustrates the importance of the first two motivations. Congress compromised on almost all of the issues Reagan opposed in the Trade Bill. Most important was

---

11. The institutional structure of Congress includes standing committees, party and committee leaders, and congressional rules and norms that give these institutional actors power to influence members' behavior.

12. Parts of this argument have been presented previously (Bond and Fleisher 1984; Fleisher and Bond 1986; Bond, Fleisher, and Northrup 1988). Edwards adopts a similar argument in his recent book (Edwards 1989).

13. In our analysis, we exclude issues on which the president's position wins by more than 80 percent in order to eliminate most of this last type. Research by Covington (1986) in the Johnson Library found that White House OCR staff bragged about inflating Johnson's presidential support scores in Congressional Quarterly's studies. The evidence in his study, however, indicates that such instances are rare; all but a few positions on issues used in the OCR's internal analysis correspond to publicly expressed positions.

removal of the Gephardt amendment, which the President viewed as protec-
tionist. Nonetheless, Reagan vetoed the Trade Bill on which he got almost
everything he wanted because it contained the plant closing notice provision.
The House overrode the veto, but the Senate failed to muster the necessary
two-thirds vote. Sensing that the plant closing provision was popular, the
Democratic leadership split the issues into two separate bills and tried again.
Both bills passed by more than two-thirds in both the House and Senate.
Reagan signed the slightly revised Trade Bill. Although he continued to oppose the Plant Closing Bill, he let it become law without his signature. Public
opinion polls revealed that the plant closing provision was very popular with
the voters, and Republican senators up for reelection pleaded with the President not to veto the bill and saddle them with an issue that Democrats could
use against them. Thus on this issue the President was motivated primarily by
his sincere preference but backed off slightly to help members of his party.

Positions of members of Congress are motivated by similar considerations. On any issue, members of Congress decide whether to vote yea, vote
nay, or be strategically absent.[14] In making this decision, they are motivated
by (1) their own sincere preferences, (2) constituency interests, and (3) other
actors both in and out of government, including members of Congress, interest groups, bureaucrats, and the president's position and his activities to influence their vote. The literature on congressional behavior clearly reveals that
party, ideology, and constituency are the dominant forces. On most issues,
there is no conflict between members' sincere preferences and constituency
interests because members share the values of their constituencies, or because
the constituency is indifferent. Members use a variety of cues to guide them in
making decisions: party leaders, committee leaders, state delegations, staff
recommendations, the president's position, etc. But the president is only one
of many competing cues, and he is clearly not the dominant actor in their
calculus.

Second, we assume that the observed policy positions of presidents and
members of Congress reflect the interaction of partisan and ideological predispositions. For both presidents and members of Congress, party and ideology are among the most powerful determinants of behavior. Thus one can
classify presidents based on their party and the types of policies they generally
favor: President Reagan was a conservative Republican; President Kennedy
was a liberal Democrat, etc. And one can classify members of Congress in a

14. This last option does not occur frequently. Most members feel it is their duty to vote on
roll calls, and attendance is typically greater than 90 percent. And when members are absent they
often express a public position by "pairing" with another member or announcing how they would
have voted in the *Congressional Record*. There is, however, evidence that a small number of
cross-pressured members of the president's party do occasionally miss votes to avoid voting
against him (Covington 1985).

similar way: Senator Arlen Specter of Pennsylvania is a liberal Republican; Congressman Sonny Montgomery of Mississippi is a conservative Democrat. While such labels are abstractions and inevitably lose some individual details, they nonetheless capture an important and useful aspect of these actors' political behavior. President Reagan, for example, did not always support the positions of conservative Republicans, but such cases were deviations from what we observed to be his normal political predisposition.

Third, we assume that the partisan and ideological predispositions of presidents and members of Congress are relatively stable. The political predispositions that these actors bring with them to the policymaking process reflect the effects of their own political values as well as their particular electoral coalitions. Senator Specter, for example, chose to be liberal and Republican. A liberal voting record is also electorally useful in an urban, industrial state like Pennsylvania. In 1986, when many of his more conservative Republican colleagues were defeated, Specter's liberalism contributed to "an unexpectedly easy reelection contest" against Congressman Bob Edgar (Cohen and Schneider 1987, 678). Because party and ideology are anchored in an actor's personal values, and because successful politicians tend to credit themselves and their issue positions for their electoral victory (Kingdon 1968, 22–24), an actor's political predispositions are likely to be stable over time. Party switches among presidents and members of Congress are rare, and drastic ideological shifts are unusual. Members of Congress who shift to the left or right probably do so in response to changing electoral circumstances such as redistricting or a strong challenge.

Finally, we assume that the interaction of party and ideology makes some members of Congress more inclined than others to vote in agreement with the president's preferences. Because both presidents and members of Congress generally take policy positions that are consistent with their partisan and ideological predispositions, and because these predispositions are stable, the outcome of many issues is determined largely by decisions of voters to elect a Congress composed of members who are more or less inclined to agree with the president's preferences.

These assumptions suggest that a theory of presidential-congressional relations should begin with a discussion of how the interaction of party and ideology in Congress is likely to affect members' propensity to support or oppose the president.

The Interaction of Party and Ideology in Congress

Both parties in congress are characterized by ideological diversity. Since the New Deal realignment, the mainstream of the Democratic party nationally has been generally liberal, while the Republican mainstream has been more conservative. Because a majority in each party hold policy views consistent with their party's ideological mainstream, party and ideology are reinforcing for most members of Congress. But each party has a minority faction composed of members who have an ideological orientation outside the mainstream of their party—i.e., conservative Democrats and liberal Republicans.

Presidents tend to be selected from the dominant ideological wing of their party. Hence, it is useful for analytical purposes to view members of Congress as falling into one of four conceptually distinct factions based on how the interaction of party and ideology affects their propensity to support the president's policy preferences. These party factions are (1) the president's party base, (2) cross-pressured members of the president's party, (3) cross-pressured members of the opposition, and (4) the opposition party base. This conceptualization is similar to James MacGregor Burns's (1963, 195–202) argument that Congress is composed of four rather than two parties: presidential Democrats, presidential Republicans, congressional Democrats, and congressional Republicans.

The president's party base is made up of individuals who have the greatest predisposition to support his policy preferences because they share with the president both a party affiliation and an ideological outlook. Among members of Congress, liberal Democrats form the party base of Democratic presidents and conservative Republicans form the party base of Republican presidents.[15]

Cross-pressured members are individuals with ideologies outside the mainstream of their party—i.e., conservative Democrats and liberal Republicans. These members often find themselves cross-pressured on presidential roll calls because their party and ideological orientation provide conflicting cues. From the perspective of the president and party leaders in Congress, this group may be subdivided into cross-pressured members of the president's party and cross-pressured members of the opposition. Although presidents frequently attract support from cross-pressured members of both parties, partisan and ideological conflicts prevent these individuals from being considered part of the party base of any president. Because the ideological split is deeper in the Democratic party than in the Republican party, the presence of cross-pressured members may be more of a problem for Democratic presidents. Al-

15. Although this conceptualization is similar to Burns's "four-party politics" argument, it differs in the definition of the Republican party base. In Burns's (1963, 199) view, liberal Republicans are the presidential wing of the party. In our framework, liberal Republicans are cross-pressured members who are expected to be less predisposed to support a Republican president than are conservative Republicans. Burns's view of Republicans seems justified for the time period he studied. The last Republican president in his study is Eisenhower. As we shall see in chapter 4, Eisenhower's relatively moderate ideological positions had strong appeal to liberal Republicans. Republican presidents after Eisenhower took more conservative stands that appealed more to the conservative mainstream of the party and created greater cross pressures for liberal Republicans.

though Democratic presidents have had the advantage of partisan majorities in Congress, this advantage is limited because there are more cross-pressured Democrats who are likely to defect and fewer cross-pressured Republicans who might be inclined to support them.

The opposition party base is the mirror image of the president's party base—conservative Republicans for Democratic presidents and liberal Democrats for Republican presidents. Because these members share neither a party label nor an ideological orientation with the president, they are the least inclined to support his preferences. Presidents occasionally receive votes from members of the opposition base, but support from this faction is sporadic and more difficult to win than is support from the president's party base or from cross-pressured members.

The relative size of the factions provides the president with a more or less favorable cast of actors with whom he must interact when he enters the legislative arena. Between elections, the number of members in each of these party factions is fixed. Every two years, however, the electoral process changes the cast of congressional characters. Although the president would like to expand the size of his political base, his capacity to do so is limited and seems to be decreasing over time. The increase in incumbency advantage in congressional elections beginning in the mid-1960s has tended to insulate congressional incumbents from national tides and to decrease the effectiveness of presidential coattails (Fiorina 1984).

Although the basic parameters of presidential success in Congress are determined by the relative size of the party factions, one must look beyond size to explain presidential success. Regardless of whether the electoral process expands or contracts the size of the president's party base, it is unlikely that his base will produce enough votes by itself to guarantee a majority on the House or Senate floor. The number of members in the president's party base rarely constitutes a majority. And more importantly, because members of Congress have different, often conflicting, institutional perspectives on policy issues, even those who are predisposed to support the president may fail to do so. Consequently, every president needs votes from members of other factions who are less inclined to agree with his preferences.

Occasionally, a president takes a position that attracts support from cross-pressured members and from the opposition. Such a strategy, however, may be counterproductive. As the president's position appeals to factions further and further from his base—cross-pressured partisans to cross-pressured opponents to opposition party base—the risk of alienating members of his party base increases. Polsby (1986, 194) observes that the president sits on the horns of an old dilemma: is it more effective to take positions to "help thy friends or woo thine enemies?"

Two empirical propositions follow from this conceptualization of congressional parties. First, if the interaction of party and ideology creates varying predispositions to support the president, then the president should attract the most support from his party base and the least support from the opposition party base. Although support from the two cross-pressured factions should fall somewhere in between, predicting which of the cross-pressured factions will be more supportive is difficult. One could make a case that cross-pressured partisans have a greater incentive to support the president than do members of the cross-pressured opposition. Despite the fact that congressional parties and party leaders are weak in comparison to their counterparts in most contemporary parliaments, the formal party organization with elected leaders is likely to exert a stronger force on members' behavior than the relatively informal ideological voting blocs, which lack a formal organization and leadership. But given that cross-pressured members won election at least in part because their ideological orientation appealed to their constituents, we may find that the pull of ideology is often as strong as the push of party.

The second proposition relates to party unity. Unity is low in American parties because (1) the parties are ideologically diverse and (2) party leaders (including the president) lack authority to control nominations and discipline members. While we can only speculate about what might happen if party leaders had more authority, our four-faction model permits us to observe the effects of reducing ideological diversity. If ideological diversity is the primary cause of the lack of discipline in American parties, then the behavior of the more ideologically homogeneous party bases should be closer to the responsible party model—that is, on most presidential roll calls, the president's party base should unify in support of his preference, and the opposition party base should unify against. Failure to observe unified behavior in the party bases would suggest that variables other than ideological diversity are more important causes of party discipline.

While party and ideology establish basic predispositions to support or oppose the president, members' decisions are not made in isolation. Instead, congressional decision making takes place within constraints imposed by the institutional structure of Congress. A theory of presidential-congressional relations, therefore, must include the effects of institutional structure.

Institutional Structure: Party and Committee Leaders

Two of the most important elements of the institutional structure of Congress are (1) the party system under the leadership of elected party leaders and (2) the committee system with each committee influenced to a great extent by committee leaders (the chair and ranking minority member) chosen on the basis of seniority.

Congressional leaders exert a significant influence on presidential-congressional relations for at least two reasons. First, congressional leaders are the primary communication link between the president and Congress. Party and committee leaders are the individuals who transmit presidential preferences to Congress and likely congressional reactions back to the president. Kingdon (1981, 190) reports that a common "set of fellow congressmen through which administration wishes are communicated is the party leadership of the president's party." Similarly, committees and committee chairs influence the fate of presidential preferences. For example, John Manley (1970, 346–47) reports that Wilbur Mills (D–Arkansas), chairman of the House Ways and Means Committee from 1958 to 1975, was the primary link between the executive branch and the committee. The passage of Medicare, a high priority of both Presidents Kennedy and Johnson, was delayed until 1965 in part because Mills opposed it. The administration decided not to try to pry the legislation out of Ways and Means because "the feeling was widespread that Mills could beat them on the floor of the House" (Manley 1970, 346). Although few committee chairs wield this much power, decisions of committee leaders to support or oppose the president's preferences on issues that come through their committees are nonetheless a major determinant of success.

Second, congressional leaders have power and authority to manipulate resources that can directly affect members' careers. While leaders in the United States Congress are weak compared to party leaders in parliamentary systems, they nonetheless have more power than the president to influence congressional behavior because congressional leaders have the power to facilitate or block members' legislation and to reward or punish members seeking assignment to a particular committee. For example, Jim Chapman (D–Texas) switched his vote on the reconciliation bill in October 1987 and gave Speaker Jim Wright (D–Texas) a one-vote victory. In the next Congress, the Speaker rewarded Chapman with a seat on the Appropriations Committee (Frazier 1988). The president has no such power. Consequently, party and committee leaders serve as voting cues on floor votes more often than does the president (Kingdon 1981; Matthews and Stimson 1975; Jackson 1974).

While it is clear that congressional leaders wield considerable power, ascertaining the effect of their actions on the rank and file is difficult. A technique frequently used to examine the impact of leaders on followers' votes is to measure the extent to which leaders and followers cast similar votes. Leaders' preferences, therefore, are observed at the same time as followers' behavior. Jackson (1974), for example, used leaders' votes as independent variables to predict followers' votes. Leaders were presumed to have had an effect on other members' votes if the regression coefficient for the leader variable was statistically significant. Inferring leader effects from similar voting patterns is problematic because there are several different causal processes that can lead to agreement between leaders and followers.

First, agreement may be the result of various forms of negotiation and bargaining between leaders and followers. Although the sanctions and benefits available to leaders in Congress are limited, party and committee leaders are not without inducements that can be used to influence members' votes. This causal process is the strongest, and usually the most interesting to political analysts, because agreement between leaders and followers results from face-to-face interactions which change the behavior of some members. But since we are unable to observe leader-follower interactions systematically across a large number of votes, we cannot determine how frequently agreement results from this cause.

Second, similar voting patterns can result from followers using leaders' positions as voting cues. Faced with the need to cast a vote for the public record on an issue about which they have little information, members may find out the position of party or committee leaders and, without necessarily engaging in any direct communication with the leader, decide to vote the same way. In two important studies, members of Congress were asked to identify where they turned for information about how to vote (Matthews and Stimson 1975; Kingdon 1981). Among the many cues mentioned were party and committee leaders, although the relative frequency with which these leaders were mentioned varied across the studies.[16] Agreement resulting from cue-taking is not as strong a causal process as direct bargaining between leaders and followers, but leaders nonetheless have influenced behavior if their votes are used as cues.

Third, leaders and followers may cast similar votes because of shared preferences that arise from similar ideologies or constituencies, just as shared values cause members to be predisposed to vote in agreement with the president. Unlike the processes involving bargaining or cue-taking, however, agreement resulting from shared values is not caused by the leader. Instead, the behavior of both leaders and followers results from some other force that causes them to share values.

Finally, leaders may anticipate and respond to preferences of rank-and-file party members. In this case, the causal direction is reversed, with followers influencing leaders' positions.

These four causal processes are not mutually exclusive. On any given

16. Kingdon (1981) found that party and committee leaders were mentioned as voting cues by only 10 percent of the members interviewed. In comparison, Matthews and Stimson (1975) report that 45 percent of the sample mentioned committee chairs as cue-givers, and 62 percent of Republicans and 48 percent of Democrats mentioned the party leader.

vote, several causal processes are likely to operate simultaneously, with each accounting for some of the agreement between leaders and followers. Since we can observe only the result, separating the different causal processes across a large number of votes over a long period of time is impossible.

Although we cannot identify the exact mix of causal processes, analyzing the extent to which leaders and followers vote together is important to understanding presidential-congressional relations. Regardless of the causal process, presidents still care about whether leaders support their preferences on roll calls. If agreement between leaders and followers results from cue-taking or from leaders' using the resources at their disposal to influence members' votes, then presidents would seek support from leaders because it might provide some additional votes that otherwise would be lost.

But even under the weakest of the causal processes—shared preferences and leaders anticipating members' reactions—the analysis of leader-follower agreement is useful. If there is a correlation between votes of leaders and followers, then knowing party and committee leaders' positions would permit the president to predict likely reactions from members of the various factions in Congress. Viewed in this light, leaders become *barometers* that can be used to test the climate in Congress. Being able to predict how particular factions will vote based on the position of key leaders provides the president with important information about whether he needs to modify his position or his timing if he is to prevail on the floor.

The actions of Senate Majority Leader Howard Baker (R–Tennessee) to help President Reagan secure congressional approval of his decision to sell AWACS (Airborne Warning and Control System) to Saudi Arabia illustrate that leaders' ability to read the mood in Congress is important to presidential success. When Reagan first announced the plan in March 1981, congressional opposition was strong. Baker advised the president to proceed slowly because he felt that the Senate would defeat the plan if it were submitted immediately. Five months later the climate was more favorable, and with Baker's help the Senate endorsed the president's decision (Davidson 1985, 245, 248). We see, therefore, that it is worthwhile for the president to solicit the advice and support of congressional leaders not only because of their influence as negotiators and cue-givers, but also because they act as barometers of likely congressional actions.

Thus we need to analyze the relationship between leader positions and presidential success. In general, we would expect presidential success to be higher when congressional leaders support the president's position. Party and committee leaders, however, do not always take the same positions on presidential roll calls. Conflicting cues from the party and committee leader are likely to reduce unity in the party.

Political Contexts

Although members' partisan and ideological predispositions operating within the institutional structure of Congress are the major determinants of presidential success or failure, the political context within which presidential-congressional relations take place may condition the effects of these variables. We need to analyze the effects of different contexts on presidential-congressional relations. Two important contexts discussed in the literature are issue salience and policy substance.

Congressional behavior might vary depending on the importance of the issue. One problem that has plagued many studies of presidential-congressional relations is the failure to control for issue salience. In most statistical analyses, all votes on which the president takes a public position are assigned an equal weight.[17] This practice leads to the criticism that such analyses combine "the significant and the trivial, the controversial and the consensual" (Ornstein et al., 1984, 171).

Although we should base our analysis of presidential-congressional relations on important issues, we must be careful not to restrict the empirical base so much that it distorts results and produces an unrepresentative picture. Our goal in this book is to develop generalizations about the causes of presidential success in Congress. To have a complete understanding, however, we must consider and test whether behavior and success vary depending on the salience of the issue involved. In the following chapter, we will discuss how we might identify a subset of more important issues that will be large enough to provide a basis for generalizations.

A second contextual variable that might affect presidential-congressional relations is the content and nature of the policy under consideration. Policies may be categorized in a number of ways. One conceptual policy distinction that seems to be especially promising for understanding presidential-congressional relations is domestic policy versus foreign and defense policy.

Aaron Wildavsky (1966) suggests the importance of the foreign/domestic distinction in his classic article, "The Two Presidencies." He presents the thesis as follows:

> The United States has one president, but it has two presidencies; one presidency is for domestic affairs, and the other is concerned with defense and foreign policy. Since World War II, presidents have had much greater success in controlling the nation's defense and foreign policies than in dominating its domestic policies. . . . The president's normal

17. Congressional Quarterly identifies the presidential roll calls and weights them equally in their presidential support score. Most statistical studies use CQ's data, sometimes ignoring their consistent warnings of its limitations. See for example, Congressional Quarterly, Inc. (1983, 2782–83).

> problem with domestic policy is to get congressional support for the
> programs he prefers. In foreign policy, in contrast, he can almost al-
> ways [get congressional support] (7).

We expect presidential success to be higher on foreign and defense policy issues because the president has greater authority and information, causing members of Congress to be more deferential to the president and less partisan in their voting. The empirical evidence supporting the thesis, however, is mixed (Wildavsky 1966; Peppers 1975; LeLoup and Shull 1979; Sigelman 1979; Edwards 1986b).

Interpreted in light of our theory of presidential-congressional relations, the two presidencies thesis suggests that the content of the policy in question might alter the predispositions of members in the various party factions. Because previous studies did not analyze support from the four party factions and from congressional leaders, we need to continue to test for differences in the two policy areas.

Presidential Variables: The Competing Explanation

Thus the theory of presidential-congressional relations presented here departs from the emphasis on presidential variables in much of the literature. If success in Congress is mainly a function of congressional variables, how do such presidential variables as popularity with the public and leadership skills fit into the theory?

Presidential popularity might be incorporated into our Congress-centered theory as a context. While our theory suggests that presidential popularity should have only a marginal effect on presidential success because it cannot alter the basic political predispositions of members of Congress, its effects might vary across the different party factions. Indeed, in earlier research we found evidence that members of the president's party respond differently to his popularity than do members of the opposition (Bond, Fleisher, and Northrup 1988; Bond and Fleisher 1980). But that research did not analyze the relationship across the different party factions.

Because members of the two party bases have reinforcing partisan and ideological values, we would expect these representatives to be influenced very little by the president's popularity. Cross-pressured members, on the other hand, are being pulled in different directions by party and ideology. In a hypothetical case in which the opposing pulls of party and ideology are equal, the president's standing in the polls might provide a basis for breaking the tie. Such a situation, of course, is not likely, but it does suggest that cross-pressured members might be influenced to support or oppose the president's position depending on which tendency is reinforced by public opinion.

Furthermore, we need to analyze presidential popularity explicitly as a contextual variable. Previous studies look at the relationship between success and percentage of the public approving of the president's job performance. Viewing popularity as a context, however, suggests that incremental changes are less relevant than the overall condition of being popular or unpopular. Thus, even if we find that variation in popularity is not strongly related to success, we still need to analyze support from the party factions and congressional leaders under different conditions of popularity.

Presidential leadership skill, therefore, remains the major competing explanation. Our theory does not deny that presidential politicking is an important aspect of presidential-congressional relations in a broad sense. Perceptions of the president's leadership skill influence how members of Congress feel about the president, and they may affect the president's electoral success and his standing in history. Furthermore, there are abundant anecdotes and case studies demonstrating that what the president does and how well he does it affect the outcome of some issues.

The debate is not whether skills matter, but rather whether skills belong at the heart or at the periphery of a theory of presidential-congressional relations. If presidential leadership skill is the key to understanding presidential-congressional relations, then we should be able to observe some general effect beyond influencing the outcome of a small number of cases. Limitations in the theory and evidence discussed earlier lead us to doubt that presidential skills can affect success in general.

Despite the inconclusive evidence, the skills explanation is nonetheless widely accepted. Because of the emphasis on skills in the literature, we will attempt to devise a more systematic test that corrects the major deficiencies of the case study approach. Before we can analyze the competing explanations of presidential-congressional relations, however, we need to discuss the issue of measuring presidential success.

CHAPTER **3**

PRESIDENTIAL SUCCESS IN CONGRESS

One thing is forever good;
That thing is success.
Emerson

Rien ne réusit comme le succès.
[Nothing succeeds like success.]
French Proverb

The relative success of the president as a legislative leader is the sine qua non of presidential-congressional relations. The emphasis on presidential success in Congress is a legacy of Franklin Roosevelt and the New Deal. In addition to fundamentally altering the scope and purpose of the national government, the "Roosevelt revolution" changed the criteria by which the nation's chief executive is judged. Since FDR, presidents have been judged more by their success as legislative leaders than by their executive ability. And all postwar presidents lead "in the shadow" of the benchmark set by FDR's legislative success.[1] The first question in the study of presidential-congressional relations, therefore, is: How should we measure presidential success in Congress?

As Bert Rockman (1984, 211) has aptly observed, the concept of presidential "success . . . is both multidimensional and frequently inextricable from dumb luck." *Legislative* success is but one of four meanings of presidential success he discusses.[2] Even legislative success, the focus in the study of presidential-congressional relations, has been defined in different ways.

Perhaps the thorniest problem concerns the meaning of the concept of legislative success: What does it mean when we observe that one president is

---

1. This is the theme of William Leuchtenburg's (1983) insightful book *In the Shadow of FDR: From Harry Truman to Ronald Reagan.*
2. The others include (1) retrospective reputation provided by experts; (2) public approval provided by mass surveys, and (3) the management of decisions that successfully solve crises and problems (Rockman 1984, 190–94).

more successful in the legislative arena than another? As noted in chapter 1, success in Congress is not influence. While presidential bargaining and arm-twisting to try to influence Congress is one process that may lead to success, a president may succeed for other reasons that have nothing to do with influence. In our view, success is a broader and more important concept than influence. To fully understand presidential-congressional relations, we must depart from the preoccupation with presidential influence and analyze the conditions under which the president's preferences succeed or fail in Congress.

If success is not influence, then what is it? Ultimately, the meaning of any indicator of legislative success involves subjective judgments about the content, complexity, and importance of the issues on which the president's preferences prevail. Is a cautious president who endorses a large number of simple, routine issues that Congress is guaranteed to pass more successful than a bold president who pushes a small number of complex, difficult issues through the legislative obstacle course? President Carter won 76 percent of votes on which he took a position during his term; President Reagan won only 62 percent during his time in office.[3] Does a higher rate of legislative victories mean that Carter was more successful than Reagan? The answer depends on one's values. Republicans, for example, would argue that Reagan was a more successful president than Carter. His overall rate may be lower, but Reagan won on issues most important to Republicans (e.g., budget and tax cuts in 1981, increases in defense spending). Furthermore, Republicans view most of Carter's policies as undesirable, so they are not inclined to count his legislative victories as successes. Democrats, in contrast, would likely have a different view. They would argue that Carter tried to deal with such difficult, complex issues as energy and environment that divided traditional coalitions. And in Democrats' view, Reagan's few legislative successes resulted in massive deficits that have gutted needed programs to help the poor and protect the environment.

MEASURES OF LEGISLATIVE SUCCESS

Because the meaning of legislative success inevitably involves subjective value judgments, no empirical indicator is completely satisfactory. We can, however, devise empirical indicators that minimize some of the problems and permit systematic comparisons over time.

Several features are necessary for an acceptable empirical measure of presidential legislative success. First, the measure must be reliable. Constructing a quantitative measure of presidential success in Congress requires

3. These numbers are the average percentage of presidential victories on roll call votes on which the president took a clear position calculated from Congressional Quarterly's analysis (Alston 1988, 3327).

one to decide how to aggregate individual and collective decisions. In order to have a measure that is comparable over time, the decision rules must be as clear and precise as possible so that different researchers will come to the same conclusion about whether to score a case as a success or a failure. Second, the measure must be valid. The activity observed must bear a close relation to what we ordinarily mean by the concept of legislative success, and it should accurately reflect major components of decision making in Congress. Third, the sample of cases must be representative of presidential-congressional relations in general, and there must be enough cases of presidential success and failure to be able to generalize the findings. Fourth, the measure should differentiate between more important and less important issues, as well as different types of policies. Finally, the measure should permit the researcher to analyze the behavior of different types of members to determine the sources of presidential support and opposition in Congress.

Students of presidential-congressional relations have used several different measures of legislative success involving different types of aggregation. Each measure has both strengths and shortcomings. Following is an evaluation of the major alternative measures and a presentation of the approach we take in this book.

Presidential Box Score

One intuitively appealing measure of success is a box score that indicates the percentage of presidential proposals approved by Congress. The measure is analogous to a batting average—number of hits as a proportion of times at bat. Since there are several ways to define how many times the president went to bat as well as how many hits he got, one can calculate several different presidential box scores. The best known and most used presidential box score is the one reported by Congressional Quarterly (CQ) from 1954 to 1975 (*Congressional Quarterly Almanac,* annually 1954–75).[4]

Two features of box scores make them appealing as a measure of presidential success. First, because a box score measures success as the percentage of presidential proposals that are approved by Congress, it gives an indication of the proportion of the president's program that is enacted into law. Thus this measure focuses the analysis on issues that are important to the president. Second, because box scores are not based exclusively on decisions made in roll call votes, the measure takes into account the multiple decision points in the legislative process. To count as a victory, a proposal must receive favorable action at each stage of the process. A proposal may fail because Congress takes some positive action to defeat it at some point in the process (committee

---

4. CQ reported box scores for Truman from 1947 to 1952 and for Eisenhower in 1953, but these are not comparable to those of other years.

action or floor vote in either chamber) or because Congress takes no action. Failure to clear either chamber for any reason counts as a defeat for the president and lowers his box score.

Despite these appealing features, box scores suffer from several serious problems and limitations. Although some of the discussion below refers specifically to CQ's box score measure, the issues raised are intended to apply to the concept of a box score in general.

One problem is the reliability of the measure. Determining what to count as presidential legislative requests and how to count them are subjective decisions. Because these subjective decisions may substantially alter the box score, the measure is unreliable. In 1954, for example, CQ identified 232 legislative requests from President Eisenhower. Of these 232 requests, Congress approved 150 by the end of the year for a box score of 64.7 percent. The White House published a different box score, calculating that Congress approved 83 percent of President Eisenhower's requests. The White House list identified 65 presidential proposals, of which 54 were checked as approved (*Congressional Quarterly Almanac* 1954, 37–46).

CQ's analysis of the differences between its tabulation and that of the White House reveals that the White House list included fifteen points that were not in the CQ tabulation. These were proposals made by other administration officials or issues that the president endorsed as they moved through the legislative process. CQ's calculation included only clear-cut requests for legislation made by the president personally. The White House list also omitted some of the president's requests. For example, the White House listed only two of ten treaties. Of the eight omitted treaties, only five were approved (*Congressional Quarterly Almanac* 1954, 37).[5]

In addition to differing in what was included, the two calculations differed in how they counted proposals. CQ divided omnibus programs into component parts, while the White House lumped programs together. On taxes, for example, CQ counted forty-three requests, of which thirty-six (or 84 percent) were approved; the White House listed the tax program as one point, and as a result it counted as a complete victory. Thus subjectivity in identifying and counting presidential proposals threatens the reliability of box scores.

One could argue that because a box score seeks to identify how much of the president's program passes, the president's subjective judgment is what

5. A similar discrepancy appeared in 1965. The White House reported that Congress had approved 84 of 88 Johnson proposals for a box score of 95 percent. The CQ box score for 1965 was 69 percent. One reason for the difference is that the White House list included twenty-one proposals made by administration officials. All twenty-one of these requests were approved, but they were not included in CQ's calculation because they were not specifically requested by the president (*Congressional Quarterly Almanac* 1965, 112).

one should use in an analysis. But presidents, like all politicians, want to look as good as possible, and they have resources to help them create a successful image. For example, Lawrence F. O'Brien, Special Assistant for Congressional Affairs to Presidents Kennedy and Johnson, was especially adept at making the president's legislative record look good. In 1964, O'Brien released the White House's evaluation of President Kennedy's legislative record. According to O'Brien's tabulation, Congress approved 62 percent of the president's program in 1961, 74 percent in 1962, and 61 percent in 1963. CQ's box scores for those same years were 48 percent, 45 percent, and 27 percent respectively (*Congressional Quarterly Almanac* 1964, 88, 96). Thus using the White House's list of proposals improves President Kennedy's legislative success rate by as much as 124 percent over the calculation of independent observers at Congressional Quarterly. While the president's perception of which issues are important is an important element of presidential-congressional relations, we should not rely exclusively on subjective lists compiled by the White House that in effect allow the president to be the judge of his own success or failure.[6] To do so is not unlike allowing the manager of a professional baseball team to call balls and strikes for his own team.

A second, closely related, reliability problem is how to handle compromises. Legislative proposals, including the president's, are frequently modified as they move through Congress. Although many changes are minor and do not fundamentally alter the original proposal, some are extensive. If a presidential proposal is adopted after extensive modification by Congress, one is forced to make a subjective judgment about whether the final version should count as a success or a failure. And the line between minor and extensive changes is not always obvious.

The editors at CQ recognized this problem. If presidential proposals were modified by Congress, "CQ tried to determine if, on balance, Congressional action was more favorable than unfavorable" (*Congressional Quarterly Almanac* 1954, 43). One example of a difficult decision involved President Eisenhower's proposal in 1954 to change the method of calculating agricultural price supports. The president requested flexible price supports ranging from 75 to 90 percent of parity for five basic commodities instead of the existing fixed level, set at 90 percent for all crops. Congress approved flexible supports between 82.5 and 90 percent of parity. Although the approved range of support differed from the president's request, CQ counted this action as favorable because Congress approved the principle of flexibility (*Congressional*

6. Even if we accept the validity of these subjective presidential assessments, the president does not publish a postsession evaluation every year. President Johnson abandoned the practice in 1969, and President Nixon did not resume it.

Quarterly Almanac 1954, 43). Most students of Congress would probably agree with CQ's decision in this case. The principle of flexible supports was clearly the important policy question, and the low end of the range of support that Congress approved (82.5 percent) split the difference evenly between the president's proposed low of 75 percent and the existing 90 percent. But what if the split had been less favorable to the president, say 83 percent? What about 85 percent? Or what if the range had been expanded to 75 to 95 percent? At what point does a change in the level of flexible supports count as unfavorable action? Because the answers to these questions will differ depending on one's subjective judgment, the measure is unreliable.

A third problem with box scores concerns the time period for aggregating congressional action on presidential proposals. CQ's box score aggregates decisions on presidential proposals for a calendar year. Proposals that are carried over to the second session of a Congress or to the second Congress of a president's term are counted in the calculation only if the president repeats his request. A proposal that eventually passes after an initial request counts as a victory in the year it is adopted, but it counts as a defeat in every year in which it failed to complete the process in both chambers of Congress. Because many proposals, especially major programs and reforms that are key elements of the president's legislative agenda, require more than a year to work their way through Congress, a yearly box score may underestimate presidential success.

Recalculating a box score for a longer aggregation period such as a Congress (two years) or a presidential term to give the president credit for proposals that take longer to pass solves the problem of underestimating success. But this procedure creates another problem for the analyst who seeks to explain variation in presidential success: it further reduces an already small number of cases. A box score measures the percentage of presidential requests that Congress approves per unit of time. The unit of time selected for the aggregation, therefore, determines the number of cases. For the period from 1953 to 1984, we can calculate box scores for thirty-two years, sixteen Congresses, eleven complete or partial presidential terms, or seven presidential administrations. Thus box scores based on a yearly aggregation may be invalid because they underestimate success, but aggregating over a longer period to increase validity reduces the number of cases to an unacceptable level.

The level of aggregation necessary for the calculation of a box score creates a fourth problem. A box score reflects the final result of a series of congressional actions and inactions over a specified period of time. The point at which a proposal passes is the same in all cases—when it clears Congress and is sent to the president. And with rare exceptions, to succeed a proposal must receive favorable *action* by Congress. The point at which a proposal fails, on the other hand, is not always clear. Different proposals die at different points and for different reasons. Some proposals fail because Congress takes some action to kill them; other proposals die because Congress takes no action and makes no decision. Thus part of the measure is the result of congressional action at discrete points in time, and part is the result of inaction for a specified period of time. Because this measure of success reflects both decisions and nondecisions that occur at different points for different proposals, one cannot match up possible explanatory variables and conditions at the time the definitive action (or inaction) occurs. Consequently, one is limited to evaluating the effects of aggregate variables, preferably aggregated to the same period as the box score.

A fifth limitation of CQ's box scores is that they miss some important cases of presidential-congressional relations that do not involve legislation. CQ includes only requests for legislation in its calculation. But presidents frequently need and request action from Congress that does not require legislation. Perhaps the best example of such a request is a presidential nomination that requires Senate conformation. The Senate confirms most presidential nominations with little opposition, but there are occasional conflicts. According to CQ, the Senate's rejection of President Nixon's nomination of Judge Clement F. Haynsworth to the Supreme Court was the president's most significant defeat in 1969 (*Congressional Quarterly Almanac* 1969, 15). A measure that omits cases such as this one may produce a misleading picture of presidential success. Although nominations could be included, doing so might not improve the validity of the measure. Because presidents make dozens of appointments, most of which are routinely approved, including nominations in the calculation would probably inflate the box scores. Furthermore, the president has more appointments to make in his first year, so including nominations would affect the box score more in some years than in others.

Finally, basing an analysis on box scores assumes that the only relevant aspect of presidential-congressional relations is the fate of legislation initiated by the president. Although the president may dominate the policymaking process by setting much of the legislative agenda, a great deal of important legislation originates in Congress. Presidents often care about these congressional initiatives and seek to influence their outcome. A measure that fails to take into account presidential-congressional interaction on congressional initiatives is not representative of presidential-congressional relations and may produce misleading results.

A case in point is the addition in 1971 of a comprehensive child development program to a bill extending the Office of Economic Opportunity (OEO) for two years. The impetus for the child development program came from Representative John Brademas (D–Indiana). Representative Brademas offered an amendment to establish a comprehensive child care program in which children of poor families would receive benefits without charge. The House accepted the Brademas amendment (with some modification) despite strong opposition from President Nixon and Republican moves to water down and defeat the proposal on the House floor. The Senate adopted a similar bill, and both chambers adopted the conference report. The child development program was the focal point of the conflict over the legislation. House Minority Leader Gerald R. Ford (R–Michigan) communicated the President's opposition as follows: "The White House is opposed to this legislation and to this conference report and it is doing as any Administration has sought to do where it differs with a legislative conclusion. . . ." President Nixon vetoed the bill because of his objections to the child development program. The president's preferences ultimately prevailed when the Senate failed to muster the necessary two-thirds vote to override the veto (*Congressional Quarterly Almanac* 1971, 512–18). Although the controversy over the child development program was an important component of presidential-congressional relations in 1971, it was not included in CQ's box score because it was not a presidential request. A complete picture of presidential-congressional relations clearly must consider issues other than those initiated by the president.

For these reasons, box scores are an unsatisfactory measure of presidential success. The editors at Congressional Quarterly certainly recognized many of these problems and ceased publishing box scores in 1975 because they "decided it was a dubious measure of the president's record" (Congressional Quarterly 1982a, 19). The two major alternative measures of presidential success are based on roll call votes. One measures the president's success in attracting roll call support across individual members of Congress; the other measures the president's success across roll call votes.

Individual Presidential Support Scores

The most commonly used measure of success is Congressional Quarterly's presidential support score. A presidential support score indicates the percentage of time during a specified period (a calendar year in CQ's measure) that each member of Congress votes in agreement with the president's preference on roll call votes on which he expresses a position. Note that a presidential support score measures a different type of presidential success than does a box score. Whereas a box score indicates the proportion of presidential proposals that succeed, a presidential support score indicates the president's relative success in attracting votes from individuals in Congress over some specified period of time. Consequently, a presidential support score does not indicate the president's programmatic success. Nevertheless, individual presidential support scores are an appropriate indicator of one type of presidential success.

Individual presidential support scores have several advantages and overcome some of the problems with box scores. One advantage is that they can be objectively and reliably computed. All that is required for the calculation is to determine the positions of members of Congress and of the president. Representatives' behavior on roll call votes is available in the public record and provides a relatively unambiguous indicator of their preferences on the issues before them. Determining the president's position on roll calls (if he expresses one) is a little more difficult, but it can be done with a fairly high degree of accuracy. CQ determines the president's position on roll call votes by analyzing his messages to Congress, remarks made in press conferences, and other public statements and documents. From these sources, "CQ tries to determine what the president personally, as distinct from other administration officials, does and does not want in the way of legislative action" (Congressional Quarterly 1982b, 20). Although CQ may miss some votes on which the president takes a position, or incorrectly attribute a position to him, there is evidence that these errors are not numerous.[7]

Once the positions have been determined, one must decide how to count pairs and absences in the calculation, but these decisions do not threaten the reliability of the measure because the decision rules can be clearly stated and consistently followed. CQ's decision rule is to count only actual votes cast in agreement with the president's position as support. Failure to vote counts as nonsupport. The rationale for this decision rule is that only yea and nay votes affect the outcome. Thus CQ's measure may be viewed as a measure of *effective* presidential support. One could calculate a support score to give credit for pairs and to not count absences as nonsupport. Each method is defensible, and the choice of one over the other is somewhat arbitrary. But so long as one states the criteria and follows them consistently, either measure will be reliable (reproducible).

Second, although modification of presidential proposals by Congress continues to pose a threat to reliability in calculating support scores, the problem is not as severe as with box scores. Frequently, issues reach the floor in a form different from the one on which the president originally expressed a position. In such cases, CQ must make a judgment about whether "on balance, the features favored by the president outweigh those he opposed or vice versa." The vote is used only if presidential support or opposition can be clearly determined. Votes are excluded if extensive floor amendments make it impossible to characterize final passage as a victory or defeat. Making this judgment is no less subjective with votes than with box scores. But unlike box scores, which

7. Cary Covington's (1986, table 1) analysis of support scores compiled by the Office of Congressional Relations under Presidents Kennedy and Johnson indicates that CQ missed between one and eight presidential votes per year between 1961 to 1967.

are based on decisions and nondecisions over a period of time, each vote used in the presidential support score represents a public decision made at a discrete point in time. CQ uses the president's position at the time of the vote in calculating support, even if the current position differs from an earlier one or if the president reverses his position after the vote was taken (Congressional Quarterly 1982b, 20). Thus, on some presidential issues that are extensively modified by Congress, it is possible to determine if the president's position has changed and to use the current position reliably in the calculation.

A third advantage of individual presidential support scores is that an adequate number of cases exists for a valid analysis. Calculating a presidential support score requires one to aggregate each representative's behavior on presidential roll calls over a period of time. CQ aggregates support over a calendar year, but shorter or longer aggregation periods are possible. Because a support score measures behavior of individuals, the number of cases is the number of individuals—435 House members and 100 senators. And adding support scores for more years increases the number of cases. Therefore, so long as one uses individual attributes and characteristics to explain why some members support the president more than others, there will be a sufficient number of cases to support a valid analysis.

Fourth, CQ's presidential support scores are based on all roll call votes on which the president expresses a public position. As a result, this measure of success includes presidential-congressional interaction on issues that do not require legislation (e.g., nominations) and legislation initiated by Congress, as well as legislation proposed by the president.

Finally, because presidential support scores reflect the behavior of members of Congress, we can identify sources of presidential support and opposition in Congress. In addition, we can analyze the effects of individual and constituency characteristics to determine why some members support the president more than others.

Hence presidential support scores in general, and CQ's in particular, provide a generally reliable and valid measure of one type of presidential success. Although individual presidential support scores offer several advantages over box scores, several limitations suggest the need for another approach.

One problem with CQ's approach is that it includes too much. Because CQ includes all votes on which the president takes a position with all votes weighted equally, its measure mixes important votes and unimportant votes, as well as different types of policy issues. Mixing such divergent votes and weighting them equally in a measure of presidential success may produce a misleading picture. CQ is aware of this limitation and typically warns readers to be cautious when using the scores. In 1981, for example, CQ pointed out that the Senate's narrow approval of President Reagan's decision to sell advanced weapons to Saudi Arabia, "his most hotly contested foreign policy initiative, counted the same as the unanimous, pro forma ratification of the U.S.–Canadian Maritime Boundary Treaty" (Congressional Quarterly 1982a, 18). They also note that issues which require many roll calls to resolve influence the scores more than do issues settled by a single vote. In some cases this added influence is desirable because issues requiring many floor votes may be more complex and important. But sometimes multiple votes distort the measure. A case in point is President Carter's Senate support score in 1978. Carter's Senate support score was dramatically increased because he won fifty-five roll calls—most of them on procedural issues—related to ratification of the Panama Canal treaties.

Students of presidential-congressional relations who have used this measure argue that equal weighting assures reliability over time and that alternative weightings would be highly subjective and unreliable (Edwards 1980, 51–52). Although this argument has merit, it is unpersuasive for two reasons. First, CQ has not been totally consistent in computing the scores over time. President Johnson's 1964 Senate support scores, for example, are not based on all votes on which he took a position. Because there were 116 roll calls on the 1964 Civil Rights Act, CQ "arbitrarily selected" 10. If all votes had been included, Johnson's Senate score would have increased from 87.6 to 92.1 percent. Most scholars would probably agree with the decision to exclude some civil rights votes (if not the particular choices) in this case, because to be consistent and include them all would produce a distorted measure. But the case reminds us that just publishing a number does not make it reliable. Second, it is possible to classify votes reliably according to importance and policy type. Each year CQ identifies several "key votes" based on their importance, and students of presidential-congressional relations have used these votes in an effort to avoid basing their analysis on "a series of essentially trivial roll calls" (Sigelman 1979, 1193–1205). In addition, William Riker (1959) has developed a quantitative method for determining the relative significance of roll call votes. A complete understanding of presidential-congressional relations requires that we continue to refine our measures to take into account differences arising from different types of votes and policy issues.

A second limitation of CQ's support scores is that they are a biased indicator of presidential success with members of Congress. As noted above, many votes included in CQ's presidential support score involve routine, noncontroversial issues on which almost all members vote in agreement with the president's position. If the proportion of nonconflictual "victories" does not vary systematically across presidents, then including these votes would not bias the measure. The proportion of nonconflictual presidential victories, however, does vary considerably across presidents. For the period 1957 through 1980, between 12 and 51 percent of the votes used in CQ's presidential support scores were nonconflictual presidential victories. And the proportion varies systematically with the party of the president: presidential support scores of Republican presidents (who were always in the minority during this period) are inflated more by these noncontroversial "wins" than are the scores of Democratic (majority) presidents (Bond and Fleisher 1984, 294).[8] Some of this partisan bias may result because minority presidents have a greater incentive to posture and endorse routine issues to improve their success rate. But much of the difference results because of simple arithmetic: support scores of opposition party members are inflated more by nonconflictual votes than are the scores of the president's partisans, and by definition the number of opposition members in Congress is larger for minority presidents. Regardless of the cause of the distortion, measures of presidential success need to exclude nonconflictual "victories" that introduce systematic error. Excluding these votes will not eliminate all bias, but it is an improvement that can be made without threatening the measure's reliability.[9]

A third limitation of individual presidential support scores is that they are inappropriate for tests of all major hypothesized explanations of variation in presidential success. Variance in presidential support scores is across individuals. Calculation requires aggregation of individual behavior over a specified period of time (a year in CQ's measure). This aggregation does not present a problem if we want to analyze the effects of individual characteristics that vary across individuals but are constant for each individual over the period of aggregation. Two of the most important influences on presidential-congressional relations, party and ideology, can be measured as individual characteristics that meet this requirement. But analyzing the effects of other possible influences, such as presidential popularity, for example, presents a problem.

Researchers who use CQ's support scores as the dependent variable are forced to use the mean yearly public approval of the president as the independent variable (Edwards 1980, 1989; Bond and Fleisher 1980). This procedure is problematical for two reasons. First, public approval and presidential support in Congress vary over the course of a year. Because annual support scores and mean yearly approval fail to reflect this variance, there is no way to match individual behavior with the president's popularity at the time the behavior occurs. If we use average public approval for the same year as the presidential support score, then part of the possible cause is observed after some of the behavior we are trying to explain. If we lag the measure of popularity one

8. Nonconflictual victories are defined as those on which more than 80 percent vote in agreement with the president.

9. Some recent studies have reconstructed individual presidential support scores to exclude nonconflictual votes (Bond, Fleisher, and Northrup 1988; Edwards 1989).

year, then it is too far removed from many of the votes used in the measure of support to have an effect.

But more importantly, presidential popularity measured as a national average is not the appropriate measure for an individual level analysis. To analyze the effects of popularity on individual decisions, we need to measure public approval at the individual level, i.e., in the representative's electoral constituency. Polls of presidential popularity for states and congressional districts are available only sporadically, if at all.[10] Substituting the national yearly average in an analysis of individual behavior is problematical because the dependent variable (individual support scores) varies across members of Congress, while the independent variable (presidential popularity) is constant across individuals within years and varies only across years.

Although this problem may appear to be a technical, statistical issue, it introduces a serious limitation into studies using analytical methods based on correlations. A correlation measures the degree to which two measures co-vary. A primary principle of statistics is, "You can't explain variance with a constant." Because national average public approval does not vary across individuals during a year, correlations of national presidential popularity with presidential support scores do not reflect individual level relationships. Instead, they reflect the extent to which variation in average public approval over time is associated with the aspect of individual presidential support scores that varies over time—i.e., the yearly average. In short, what appears to be an analysis of individuals is, in effect, a correlation of average popularity for the year with the average presidential support score for the year. Thus using national averages not only masks a great deal of variance in presidential popularity and presidential support scores within years; it also severely limits the number of cases. The *effective* number of cases in such an analysis is not the number of individuals times the number of years, but the number of years.[11]

A final limitation of presidential support scores is more conceptual. It concerns which questions in the study of presidential-congressional relations are most important, and the units of analysis appropriate to answer those ques-

10. Some researchers have measured the president's state or district popularity with his electoral performance. This approach provides a defensible measure of constituency opinion, but it is available only once every four years, and there is little reason to expect election returns to influence individual decisions after the midterm elections, or perhaps sooner. Thus, election returns are not a satisfactory substitute for district opinion polls.

11. This discussion argues that correlating individual support scores with an independent variable aggregated across individual constituencies to a national average is *conceptually* the same as correlating averages with averages. It can be shown that the two procedures are *mathematically* equivalent. The slopes and intercepts of the regressions are identical; the correlations differ depending upon how much variance there is around the mean of the true individual level variable within each year. As variance around the mean decreases, the mean more accurately reflects the individual behavior, and the correlations from the two procedures get closer.

tions. As noted in chapter 1, the basic issue in the study of democratic linkage in a system of separate institutions sharing powers is policy responsiveness. The most important reason to study presidential-congressional relations is to learn what conditions and agents bridge the inevitable conflict between the president and Congress and permit the formation of policy in response to popular preferences. Discovering what variables cause individual members of Congress to increase or decrease their support for the president is an important first step, but this approach provides an incomplete picture because it does not tell us much about policy success. Policymaking in Congress requires collective decisions. Consequently, a variable may systematically increase support from individuals but fail to increase the president's programmatic success: the variable's effect on each individual may be too small to result in more presidential victories, or it may cause more individuals to support the president on issues he would have won without the additional support. A complete understanding of presidential-congressional relations, therefore, requires analysis of presidential success and failure across collective policy decisions as well as analysis of presidential support across individuals.

Fortunately, there is another approach to measuring presidential success that focuses on policy success, preserves the necessary qualities of reliability and validity, and overcomes many limitations of other measures. This approach uses roll call votes as the unit of analysis, and it is the one we adopt for this study.

Roll Call Votes

As noted previously, votes are the basic commodity of presidential-congressional relations (King 1983, 247). Roll call votes, of course, are not the only important decision point in the congressional policymaking process. Actions of congressional leaders and standing committees often determine whether legislative proposals of interest to the president will ever come to the floor for a vote. Occasionally, intense conflict between the president and Congress is compromised or finessed so that the issue never reaches the floor for a vote.

A case in point is the conflict in 1985 between President Reagan and Congress over the issue of imposing economic sanctions against South Africa. President Reagan strongly opposed sanctions, arguing that his policy of "constructive engagement" was a more effective strategy to encourage the end of apartheid. But despite the president's repeated threats to veto legislation imposing sanctions, the legislation had widespread bipartisan support in Congress and continued to move easily toward passage, even in the Republican-controlled Senate. The sanctions issue was so popular that Congress probably would have been able to override a presidential veto. The confrontation was especially troublesome for Senate Republicans. On the one hand, they wanted to support their president, and they did not relish the idea of helping the

Democrats hand him a major legislative defeat. On the other hand, the American public strongly supported imposing sanctions directed at the racist apartheid policy, and Republicans (especially senators up for reelection) could not afford to be on the wrong side of this intense moral issue. President Reagan managed to avoid a major legislative defeat and the further embarrassment of an almost inevitable veto override by imposing a set of milder sanctions by executive order. The president's action satisfied Republicans in Congress; although Democrats continued to argue that Congress should impose stronger sanctions, without Republican support there was little chance of overriding a presidential veto.

Measures of presidential success based on roll call votes miss cases such as the one just discussed, as well as others that never get to the floor because they are bottled up in committee or blocked by actions of party leaders who regulate scheduling. Although we recognize that some important interactions between the president and Congress occur at times and places other than floor votes, several considerations justify using roll call votes as the basis for a measure of presidential success.

First, a roll call vote may not be the only important decision point in the legislative process, but it is one of the important points. Most important policy issues show up on the floors of the House and Senate for resolution by roll call vote.[12] Analyzing interaction at the roll call vote stage of the process, therefore, is likely to produce a representative picture of presidential-congressional relations. Although cases such as the South Africa sanctions issue are interesting and important, they are relatively unusual and unrepresentative of the normal pattern of interaction between the president and Congress. And President Reagan's finesse on the sanctions issue only temporarily postponed defeat on the floor of Congress. Congress passed a sanctions bill in 1986 and overrode the president's veto. This action "marked the most serious defeat Reagan . . . suffered on a foreign issue and one of the most stunning blows of his presidency" (Felton 1986, 2338). Thus, while the sanctions issue would have been missed with this method in 1985, like most important issues it eventually came to the floor for resolution. A political science that seeks to provide general explanations must base its analysis on cases that are typical and must deal with idiosyncratic events on a case by case basis.

Second, behavior on roll call votes is the only point in the process where we can observe the preferences of both the president and members of Congress on a large number of cases. The point here is not that we should analyze roll call votes simply because we can observe them, like the drunk who

---

12. Mark Peterson's (1986) study of presidential initiatives from 1953 to 1981 reveals that congressional inaction on presidential proposals is not common. Only 8 percent of "major" presidential proposals in his sample failed to receive action in Congress.

searched for his car keys under the streetlight where the light was good instead
of in the dark part of the block where he dropped them. Roll call votes are a
fundamental part of a democratic process and therefore are *exactly the right
place to look* to find explanations of presidential-congressional relations. Roll
calls require members of Congress to express publicly a position for or against
an issue. On a significant number of roll calls, the president also publicly expresses his personal position. If we seek to understand how elected policymakers in the presidency and Congress interact in a democratic process, then
it is appropriate to analyze behavior that is readily observable to the public
and to the analyst. Of course, all public behavior is not relevant. As noted
above, presidential positions on nonconflictual roll calls may result from posturing or the routine nature of the issue. But within the universe of roll call
votes on which the president expresses a public position, there is an identifiable
subset that is appropriate to use for analysis. And this subset of appropriate
votes is large enough to provide a basis for reliable and valid generalizations.

A third consideration which justifies using roll call votes to measure success is that presidents and other political actors such as interest groups use roll
call votes to identify supporters and opponents. A large number of political
interest groups publish ratings of members of Congress that indicate the percentage of the time each member votes in agreement with the group's position
on roll call votes occurring over a period of time, usually a calendar year or a
Congress. Interest groups use these ratings as a basis for electoral support and
urge their members to do likewise. One such group is one of the nation's
largest labor unions, the AFL-CIO. The introduction to the group's highly
critical report on the 98th Congress (1983–84) includes the following admo-
nition: "In the future, labor's legislative successes or failures will depend in
large measure upon the willingness of rank-and-file union members and local
union leaders to hold members of Congress accountable for their votes" (Denison 1985, viii).

But more important for the analysis in this book, presidents also use roll
call support as a basis for distributing rewards and punishments to members of
Congress. In a careful study of the activities of the Office of Congressional
Relations (OCR) under Kennedy and Johnson, Cary Covington discovered that
OCR was not able to avoid relying on roll call votes to identify congressional
supporters and opponents. Moreover, OCR used this measure of support to
make decisions about how to respond to members' requests for presidential assistance. White House aides were intimately aware that because many important decisions in Congress are made in places other than floor votes and by
means other than roll calls, this measure might miss some important actions of
support and opposition. If the measure based on roll call votes were invalid,
then the White House risked making mistakes in deciding whom to reward
and whom to punish, mistakes that it could not afford to make. Hence, Cov-

ington concludes that "OCR's reliance on them provides a strong rationale for the use of roll call votes to measure support" (Covington 1986, 721). These considerations suggest that roll call votes provide a reliable and valid basis for measuring presidential success in Congress.

Using roll call votes as the unit of analysis offers several advantages for the study of presidential-congressional relations. First, this approach focuses on the most important component of presidential success—whether the president wins or loses on policy decisions in Congress. Although presidents care about and keep track of which individuals support them, the more important issue for the president is the collective result. The outcomes of votes can be aggregated over different periods of time to give a partial indication of the president's programmatic success, but because each vote is a case, presidential success can always be disaggregated. Thus this approach incorporates an element of the principal advantage of box scores while overcoming some of the major limitations that make box scores an unsatisfactory measure.

Second, on each roll call we can identify which types of individuals (e.g., liberal Democrats, conservative Democrats, liberal Republicans, and conservative Republicans) voted in agreement with the president's position and analyze variation in support from different coalitions of members. This approach is not the same as analyzing support across individuals, but it permits us to answer some of the same questions addressed in studies of individual support.[13]

Third, because the result of a roll call vote indicates presidential success or failure at a discrete point in time, we can analyze the effects of possible influences at the time the decision is made. Of particular importance is being able to match up presidential success or failure with presidential popularity at the time of the vote or a short time before. We still do not have popularity measured for each member's constituency, but since we are analyzing the behavior of aggregations of individuals, it is appropriate to use aggregate public approval.

In addition to analyzing the effects of presidential popularity at the time of the vote, we can analyze the effects of support from party and committee lead-

13. Edwards (1989, 33.) argues that individual support scores are preferable to "aggregate measures" if we want to investigate "theoretically significant questions about presidential success in Congress. . . ." He seems to include both box scores and success on roll call votes in his critique of "aggregate measures" and argues that we cannot tell whether different types of members respond differently (17). This criticism is true of box scores, but it is clearly possible to analyze the behavior of different types of members (Democrats, Republicans, liberals, conservatives, leaders, etc.) on roll call votes. A unique advantage of individual support scores, however, is that we can analyze the effects of various constituency characteristics (e.g., the member's margin of victory, how well the president ran in the district, seniority of the member, etc.) on presidential support. Although Edwards (1989) has corrected some limitations of CQ's presidential support scores, unfortunately he does not analyze relationships between individual characteristics and individual behavior. Instead, he presents only aggregate analyses which fail to exploit the major advantage of presidential support scores.

ers on the behavior of different groups of members, as well as on whether the president's position succeeds or fails. Party and committee leader support or opposition is often a key determinant of legislative floor success. But analyzing the effects of leader behavior is not possible with measures such as box scores and individual support scores because these measures aggregate decisions and behavior over time.

Finally, this approach permits us to analyze all votes or particular subsets classified according to policy type or importance. The substance and importance of roll call votes vary greatly. Although classifying votes according to substance or importance poses some difficult reliability issues, these problems are not insurmountable.

One important policy division is domestic policy versus foreign/defense policy. Several presidency scholars have debated the issue of whether the president has more power over foreign policy than over domestic policy (Wildavsky 1966; Peppers 1975; LeLoup and Shull 1979; Sigelman 1979; Edwards 1986b). Hence we classify votes in our study according to whether they involve foreign/defense policy or domestic policy issues.

Classifying votes according to importance is more problematic, but perhaps more crucial for a valid analysis. As suggested above, nonconflictual votes should be excluded. Congressional scholars normally exclude unanimous or near unanimous votes from roll call studies. A common practice is to exclude votes on which 80 percent or more members vote the same way. Following this practice, we exclude all votes on which 80 percent or more voted in agreement with the president. But we leave near unanimous presidential losses in the analysis on the ground that the president's disagreement has injected conflict into the decision.[14] Although this procedure eliminates most trivial and routine cases, it is only the first step in addressing the importance issue.

Among controversial issues, some votes are more important to the president than others. The question is whether subjective importance to the president is the only, or even the primary, criterion for selecting cases of presidential-congressional relations. We argue that it is not. The president's perception of which votes are important to him is without question one consideration, but only one. An equally legitimate consideration in determining importance is the perception of members of Congress. In short, the best judges of the importance of a roll call vote in Congress are the members who cast the votes. Because the president and the Congress are coequal branches in the American system, a case viewed as important by *either* one should be included in an

14. There are a relatively small number of votes in which the president stands virtually alone against Congress.

analysis. Regardless of the importance of an issue to the president or to his program, when he takes a position he wants congressional support and must receive it if his preference is to prevail. Therefore, if an issue on which the president takes a position is important to members of Congress, then it is a legitimate case of presidential-congressional relations that should be included in an analysis.

Members' judgments of importance are reflected in their behavior on the vote. Member behavior is the basis of Riker's (1959, 379) method of determining the importance of votes. His method defines the most important votes as those (1) on which all members vote and (2) in which the difference between the majority and minority is the minimum possible under the decision rule.

Another method of identifying important votes is the subjective judgment of an outside observer. Congressional Quarterly, for example, identifies a small number of "key votes" each year. CQ designates a roll call as a key vote if it meets one or more of the following criteria: (1) "a matter of major controversy"; (2) "a test of presidential or political power"; or (3) "a decision of potentially great impact on the nation and lives of Americans" (*Congressional Quarterly Almanac* 1953–84). There is no guarantee, of course, that votes perceived as important to CQ are important to either the president or Congress. But CQ has an excellent reputation for making sound and accurate judgments about congressional politics. CQ's judgment may vary from that of other observers, but its key votes are a set of votes perceived to be important by one set of informed political observers.

As the preceding discussion illustrates, several approaches to measuring presidential success are available, all of which require some type of aggregation. Box scores aggregate individual and collective decisions and nondecisions over time. Presidential support scores aggregate individual behavior over time. Roll call votes aggregate individual behavior at a discrete point in time. Of the available measures, we believe that the analysis of roll call votes offers the most advantages and the fewest problems. It does not solve all of the problems, but it improves the basis for systematic quantitative analysis of the major explanations of presidential-congressional relations. The following section describes trends in presidential success from Eisenhower to Reagan using our measure.

TRENDS IN PRESIDENTIAL SUCCESS

Overall Success

Table 3.1 compares presidential success rates on roll call votes using CQ's measure, which includes all presidential votes, and our measure, which ex-

Table 3.1 Presidential Victories on Roll Call Votes, 1953–84

	ALL VOTES				CONFLICTUAL VOTES			
	House		Senate		House		Senate	
PRESIDENT AND YEAR	%	(N)	%	(N)	%	(N)	%	(N)
DDE								
1953	91.2	(34)	87.8	(49)	88.5	(26)	84.6	(39)
1954	78.9	(38)	77.9	(77)	61.9	(21)	72.1	(61)
1955	63.4	(41)	84.6	(52)	44.4	(27)	68.0	(25)
1956	73.5	(34)	67.7	(65)	55.0	(20)	61.1	(54)
1957	58.3	(60)	78.9	(57)	47.9	(48)	69.2	(39)
1958	74.0	(50)	76.5	(98)	65.8	(38)	69.3	(75)
1959	55.6	(54)	50.4	(121)	45.5	(44)	35.5	(93)
1960	65.1	(43)	65.1	(86)	61.5	(39)	55.9	(68)
Mean	68.4		70.7		57.4		61.0	
JFK								
1961	83.1	(65)	80.8	(125)	78.0	(50)	77.4	(106)
1962	85.0	(60)	84.9	(126)	79.1	(43)	79.6	(93)
1963	83.1	(71)	88.8	(116)	77.8	(54)	84.5	(84)
Mean	83.7		84.7		78.2		80.2	
LBJ								
1964	88.5	(52)	91.2	(203)	84.6	(39)	90.4	(167)
1965	93.8	(112)	91.9	(162)	90.7	(75)	89.4	(123)
1966	89.4	(104)	68.0	(125)	84.5	(71)	55.1	(89)
1967	75.6	(127)	81.4	(167)	62.2	(82)	71.0	(107)
1968	83.5	(103)	69.1	(165)	72.1	(61)	58.5	(123)
Mean	85.5		81.6		78.0		75.2	
RMN								
1969	72.3	(47)	74.6	(71)	61.8	(34)	64.7	(51)
1970	84.6	(65)	71.4	(91)	73.0	(37)	53.6	(56)
1971	82.1	(56)	69.5	(82)	77.8	(45)	60.3	(63)
1972	81.1	(37)	54.3	(46)	76.7	(30)	38.2	(34)
1973	48.0	(125)	52.4	(185)	38.7	(106)	30.7	(127)
1974	67.9	(53)	54.2	(83)	57.5	(40)	47.2	(72)
Mean	68.1		61.3		58.2		46.4	

Table 3.1 (*Continued*)

PRESIDENT AND YEAR	ALL VOTES				CONFLICTUAL VOTES			
	House		Senate		House		Senate	
	%	(N)	%	(N)	%	(N)	%	(N)
GRF								
1974	59.3	(54)	57.4	(68)	43.6	(39)	44.2	(52)
1975	50.6	(89)	71.6	(95)	43.6	(78)	57.8	(64)
1976	43.1	(51)	64.2	(53)	37.0	(46)	50.0	(38)
Mean	51.0		65.3		41.7		51.3	
JEC								
1977	74.7	(79)	76.4	(89)	66.1	(59)	65.0	(60)
1978	70.2	(114)	84.8	(151)	64.2	(95)	81.6	(125)
1979	71.7	(145)	81.4	(161)	66.4	(122)	75.4	(122)
1980	76.9	(117)	73.3	(116)	69.7	(89)	65.2	(89)
Mean	73.2		79.7		66.6		73.5	
RWR								
1981	72.4	(76)	88.3	(128)	66.7	(63)	82.1	(84)
1982	55.8	(77)	82.5	(120)	41.4	(58)	77.7	(94)
1983	47.6	(82)	85.7	(84)	46.3	(80)	82.6	(69)
1984	52.2	(113)	85.7	(77)	44.3	(97)	81.0	(58)
Mean	56.3		85.6		49.0		80.7	

Source: *Congressional Quarterly Almanac, 1953–84* (annual editions). Percentages recalculated in years in which the number of presidential wins and losses in *CQ*'s summary did not match the numbers found in the roll call votes.

cludes nonconflictual presidential victories.[15] Excluding nonconflictual presidential wins lowers the president's success rate in each year, but the two methods produce similar trends.

Figure 3.1 plots the trends for the House and the Senate using both measures. A cursory inspection of the trends suggests that excluding nonconflictual wins merely shifts the trends slightly downward, but otherwise the two measures seem to track the ebb and flow of presidential success in essentially

15. In a few years our calculation of the success rate based on all votes does not match the percentage reported by CQ. The largest difference occurs in the Senate in 1964, when CQ used only 10 of 116 presidential roll calls on the 1964 Civil Rights Act. In fifteen other years we found that CQ's summary miscounted between one and three votes, which altered the success rate a small amount (less than 1 percent in each case except the 1966 House score, in which the correction lowered the score from 91.3 to 89.4).

Figure 3.1 Presidential Victories on Roll Call Votes in the House and Senate

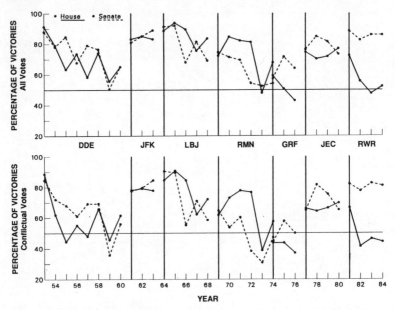

the same way for all presidents. A closer analysis of the two measures, however, reveals a systematic difference. The percentage change in success rates with and without nonconflictual votes is systematically related to whether the president's party controls the chamber—the scores of minority presidents are inflated more by nonconflictual wins than are those of majority presidents. The correlations (Pearson's r) between party control of the chamber and the presidency (1 = same, 0 = different) and percentage change in success rates with and without nonconflictual wins are $-.41$ in the House and $-.61$ in the Senate. Thus excluding noncontroversial issues removes some systematic partisan bias from the measure of support.

The aggregate trends from 1953 to 1984 reveal that presidential success on conflictual roll calls varies substantially across presidents, and over time and across chambers within administrations. Comparing across presidents, we see that presidents tend to win more votes if their party controls the chamber, but there is substantial variation for both majority and minority presidents. Based on the experience of the seven presidents in this study, if the president's party has a majority, he wins an average of 74.7 percent of House roll calls and 76.3 percent of Senate roll calls. The standard deviations around these

Table 3.2 Ranking of Presidents according to Success Rate on Conflictual Votes

	HOUSE			SENATE	
Rank	President	Mean % Wins	Rank	President	Mean % Wins
1	JFK	78.2	1	RWR	80.7
2	LBJ	78.0	2	JFK	80.2
	(DDE—83rd	76.6)*		(DDE–83rd	77.0)*
3	JEC	66.6	3	LBJ	75.2
4	RMN	58.2	4	JEC	73.5
5	DDE	57.4	5	DDE	61.0
6	RWR	49.0	6	GRF	51.3
7	GRF	41.7	7	RMN	46.4

Source: Table 3.1.
*Eisenhower's success rate in the Republican-controlled 83rd Congress.

means are 9.9 percent in the House and 10.0 percent in the Senate. If the opposition party controls the chamber, the president's success rate drops to an average of 54.1 percent in the House and 53.7 percent in the Senate, and the standard deviations increase to 13.2 percent in the House and 12.5 percent in the Senate. Thus majority status gives the president an advantage, but it does not guarantee consistent victories. Conversely, minority presidents are frequently able to secure majority support on the House and Senate floors.

Table 3.2 ranks the presidents according to their average success rates in the House and Senate. As expected, majority presidents cluster in the top half and minority presidents fall into the bottom half. The rankings within party are mostly as expected, but there are some surprises. Contrary to the general perception that Johnson was more successful than Kennedy in dealing with Congress, we find that Kennedy was the most successful Democratic president in both chambers. In the House the difference between Kennedy and Johnson is trivial, but in the Senate Johnson is five points lower. It is important to remember, however, that the data here reflect success on conflictual issues that reached the floor. President Johnson may have been more successful than Kennedy in getting his policies to the floor, and Johnson may have won more votes by lopsided margins. Consistent with conventional wisdom, President Carter was less successful than his Democratic predecessors, but the difference is mainly in the House. Carter's success rate in the House is about eleven points below those of Kennedy and Johnson and about eight points above that of the most successful minority president (Nixon); in the Senate, however, his success rate is only slightly lower than Johnson's.

Eisenhower and Reagan are the only Republican presidents in our study who enjoyed majority status, but Republican control of Congress during their administrations was brief or incomplete: Republicans controlled both chambers by narrow margins during the first two years of Eisenhower's presidency (the 83rd Congress), and Republicans controlled only the Senate during Reagan's first term. When Eisenhower and Reagan enjoyed majority status, their success rates were typical of those of Democratic presidents. Eisenhower's success in the 83rd House is 76.6 percent, only slightly lower than Kennedy and Johnson and ten points above Carter. His success rate of 77 percent in the 83rd Senate is slightly above Johnson's and Carter's and slightly below Reagan's and Kennedy's. President Reagan won slightly more often than Kennedy in the Senate for the top ranking.

Republican presidents are less successful when their party is in the minority, but the effects of minority status vary greatly. In the House, Reagan was less successful than both Nixon and Eisenhower; only President Ford had a lower success rate in the House. President Nixon was the most successful minority president in the House and the least successful in the Senate. President Eisenhower, who was a minority president for six of his eight years in office, was about equally successful in both chambers, ranking as the most successful minority president in the Senate and second in the House.[16] President Ford won less than half of the conflictual roll calls in the House and only slightly more than half in the Senate.

The trends over time within administration also exhibit substantial variation. There is a tendency for success to decline over the course of a president's term. Eisenhower, Johnson, Nixon, and Reagan (in the House) experienced declining success over the course of their terms. Kennedy, Carter, and Reagan (in the Senate) experienced relatively constant success rates over time. In general, it seems that minority presidents are more subject to declining support over the course of their term, while the trends for majority presidents (except President Johnson) are flatter and in some cases increasing. Johnson's success rates in both chambers deteriorated from levels higher than any other president in the study to levels more typical of minority presidents. President Reagan's record during his first term illustrates the generalization well. In the Democrat-controlled House he experienced sharply declining support; in the Republian-controlled Senate he experienced slightly increasing support.

16. Excluding the 83rd Congress from the calculations lowers Eisenhower's scores but does not change the ranking.

Comparisons across chambers reveal no consistent pattern. Except in the case of Reagan, who faced a divided Congress, success rates in the two chambers tend to start out at similar levels at the beginning of the president's term and then diverge over time. Even with the same party in control of both chambers, the House and Senate do not respond to the president in the same way. Kennedy tended to do better in the Senate over the course of his three years in office, but the differences are small. Johnson and Nixon, both with extensive Senate experience, tended to win less often in the Senate, and the precipitous decline in success for both started first in the Senate. Ford, whose congressional experience was limited to the House, and Carter both had greater success in the Senate. Eisenhower was generally more successful in the Senate during the first six years of his presidency and more successful in the House during his last two years.

Important versus Less Important Issues

Thus far we have looked at trends in success using all conflictual votes. While focusing on conflictual votes eliminates most trivial and routine issues, some controversial issues are more important than others. We need to consider whether presidential success is systematically different on important issues.

The previous section discussed two ways to identify important votes: (1) CQ's key votes and (2) Riker's method based on turnout and closeness of the vote. Neither of these methods focuses exclusively on votes that are important to the president or to his program. But as we argued previously, the president's subjective evaluation of importance is only one criterion for defining significant issues involving interaction between the president and Congress. The combination of CQ's key votes and votes identified as most important using Riker's method based on congressional behavior yields a reasonable subset of important issues on which the president and Congress interact.[17] These roll calls are likely to include most issues that are important to the president and on which presidential activity is high. Even though some of these votes may not be part of the president's program, they are votes that are important for other reasons, and the president has expressed a public position on them.[18]

17. Riker (1956) presents a formula for calculating a coefficient of significance (s) that ranges between zero and one with values closer to one indicating the most significant roll calls. Following Riker's illustration we included all presidential roll calls with significance coefficients greater than or equal to .90 in our subset of more important issues. Thus, we define important issues as all key votes and other roll calls with s-coefficients of .90 or greater. With this definition, 21 percent ($n = 388$) of House votes and 14 percent ($n = 360$) of Senate votes are included in the more important category. This division between more important and less important votes is reasonable and still identifies enough votes for analysis.

18. A spot check of some of the specific votes suggests that this method picks up issues of great importance to the president (e.g., the two Gramm-Latta votes and the tax cut vote in 1981) but excludes the more routine issues on which the president takes a stand.

Table 3.3 Presidential Success on Important Roll Calls in the House and Senate, 83rd–98th Congresses

PRESIDENT AND CONGRESS	HOUSE				SENATE			
	Important		Other		Important		Other	
	%	(N)	%	(N)	%	(N)	%	(N)
DDE								
83rd (1953–54)	78.6	(14)	75.8	(33)	70.0	(10)	77.5	(89)
84th (1955–56)	40.0	(15)	53.1	(32)	47.1	(17)	67.7	(62)
85th (1957–58)	55.6	(18)	55.9	(68)	78.6	(14)	68.0	(100)
86th (1959–60)	82.4	(17)	45.5	(66)	57.1	(21)	42.1	(140)
JFK								
87th (1961–62)	65.4	(26)	83.6	(67)	70.0	(20)	79.3	(179)
88th (1963)	84.6	(13)	79.3	(29)	67.7	(6)	83.8	(68)
LBJ								
88th (1964)	83.3	(12)	79.5	(39)	69.2	(13)	92.3	(164)
89th (1965–66)	81.5	(27)	87.4	(119)	71.4	(46)	75.4	(191)
90th (1967–68)	57.1	(21)	68.0	(122)	70.8	(24)	63.6	(206)
RMN								
91st (1969–70)	76.5	(17)	64.8	(54)	57.9	(19)	59.1	(88)
92nd (1971–72)	69.2	(13)	79.0	(62)	46.2	(26)	54.9	(71)
93rd (1973–74)	41.7	(24)	45.1	(122)	70.8	(24)	33.7	(178)
GRF								
93rd (1974)	50.0	(4)	41.2	(34)	66.7	(3)	37.8	(45)
94th (1975–76)	48.2	(27)	39.2	(97)	63.2	(19)	53.0	(83)
JEC								
95th (1977–78)	75.0	(28)	62.7	(126)	64.7	(17)	77.4	(168)
96th (1979–80)	72.7	(33)	68.0	(178)	67.7	(34)	71.8	(177)
RWR								
97th (1981–82)	70.0	(30)	49.5	(91)	74.4	(39)	81.3	(139)
98th (1983–84)	57.1	(49)	38.3	(128)	81.8	(33)	81.9	(94)

Table 3.3 presents presidential success on our subset of more important votes. In general, the forces that cause success on important votes are the same as those that cause success on less important votes. The effect of party control is similar on both types of issues. In the House, majority presidents win an average of 74.8 percent of important votes, while minority presidents win an aver-

Table 3.4 Ranking of Presidents according to Success Rate on Important Votes

HOUSE			SENATE		
Rank	President	Mean % Wins	Rank	President	Mean % Wins
	(DDE—83rd)	78.6)*	1	RWR	77.8
1	JEC	73.8	2	LBJ	71.1
2	LBJ	73.3		(DDE—83rd)	70.0)*
3	JFK	71.8	3	JFK	69.2
4	DDE	64.1	4	JEC	66.7
5	RWR	62.0	5	GRF	63.6
	(DDE—minority	60.0)**	6	DDE	61.3
6	RMN	59.3		(DDE—minority	59.6)**
7	GRF	48.4	7	RMN	58.0

*Eisenhower's success rate in the Republican-controlled 83rd Congress.
**Eisenhower's success rate in Democratic-controlled Congresses.

age of 60.1 percent. In the Senate, the average for majority presidents is 70.7 percent, compared to 60.2 percent for minority presidents.

Furthermore, we find no tendency for presidents to be more successful on important votes than on other votes. One might expect that success would be higher on important issues because the president's effort to influence the outcome is greater. Although we do not have a direct measure of presidential activity on these roll calls, it is reasonable to infer that important votes on which the president expresses a position are also ones on which he actively seeks to influence the outcome.[19]

Even though the average level of presidential activity across our subset of important votes is probably higher than the average on other votes, the success rate is not consistently higher on important issues. Every president in our study experienced greater success on important votes in some Congresses and greater success on less important votes in other Congresses. The only apparent systematic difference is that minority presidents tend to do slightly better on important issues than on less important issues. In the House, the average difference between success on important votes and success on other issues is

19. Recall that our important votes include key votes and close votes on which turnout is high. One of CQ's criteria for designating a roll call a key vote is that it is "a test of presidential . . . power." And Covington (1987a) has shown that presidents often mobilize their supporters on votes that are important to them, thereby increasing turnout.

6.8 percent for minority presidents and −0.7 percent for majority presidents. In the Senate, the average differences are 6.9 percent for minority presidents and −7.7 percent for majority presidents. These differences, however, are not great, and the variance around the means is large. Thus variation in the importance of issues does not provide a strong explanation of variation in presidential success.

Success on important issues, however, is not the same as success on all conflictual votes. The correlations between the two measures are .59 in the House and .39 in the Senate, indicating that, although success on important votes is related to overall success, other forces come into play on important issues. These differences might lead to different conclusions about the relative success of presidents. For instance, the ranking of presidents on important votes is slightly different than the ranking based on all conflictual votes.

Table 3.4 ranks the presidents according to success on important votes. Although the rankings here are similar to the rankings based on all votes ($r =$ .75 in the House and .93 in the Senate), there are some important differences. The greatest difference occurs in how Carter compares to other majority presidents. In the Senate his position in the ranking is the same as in table 3.2, but in the House Carter is the most successful Democratic president on important votes. And Eisenhower's success on important votes in the Republican-controlled 83rd Congress ranks him as the most successful president in the House. In addition, Johnson ranks slightly ahead of Kennedy in both chambers, a result more consistent with conventional evaluations of the Kennedy and Johnson presidencies. Looking back to table 3.3, we see that the change in rankings in this case occurs because Kennedy was much less successful on important votes than on other conflictual issues in the 87th Congress (1961– 62). But by the 88th Congress, Kennedy's success rate was about the same on both types of votes. Otherwise, the rankings based on important votes are the same as the rankings based on all conflictual issues.

In conclusion, our analysis of important presidential roll calls revealed some small yet notable differences. Although the importance of issues per se does not explain differences in presidential success, the findings suggest that this variable should be incorporated as a control in the analysis to determine if the importance of the issue alters or conditions the relationships.

Hence inspection of aggregate trends in presidential success reveals substantial variation. We now turn our attention to analyzing the impact of each of the linkage agents on presidential success, beginning with the partisan and ideological makeup of Congress.

CHAPTER 4

PARTY, IDEOLOGY, AND PRESIDENTIAL SUCCESS

The inauguration of John Kennedy as president in 1961 was accompanied by much optimism. Democrats had recaptured control of the White House after eight years of lackluster Republican leadership and maintained large majorities in both houses of Congress. The youthful idealism of the new president was contagious as he promised to "get this country moving again" and called upon all Americans "to bear the burden of a long twilight struggle . . . against the common enemies of man: tyranny, poverty, disease and war itself." [1]

During the next two years, the Democrat-controlled 87th Congress translated some of this idealism into programs. Some of Kennedy's major legislative accomplishments include permanent authorization of the Peace Corps, minimum wage increases and extension, increases in Social Security benefits, a $4.9 billion housing bill, approval of a United States Arms Control and Disarmament Agency, five-year authorizations for foreign aid, Senate ratification of the Organization for Economic Cooperation and Development convention, and passage of the Trade Expansion Act of 1962 (Congressional Quarterly 1965, 45).

Yet despite the idealism and the political advantages of unified party control, relations between Kennedy and the 87th Congress were not always smooth. "Congressional apprehension about use of political power by the new Administration, and a continuing 'conservative coalition' between Southern Democrats and Republicans . . . tended to slow down if not wreck parts of Kennedy's program" (Congressional Quarterly 1965, 43).

Kennedy's experience with Congress is typical. For example, Congressional Quarterly similarly summed up Carter's first year in office: "Abrasive confrontation with Congress seemed to be the norm—not the harmony expected from having a president and a congressional majority of the same party in Washington for the first time in eight years" (Congressional Quarterly 1981, 957). Unlike executives in parliamentary systems, the United States president

---

1. From Kennedy's inaugural address, quoted in Congressional Quarterly, Inc. (1965, 41).

cannot count on members of his party to support his policy preferences. Even with unified party control, the American system guarantees conflict between the president and Congress. As Neustadt (1960, 33) says, "What the Constitution separates our political parties do not combine."

Yet few would go so far as to argue that majority status is irrelevant to presidential success. Certainly Lyndon Johnson's success in winning passage of the Great Society from an overwhelming Democratic majority in Congress and, at the other end of the continuum, Gerald Ford's frustration at having to resort to the veto as the only effective strategy for dealing with a Congress dominated by the opposition party are images that most observers remember. Previously we noted that shared partisan interests serve to link the president and members of Congress. Congress is a partisan institution, and according to Paul Light, party support "is the chief ingredient in presidential capital; it is the 'gold standard' of congressional support" (Light 1983, 27). A member of President Johnson's legislative liaison staff noted, "The President's legislative success starts with party. It's that simple" (quoted in Light 1983, 27).

While there is no denying that parties link the interests of the president and members of Congress, compared to that in most western democracies, the partisan linkage in the United States is weak. The president's success rate increases as the size of his party increases, but the relationship is not especially strong.[2] Despite the party link, Congress and the presidency remain separate, autonomous institutions.

In modern European parliamentary systems, legislatures have tended to lose autonomy to the executive. Malcolm Jewell (1973, 204) argues that the lack of legislative autonomy in parliamentary democracies "is largely because a single party with a majority in the legislature has a high degree of cohesion and provides consistent support to its leader—the prime minister." Cohesion is high in parliamentary systems because members of a given party tend to share the prevailing ideology of their party. Party leaders have authority to discipline defectors, but coercing party members in parliament to support the prime minister is typically unnecessary. Because party leaders control nominations, most candidates with incompatible ideologies are filtered out before the election.

---

2. The correlations (Pearson's r) between the percentage of presidential victories in a Congress and the number of seats held by the president's party are .64 in the House and .49 in the Senate. These correlations measure the association between party seats and variation in aggregate success across Congresses. But presidential success also varies from one vote to another within a Congress. Because party seats in each chamber are constant between elections (except for relatively minor variation resulting from absences and vacancies), percent party cannot explain variation in presidential wins and losses within a Congress. Thus, the correlations between the president's success on each roll call (win/lose) and number of party seats are much weaker ($r =$ .23 in the House and .11 in the Senate).

American parties, in contrast lack cohesion and discipline. The president is the nominal head of his party, but members of his party in Congress have little to say about his selection or the policy positions he takes. And the reverse is also true: the president has little control over who wears his party's label in Congress or the policies they support. To be nominated, elected, and reelected, members of Congress must satisfy local political preferences. Supporting positions of the national party and the president that conflict with local interests can be costly; the costs of opposing the national party and the president are minimal. This electoral system produces ideological diversity within each party and low levels of party cohesion and discipline.

This chapter explores the extent to which undisciplined, ideologically diverse parties link the policy preferences of the president and members of Congress. The discussion above suggests that the low level of party cohesion in Congress is a function of (1) ideological diversity in the parties and (2) the absence of formal authority to control nominations and discipline members. Although we can only speculate about the effects of increasing party leaders' authority to control nominations and discipline members, the theoretical framework described in chapter 2 permits us to observe the effects of ideological diversity on presidential success in Congress.

CONGRESSIONAL PARTIES: FOUR-PARTY POLITICS

To review briefly, our theoretical framework accounts for ideological diversity in Congress by dividing members into four ideologically homogenous party factions ("four-party politics").[3] Nationally, the mainstream of the Democratic party is generally liberal; the mainstream of the Republican party is more conservative. But each party has a minority faction composed of members who have a general ideological orientation different from most of their fellow partisans—i.e., conservative Democrats and liberal Republicans.

There is a geographical cast to the party factions—many conservative Democrats are from the south; many liberal Republicans are from the northeast. Consequently, a common method of dealing with the ideological diversity in the parties is to divide members along regional lines. As a measure of ideology, however, region is an indirect and imprecise indicator. We have the ability to measure the ideological orientation of members of Congress more precisely in order to identify the members of the minority factions regardless of the region from which they come.

The interaction of party and ideology affects members' propensity to support the president's positions on roll call votes. Members of Congress, there-

3. Apologies to James MacGregor Burns. See his *The Deadlock of Democracy: Four-Party Politics in America* (1963).

fore, may be viewed as falling into one of four conceptually distinct party factions: (1) the president's political base, (2) cross-pressured members of the president's party, (3) cross-pressured members of the opposition party, and (4) the opposition political base.

The president's political base includes those members who have the greatest predisposition to support his preferences, because they share with the president both a party affiliation and an ideological outlook (i.e., liberal Democrats for Democratic presidents and conservative Republicans for Republican presidents). Cross-pressured members are individuals with ideologies outside their party's mainstream (i.e., conservative Democrats and liberal Republicans). For these members, party and ideology often provide conflicting cues, and the resulting cross-pressure prevents them from being considered part of the political base of any president. The opposition political base is the mirror image of the president's base (i.e., conservative Republicans for Democratic presidents and liberal Democrats for Republican presidents).[4]

In chapter 2, we suggested that the four-faction conceptualization of congressional parties yielded two empirical propositions. First, among their own partisans, presidents should receive more support from the base than from the cross-pressured. Among opposition party members, presidents should receive less support from the base than from the cross-pressured group. The second and more important proposition relates to party unity. If ideological diversity is the primary cause of the lack of discipline in American parties, then the behavior of the more ideologically homogeneous party bases should be closer to the responsible party model—i.e., the president's party base should unify in support of his preferences, and the opposition base should unify against.

Before examining the behavior of the party factions and the consequences of such behavior for presidential success, we need to consider how deep the ideological divisions in congressional parties actually are. The following section describes the sizes of the party factions during the period of our study.

THE FOUR PARTY FACTIONS

Definition and Measurement

To define the party factions operationally, we use the mean liberalism score for each party to determine the party mainstreams in each Congress. Using the mean party liberalism in each Congress permits the measure to reflect any

---

4. As noted in chapter 2, while this conceptualization is similar to the four-party politics argument in Burns (1963), our framework views Republicans differently. Burns viewed liberal Republicans as the "presidential wing" of the party; our framework views them as the cross-pressured faction that is expected to be less supportive of Republican presidents than is the conservative Republican base.

changes in the ideological positions of the parties over the three decades covered in this study. Cross-pressured members are defined as those who have liberalism scores closer to the mean of the opposition party than to the mean of their party. Members of the political bases are those who have liberalism scores closer to the mean of their party than to the opposition party mean.[5]

Two potential problems arise from operationalizing the party factions in such a manner. First, the use of the party means to define whether or not a member is cross-pressured is an arbitrary decision rule. If some other value had been used, the placement of members might have been different. Second, the division of each of the parties into two factions still results in groups that are ideologically heterogeneous.

In terms of the first problem, using the mean as the basis for placing members into factions is no more arbitrary than other alternatives. Another reasonable measure is the median ideological position in each party. While the mean tends to be slightly lower for Democrats and higher for Republicans than the corresponding medians, our decision rule uses the midpoint between the two values to determine whether a member's ideology is closer to the other party's ideological mainstream. Because the midpoint between the party means is not much different than the midpoint between the two medians, either measure results in a similar placement of members. Another solution would have been to define cross-pressured members as those who are more than one (or two) standard deviations away from their party mean. This operationalization is also arbitrary. Moreover, using the standard deviation would not necessarily produce a more valid measure of cross-pressures, because members who are more than one standard deviation away from their party mean could still be closer to their party's ideological mainstream than to the opposition party. After carefully considering these alternatives, we decided that the midpoint between the means provided a reasonable dividing line between a party's base and its cross-pressured members.[6]

The second problem is potentially more serious. Even after eliminating the members of the party who are cross-pressured, we are still left with party bases that are ideologically heterogeneous, although less so than the party as a whole. We believe, however, that the partisan groupings are not so heterogeneous that it makes comparison to parliamentary parties unwise. Even parliamentary parties are made up of individuals who hold a range of ideological viewpoints. Kenneth Janda's (1980) cross-national study of political parties revealed that ideological factionalism was not uncommon in Western par-

---

5. A discussion of the votes used to define a member's ideology can be found in appendix A.
6. In a typical Congress, the midpoint between the party means is approximately fifty on a zero to one hundred scale.

liamentary democracies. For example, the British Labour party, the Canadian Progressive Conservative party, and the French Radical Socialist party scored as high on his measure of ideological factionalism as did congressional Democrats and Republicans. And note that Janda's measure was across the full ideological range of the parties, so the party bases in our analysis are less ideologically diverse than these parliamentary parties. Furthermore, the standards that we will use to judge whether the party bases are acting consistently with the model do not require unanimity or even near unanimity. Although the division of the parties into two factions does not completely eliminate ideological diversity, we do not believe that the remaining heterogeneity biases the analysis against finding party cohesion.

Having dealt with how we defined and measured the party factions, we can now turn out attention to describing the sizes of the party factions over the period of the study.

Size of the Party Factions

The relative size of the party factions in Congress determines whether the president will interact with a more or less favorable cast of actors when he enters the legislative arena. At any given time, the number of members in each party faction is fixed. Every two years, however, the electoral process changes the cast of congressional actors. One of the most persistent patterns in American politics is the tendency for the president's party in Congress to pick up seats during the presidential election but to lose them in the midterm elections. During the period of our study, the president's party lost House seats in every midterm election and Senate seats in five of the eight midterms. Compared to those in earlier periods in American history, partisan seat swings in Congress during the post–World War II period have been relatively small.

In the Senate, the tendency for the president's party to gain seats during the presidential election but to lose seats during the midterm has not been nearly as strong in the House. The lack of a pattern in the Senate is probably the result of the staggered election years and six-year terms. Only one-third of Senate seats are up for election at a time, and the seats that are up at midterm often come disproportionately from one party. Sometimes the president's party has the most seats at stake; at other times the opposition party has more. Because the party with the most seats up for election is likely to suffer the greater loss, the president may be protected from losing Senate seats if his party does not have many at stake.[7]

Table 4.1 presents the number of members in each party faction in the

---

7. A recent analysis of seat change in Senate elections demonstrates that the relative number of seats at stake is a strong predictor. Other things being equal (e.g., the condition of the economy), the president's party will lose about one seat for every three seats it has at stake over the opposition party (Abramowitz and Segal 1986, 436–37).

Table 4.1 Sizes of the Party Factions

PRESIDENT AND CONGRESS	HOUSE				SENATE			
	President's Base	Cross-Pressured Partisans	Cross-Pressured Opposition	Opposition Base	President's Base	Cross-Pressured Partisans	Cross-Pressured Opposition	Opposition Base
DDE								
83rd	201	19	43	170	36	12	13	35
84th	129	74	74	157	44	3	12	36
85th	178	22	37	196	34	13	15	34
86th	141	12	33	248	23	11	21	45
JFK								
87th	188	74	31	143	42	22	11	25
88th	166	90	32	146	45	22	8	25
LBJ								
89th	203	91	19	121	51	16	4	29
90th	180	65	16	173	44	20	9	27
RMN								
91st	160	31	81	162	31	11	17	41
92nd	146	34	75	179	32	12	18	38
93rd	157	35	62	180	28	14	15	43
GRF								
94th	120	22	68	224	25	13	15	47
JEC								
95th	223	66	21	124	44	18	12	26
96th	230	45	16	143	51	8	7	34
RWR								
97th	168	24	51	191	43	10	13	34
98th	150	17	25	242	43	11	9	37

Note: Entries are number of members in each party faction. Numbers may not sum to the total for the chamber because of vacancies.

83rd to the 98th Congresses (1953–84). The size of presidential political bases in Congress varies considerably. One source of variation is majority or minority status. As one would expect, majority presidents typically have larger bases than minority presidents. The average size of the political base for majority presidents is 199 in the House and 44 in the Senate, compared to average bases for minority presidents of 150 in the House and 31 in the Senate.

But there is substantial variation around the average base sizes of both majority and minority presidents. The upper size of the base for minority presidents (e.g., Eisenhower in the 84th Senate and the 85th House) was larger than the smallest base for majority presidents (e.g., Kennedy in the 87th Senate and the 88th House). The largest political bases exceeded an absolute majority, but this situation occurred only twice in each chamber (the 95th and 96th Houses and the 89th and 96th Senates). The smallest political base in each chamber (Ford's in the 94th Congress) constituted only about one-fourth of the seats.

Thus ideological diversity in both parties reduces the number of members of the president's party who are most predisposed to support his positions. Does the degree of ideological diversity vary across the parties?

Ideological Diversity of Democrats and Republicans

Conventional wisdom argues that the ideological split is much worse in the Democratic party than in the Republican party. In terms of actual numbers of members, cross-pressured Democrats typically outnumber cross-pressured Republicans. Democratic presidents normally interacted with an average of seventy-two conservative Democrats in the House and less than one-third that many liberal Republicans (mean = 27). In the Senate, Democratic presidents usually interacted with twice as many conservative Democrats (mean = 18) as liberal Republicans (mean = 9). Republican presidents were less disadvantaged by ideological spits. In the House, Republican presidents had nearly twice as many conservative Democrats (mean = 55) to make up for votes lost from liberal Republicans (mean = 29). In the Senate, Republican presidents had about equal numbers of conservative Democrats (mean = 13) and liberal Republicans (mean = 11).

As a proportion of party members, however, the ideological split is worse for Democrats only in the House. An average of 25 percent of House Democrats are cross-pressured compared to an average of 15 percent of House Republicans. In the Senate, the proportion of cross-pressured members is similar for both parties—25 percent of Republicans and 27 percent of Democrats. Thus in the Senate, Republican and Democratic presidents typically interact with parties of similar ideological diversity.

Furthermore, the ideological splits have declined over time in both par-

Table 4.2 Average Percentage of President's Party in the Cross-Pressured Faction

Party and President	House %	House (N)*	Senate %	Senate (N)*
Democrats				
JFK	32	(82)	34	(22)
LBJ	28	(78)	28	(18)
JEC	20	(56)	22	(13)
Republicans				
DDE	16	(32)	23	(10)
RMN	18	(33)	29	(12)
GRF	15	(22)	34	(13)
RWR	11	(21)	20	(11)

*Average number of cross-pressured partisans.

ties. Table 4.2 reports the average proportion of each president's party in the cross-pressured faction. Among Democratic presidents, Kennedy was disadvantaged the most by the ideological diversity of American parties. Although Kennedy had large Democratic majorities in both chambers, about one-third were conservatives with ideologies closer to the average Republican. Subsequent Democratic presidents also had large majorities, but the proportion of conservative Democrats declined monotonically over time. Johnson's Democratic majorities contained about 28 percent conservatives; Carter's majorities contained about 20 percent conservatives.

Although the trend in the proportion of cross-pressured Republicans over time is less pronounced, there was a decline during the Reagan administration. There were only 11 percent liberal Republicans in the House and 20 percent in the Senate during Reagan's first term. These proportions are lower than the averages of 17 percent in the House and 27 percent in the Senate for the three previous Republican presidents. Until Reagan's first term, however, the ideological diversity among Senate Republicans increased from less than one-fourth in the cross-pressured faction under Eisenhower to about one-third under Ford.

Also note that in the House, all three Democratic presidents had cross-pressured factions proportionally greater than those of Republican presidents. But Kennedy is the only Democrat who had a cross-pressured faction larger than that of most Republican presidents in the Senate as well as the House.

Table 4.3 Average Percentage of Party Factions Supporting the President

PRESIDENT	House				Senate			
	President's Base	Cross-Pressured Partisans	Cross-Pressured Opposition	Opposition Base	President's Base	Cross-Pressured Partisans	Cross-Pressured Opposition	Opposition Base
DDE	63	65	31	45	75	66	43	35
JFK	90	52	46	23	81	52	52	27
LBJ	87	42	57	24	74	40	71	42
RMN	67	55	52	35	71	44	50	26
GRF	64	48	47	28	73	43	52	25
JEC	70	38	56	27	72	52	69	30
RWR	68	45	53	26	78	62	53	27

Note: Entries are the average percentage of faction members voting in agreement with the president's position.

BEHAVIOR OF THE PARTY FACTIONS

Our analytical framework assumes that the interaction of members' party and ideology creates different predispositions to support the president's preferences on roll call votes. Furthermore, we hypothesized that each of the party bases would provide levels of support and opposition more similar to that of cohesive parliamentary parties. In the American system, however, even members of Congress who are predisposed to support the president may fail to do so. Thus, before analyzing unity of the party factions, we need to look at average levels of presidential support provided by the four party factions to determine if behavior is consistent with our assumptions about members' predispositions.

Average Levels of Support

Table 4.3 reports average levels of support for the president from each party faction. In general, the members of the various party factions behave as expected. The president typically attracts the most support from his political base and the least support from the opposition base. Cross-pressured members of both parties are usually quite divided, and average support from these two factions is normally somewhere in between that of the two party bases. Support is sometimes higher from the president's cross-pressured partisans and sometimes higher from cross-pressured members of the opposition, but there is no regular pattern.

There are, however, some exceptions to the expected patterns of support form the various party factions. Eisenhower, for example, attracted slightly more support from cross-pressured liberal Republicans (mean = 65%) than from the conservative Republican base (mean = 63%) in the House. And support from the liberal Democratic base in the House was higher (mean = 45%) than support from cross-pressured conservative Democrats (mean = 31%). In the Senate, the patterns of support for Eisenhower are as expected, but he did well with liberals in the upper chamber also. Levels of support for Eisenhower from liberal Republicans (mean = 66%) and from liberal Democrats (mean = 35%) were higher than for other Republican presidents.

Eisenhower's moderate ideology may account for this pattern of support. While he was no liberal, he was considerably less conservative than the average Republican member of Congress.[8] Eisenhower's moderate policy positions may have created a climate in which the predispositions of members of the party factions were altered—conservative Republicans and liberal Democrats may have been more cross-pressured than under other Republican presidents; liberal Republicans and conservative Democrats may have been less cross-pressured. Relative to other Republican presidents, therefore, Eisenhower tended to attract more support from liberals and less support from conservatives.

Both Democratic and Republican presidents experience defections in their political bases. Although conventional wisdom suggests that Republicans in Congress are more cohesive than Democrats, we find that liberal Democrats are often more supportive of Democratic presidents than conservative Republicans are of Republican presidents. In the Senate, the averages are only 2 percent higher for Democrats—Democratic presidents receive votes from an average of 76 percent of their base; Republicans receive an average of 74 percent of theirs. In the House, however, levels of support from the president's base are an average of 16 percent higher for Democratic presidents—Democratic presidents receive an average of 82 percent of their base compared to an average of 66 percent for Republican presidents. And while liberal Democrats were unusually supportive of Kennedy and Johnson, even Carter had a higher average support rate from his political base than did any Republican president.

Defections in the president's political base reduce its *effective* size. The effective size of the president's political base is indicated by the number of

8. We used ADA and ACA votes on which the president expressed a position to calculate how often each president took a liberal position. Note that these presidential roll calls were excluded from the calculations of representatives' ideology used to define the four party factions. A liberal position is agreement with ADA or disagreement with ACA.

Table 4.4 Effective Size of the President's Party Base

PRESIDENT AND CONGRESS	HOUSE		SENATE	
	Average Number of Votes	% of Majority	Average Number of Votes	% of Majority
DDE				
83rd	127	58%	27	55%
84th	81	37%	33	67%
85th	112	51%	26	53%
86th	89	41%	17	35%
JFK				
87th	169	78%	34	69%
88th	149	68%	36	71%
LBJ				
89th	177	81%	38	75%
90th	157	72%	32	63%
RMN				
91st	107	49%	22	43%
92nd	98	45%	23	45%
93rd	105	48%	20	39%
GRF				
94th	77	35%	18	35%
JEC				
95th	156	72%	32	63%
96th	161	74%	37	73%
RWR				
97th	114	52%	34	67%
98th	102	47%	34	67%
Mean	124	57%	29	57%

votes it normally produces in support of the president's position (number of members × average support). Table 4.4 shows the effective size of the president's political base in the 83rd to the 98th Congresses.

Discounting the size of the president's base with the normal behavior of its members does not diminish differences between majority and minority presidents. In fact, the differences are accentuated in the House. Majority presidents in the House received an average of 157 votes from their political base; minority presidents received an average of 98 votes from theirs. Thus, compared to minority presidents, majority presidents had an average of 49 more members in their political base, but they received an average of 59 more votes. In the Senate, majority presidents received an average of 34 votes from their base compared to an average of 23 votes for minority presidents. This eleven-vote advantage for majority presidents is about the same as the thirteen-seat advantage.

The political base of majority presidents usually yields between two-thirds and three-fourths of the votes needed to assure victory on the floor; the average is 72 percent of the votes required for a majority in the House and 67 percent in the Senate. Minority presidents receive between one-third and two-thirds of the votes needed to win from their political base; the average is 45 percent in both chambers. Thus even majority presidents normally must take positions that appeal to members outside of their political base.

Support from the party bases is relatively stable over time. Liberal Democrats in the House, however, have become less supportive of presidents of both parties. Carter received considerably less support from liberal Democrats than Kennedy and Johnson. And liberal Democrats' support for Republican presidents declined in a linear fashion across the four Republican administrations. Previous research suggests that new issues (e.g., energy and environment) on the political agenda may have contributed to this trend by fragmenting the traditional liberal Democratic coalition (Sinclair 1981).

Cross-pressured members occupy a middle position between the two party bases. Conservative Democrats and liberal Republicans divide almost evenly in their support of both Democratic and Republican presidents. In the House, average presidential support from conservative Democrats is 44 percent for Democratic presidents and 46 percent for Republican presidents. Average presidential support from liberal House Republicans is 53 percent for both Democrats and Republicans. In the Senate, average presidential support from conservative Democrats is 48 percent for Democrats and 50 percent for Republicans. Liberal Republicans in the Senate are the only faction that tends to be more supportive of one party—Democratic presidents receive support from an average of 64 percent of liberal Senate Republicans compared to an average of 54 percent for Republican presidents.

At the beginning of this chapter we noted that despite Democratic control of Congress, President Kennedy was frequently frustrated by a conservative coalition of Republicans and cross-pressured conservative Democrats. President Johnson, in contrast, seemed to have more success in overcoming defections from cross-pressured Democrats. The analysis in table 4.3 reveals that Kennedy attracted more support from conservative Democrats than did Johnson. Kennedy typically received support from slightly more than half of conservative Democrats, while Johnson received support from only about 40 percent. In the House, however, the average for the Kennedy administration disguises differences in behavior in the 87th and 88th Congresses. Kennedy had more trouble with conservative Democrats in the 87th Congress (1961– 62) than in the 88th (1963).[9] Thus, while Kennedy's dealings with conservative Democrats were beginning to improve when his presidency was cut short by assassination, perceptions set by early conflicts have persisted.

Party Bases as Loyal Opposition

Our theoretical framework assumes that the behavior of a party base in its role as the loyal opposition is the mirror image of its behavior as the president's political base. That is, when a change in party control of the White House transforms a party faction's role from president's political base to the base of the loyal opposition, cohesion in opposition should be similar to cohesion in support. The figures presented in table 4.3 reveal that, although this assumption is generally accurate, there are differences across parties and chambers.

Liberal Democrats are less cohesive in their role as loyal opposition in both chambers. The difference in the Senate is small—an average of 76 percent support Democratic presidents; an average of 72 percent oppose Republican presidents.[10] The difference in the House, in contrast, appears considerably larger—an average of 82 percent support Democrats compared to an average of 67 percent in opposition to Republicans. The difference in the House, however, is due in part to liberal Democrats' unusually high levels of support for Kennedy and Johnson. The cohesion of liberal Democrats in their role as loyal opposition is fairly typical.

Conservative Republicans are less cohesive in their role as the loyal opposition only in the Senate—an average of 74 percent support Republican presidents; an average of 67 percent oppose Democratic presidents. In the House the pattern is reversed—an average of 66 percent support Republican presidents, and 75 percent oppose Democratic presidents.

Thus lack of cohesion in the party bases is common on conflictual issues. Perhaps the factions behave differently on the subset of more important issues.

Support on Important Votes

Table 4.5 reports average levels of support for the president on our subset of important votes. The behavior of the party factions on important votes is basi-

9. Kennedy attracted support from an average of 49 percent of conservative House Democrats in the 87th Congress. By the 88th Congress, support from conservative Democrats increased to 59 percent. In the Senate, support from the conservative Democrats was the same in both the 87th and 88th Congresses.

10. Percent opposing the president is calculated as one hundred minus the percentage supporting the president as reported in table 4.3.

Table 4.5 Average Percentage of Party Factions Supporting the President on Important Votes

PRESIDENT	HOUSE				SENATE			
	President's Base	Cross-Pressured Partisans	Cross-Pressured Opposition	Opposition Base	President's Base	Cross-Pressured Partisans	Cross-Pressured Opposition	Opposition Base
DDE	66	70	30	46	75	59	44	30
JFK	92	46	39	12	84	39	49	17
LBJ	89	29	58	20	77	35	73	37
RMN	72	52	53	27	81	42	65	22
GRF	75	49	55	21	86	46	61	20
JEC	69	39	56	25	74	51	61	23
RWR	80	51	65	21	83	53	48	16

Note: Entries are the average percentage of faction members voting in agreement with the president's position.

cally the same as on all conflictual issues. Usually, the president's base is the most supportive; the opposition base is the least supportive; and support from the two cross-pressured factions is in between.

The party bases tend to be more cohesive on important votes than overall. Nixon, Ford, and Reagan attracted considerably more support from conservative Republicans and less support from liberal Democrats on important votes. Kennedy and Johnson attracted only slightly more support from liberal Democrats on important votes, in part because base support on all votes was relatively high. Conservative Republicans behaved more consistently in opposition on important votes, especially during Kennedy's presidency. The behavior of the party bases toward Eisenhower and Carter is not much different on important issues.

The behavior of the cross-pressured factions is not systematically different on important issues. Both factions are typically divided fairly evenly in support of both Democratic and Republican presidents. The behavior of conservative Democrats changes the most on important issues. They are 5 to 6 percent more supportive of Republican presidents and 5 to 6 percent less supportive of Democratic presidents in both chambers.[11]

11. The difference discussed above in conservative Democrats' support for Kennedy in the 87th and 88th Houses is greater on important votes. An average of 39 percent of conservative Democrats supported Kennedy in 1961–62; an average of 62 percent supported him in 1963.

Thus the behavior of members of Congress is generally consistent with the expectations derived from our theoretical framework. Although this evidence supports the view that the lack of unity in American parties results from ideological diversity, ideology is only part of the explanation.

After controlling for ideological diversity, we find that partisan behavior in the United States Congress seldom approaches the responsible party model of most parliamentary democracies. Our analysis reveals generally low levels of cohesion even among members of the same ideological wing of the party. Only Kennedy and Johnson received levels of support from their political base high enough to be called cohesive by parliamentary standards, and this unusually high cohesion was limited to the House. The president normally fails to get the support of 20 to 25 percent of the members who have the greatest predisposition to support his position, but he typically gets the support of 25 to 33 percent of those with the least predisposition to support him. While cohesion of the party bases on important issues tends to be slightly higher than in the entire sample, cohesion still fails to approach the responsible party model.

Thus the average levels of support reveal that a sizeable minority of each party's base typically defects from the party position. This finding helps us understand why the relationship between majority party status and presidential success is not stronger. Majority party status provides a definite advantage because there are more members of the legislature who are predisposed to support the president. But there is great uncertainty surrounding this advantage. The base rarely constitutes a majority of the chamber, and on any given vote defections reduce the effective size of the base. As a result, even majority presidents must get votes from other factions. For minority party presidents, the uncertainty means that on any given vote there may be a majority coalition willing to support the president's position, but the probabilities of winning are less because a minority president must attract more votes from factions outside his base.

Average levels of support, however, do not tell us *how often* the parties were unified. Statistically we can get similar mean scores from fundamentally different distributions of behavior. For example, a mean cohesion level of 60 percent would result if 60 percent of the president's party supported his position on every vote. A 60 percent average would also result if all party members supported the president on 60 percent of the votes and all opposed him on 40 percent. Although the two means are the same, the substantive implications for presidential success are fundamentally different. In the first case, members are never totally unified, and the president would always be in need of additional votes even if his party controlled the chamber. In the second case, members are always totally unified, and a majority president would win 60 percent of time without any votes from the other party. Because previous research suggests that party unity may be the key to presidential success in Congress (Fleisher and Bond 1983), we now turn our attention to the unity of the party factions. The following section analyzes the frequency of unified support within the president's party and unified opposition within the opposition party.

PARTY UNITY

Party unity in parliamentary democracies is nearly perfect. On most votes, more than 90 percent of the members of one party vote against 90 percent of the members of the other parties (Harmel and Janda 1982, 88–89). In the United States, party unity rarely reaches these levels, even within the same ideological party faction.

Defining Unity

The concept of party (or faction) unity assumes the formation of a coalition resulting from conscious, coordinated behavior.[12] Since we cannot observe meetings, strategies, and leadership activities usually associated with building coalitions, we must rely on indirect means to distinguish the conscious formation of coalitions from the accidental formation of voting blocs.

Following Hinckley (1981a, 115), we define unified behavior as more than 75 percent of the members of a faction voting together. While 75 percent is an arbitrary cut-point, it has the intuitive appeal of being midway between the limiting conditions of majority voting blocs and perfectly unified blocs. Because members vote only yea or nay, a majority could vote together by random chance with no conscious coordination. The other extreme of perfect (or near perfect) unity is unnecessarily restrictive and occurs so seldom in the United States Congress that there are too few cases for analysis. When more than 75 percent of the members of a party faction vote together, it is reasonable to infer that some minimal level of conscious, coordinated behavior has occurred. And such blocs occur often enough to produce a sufficient number of cases for analysis.

The responsible party model implies something about the behavior of both the chief executive's party and the loyal opposition—i.e., members of the chief executive's party should unify in support of the government's position and members of the loyal opposition should unify against that position. While behavior in the United States Congress does not approach this responsible party model (and we are not advocating it), it is useful for analytical purposes to see how often it occurs within the context of the four party factions in Con-

12. These are essential elements in the definition of a coalition (Brady and Bullock 1980; Hinckley 1981a).

Table 4.6 Percentage of Votes on Which Party Bases Unified for or against the President

President and Congress	HOUSE			SENATE		
	President's Base Unified For	Opposition Base Unified Against	(N)	President's Base Unified For	Opposition Base Unified Against	(N)
DDE						
83rd	62	36	(47)	70	39	(98)
84th	32	49	(47)	53	52	(79)
85th	29	23	(86)	55	40	(114)
86th	53	43	(83)	58	58	(161)
Mean	43	37		59	48	
JFK						
87th	88	55	(93)	78	60	(199)
88th	95	74	(42)	64	54	(74)
Mean	90	61		74	59	
LBJ						
88th	92	69	(51)	80	27	(177)
89th	93	67	(146)	63	42	(212)
90th	80	51	(143)	44	43	(230)
Mean	87	61		61	38	
RMN						
91st	30	41	(71)	56	51	(107)
92nd	64	40	(75)	73	61	(97)
93rd	52	61	(147)	56	72	(203)
Mean	49	51		60	64	
GRF						
93rd	18	66	(38)	42	63	(48)
94th	53	60	(124)	69	58	(102)
Mean	45	61		60	59	
JEC						
95th	57	60	(154)	65	65	(185)
96th	58	59	(210)	50	48	(211)
Mean	57	60		57	56	

Table 4.6 (*Continued*)

	HOUSE			SENATE		
PRESIDENT AND CONGRESS	President's Base Unified For	Opposition Base Unified Against	(N)	President's Base Unified For	Opposition Base Unified Against	(N)
RWR						
97th	41	53	(121)	72	53	(178)
98th	49	59	(177)	61	58	(127)
Mean	46	56		68	55	

Note: Entries are the percentage of votes on which more than 75 percent of faction members voted for or against the president's position.

gress. Hence we will analyze how often the president's political base is unified in support of his position and how often the opposition base is unified against the president. Since the two cross-pressured factions may join either the president's coalition or the loyal opposition, we will analyze unified support and unified opposition from cross-pressured members.

Unified Support and Opposition from the Party Bases

Table 4.6 shows how often the president's base unified in support of his position and how often the opposition party base unified in opposition. The major finding of this analysis is how often the party bases fail to unify.

Looking first at support from the president's political base, we find that the president's party base unified in support of his position on an average of about 60 percent of conflictual roll calls. There is, however, considerable variation around the average frequency of base unity.

The variation is greatest in the House. On the high end, Kennedy and Johnson received unified support from liberal House Democrats on nearly 90 percent of conflictual roll calls. This level of unity is unmatched in any other administration, and this extraordinary cohesion was not repeated in the Senate even for Kennedy and Johnson. On the low end, Ford received unified support from conservative Republicans on only 18 percent of roll calls in the last months of the 93rd Congress (August to December 1974). This unusually low cohesion no doubt reflects the unique circumstances of Ford's assuming the presidency. Conservative Republicans failed to rally around Ford in the wake of the Watergate scandal, the unpopular pardon of Nixon, and the pressure of rapidly approaching midterm elections that promised to be especially hard on Republicans. But even in more normal circumstances, unified support was relatively rare in several Congresses. The president's base unified on less than one-third of roll calls in the 84th, 85th, and 91st Congresses.

There is less variation in unity in the Senate. The frequency of unified support ranges from a high of 80 percent for Johnson in the 88th congress to a low of 42 percent for Ford in the 93rd Congress. The only other instance in which the president's political base unified less than half the time occurred in the 90th Senate during the Johnson administration. Thus the behavior of liberal Democrats during the Johnson presidency spans almost the entire range. Johnson attracted the most unified support from liberal Senate Democrats in the 88th Congress after the assassination of President Kennedy. These are the same members that unified behind Kennedy only 64 percent of the time in 1963. By the 90th Congress (1967–68), Johnson's base of liberal Democrats unified less than half the time.

Comparing unity in the House and Senate, we see that the president's political base unified more often in the Senate than in the House. The difference across chambers, however, is primarily partisan. Republican presidents received unified support from conservative Republicans more often in the Senate in every Congress. Democratic presidents, in contrast, received unified support from liberal Democrats more often in the House. Only Carter in the 95th Congress attracted unified support more often in the Senate.[13]

Within each chamber, variation in the unity of the president's base is related to majority or minority status—majority presidents receive unified base support more often than do minority presidents. In the House, majority presidents receive unified support an average of 78 percent of the time compared to an average of only 42 percent for minority presidents. In the Senate, the bases of majority presidents are unified an average of 65 percent of the time, while the bases of minority presidents are unified an average of 58 percent of the time.

The cases of Republican majorities reveal that the difference is a function of majority or minority status rather than party per se. Eisenhower's base in both chambers of the Republican controlled 83rd Congress was unified more often than in subsequent Congresses controlled by Democrats. And Reagan's political base in the Republican-controlled Senate was unified more often than his base in the Democrat-controlled House.

Greater unity under majority presidents may result from two advantages of majority control. First, because majority presidents have more partisans to cast votes, they have an advantage in bargaining and compromise. The Ameri-

13. It is not clear why conservative Republicans unify more often in the Senate than in the House. The differences in behavior across the chambers does not appear to result from minority status, since the pattern is present in the 83rd Congress (when Republicans controlled both chambers) and in the 97th and 98th Congresses (when Republicans controlled the Senate). And since the liberal Demoratic base unifies more often in the House, different rules across the chambers cannot explain the pattern.

can system requires any president to compromise with Congress (Neustadt 1960, passim). But majority presidents can bargain and compromise within their party and still have enough votes to win on the floor. Minority presidents, in contrast, have no choice but to bargain and compromise with members outside their party. As the president moves further away from the policy preferences of his base to attract support from other factions, it may become more difficult to keep the base unified. We will analyze the trade-offs the president faces below.

Second, majority presidents have an advantage because their partisans control the committee system. Given the importance of committee recommendations in Congress, unity is more difficult to achieve if the president opposes the committee, and positions of minority presidents may be more likely to conflict with committee recommendations. We analyze presidential support form committee and party leaders in the next chapter.

The analysis of average levels of support in the preceding section suggested that the liberal Democratic base is more cohesive than the conservative Republican base. The more detailed analysis of faction unity in table 4.6 suggests that this partisan difference is also a function of majority and minority status. Partisan breakdowns in the frequency of unified support reveal patterns similar to those seen in the earlier analysis of average levels of support. In the Senate, the difference in unity of the parties is small—liberal Democrats were unified an average of 63 percent of the time; conservative Republicans were unified an average of 60 percent of the time. In the House, the difference is more dramatic—liberal Democrats were unified an average of 80 percent of the time compared to an average of 44 percent for conservative Republicans.

The difference between Democratic presidents, who were always in the majority, and majority Republican presidents, however, is less. In the Senate, Eisenhower's base in the 83rd Congress was unified on 70 percent of conflictual roll calls, and Reagan's base was unified an average of 68 percent of the time. Thus when Republicans controlled the Senate, conservative Republicans unified more often than did liberal Democrats under every Democratic president except Kennedy. In the House, Eisenhower's base in the Republican-controlled 83rd Congress was unified 62 percent of the time. While this level is much lower than liberal Democrats' unity under Kennedy and Johnson, it is higher than their unity under Carter.

While the unity of the president's base varies considerably over time, there are no consistent trends. The unity of conservative Republicans in the House is surprisingly stable across Republican administrations. The Republican base unified slightly more often in the Senate during Reagan's first term, but this increase is probably the result of majority status. Note that the average for Reagan is about the same as for Eisenhower in the 83rd Senate.

Liberal Democrats have tended toward less unity over time. In the House, the major decline occurred during Carter's presidency. In the Senate, the largest drop-off occurred during Johnson's presidency, and unity under Carter was only slightly lower. This tendency is consistent with the finding in the previous section that average support from liberal Democrats declined over time. Not only did Carter receive less support from his base on average, the base unified less often than under previous Democratic administrations.

The causes of fragmentation in the liberal Democratic base under Carter are difficult to pinpoint. Conventional wisdom pins the blame squarely on Carter and his lack of political skill in dealing with Congress. While there is no question that Carter's lack of understanding of Congress and his aversion to engaging in the usual political "horsetrading" led to strained relations on the Hill, other forces beyond his control may have made it more difficult to unify liberal Democrats in support of his policy preferences.

First is the change in the political agenda. Charles Jones (1988) argues that there was less agenda congruence between Carter and his base than was previously the case. The issues on the agenda during the Kennedy and Johnson administrations involved enlarging the scope of governmental power to reduce poverty, unemployment, and racial discrimination. These "bread and butter" issues could unite the liberal Democratic base. The issues on the political agenda in the mid-1970s—high inflation and high unemployment, an energy crisis, and environmental protection—are more likely to split liberal Democrats.

Second, congressional reforms in the 1970s that made the legislative process more open and subject to public scrutiny reduced the power of congressional leaders. Presidents can no longer deal with party leaders and a handful of committee chairs with power to deliver votes on the floor. The Democratic caucus now votes on committee chairs with secret ballots, which forces committee leaders to be more responsive to the rank and file. Subcommittees have become more important with the adoption of the "subcommittee bill of rights." Limitations on the number of leadership positions a member can hold made leadership positions available to most Democrats. In the 96th Congress, a majority of House Democrats (52.2 percent) and virtually all Senate Democrats (98.3 percent) chaired at least one standing committee or subcommittee (Smith and Deering 1984, 51). Open committee meetings and recorded teller votes forced members to go on the record more often. As a result, members have less leeway to maneuver and to respond to requests from party leaders or the president, because they know that their actions will be monitored by increasingly sophisticated interest groups (Crotty and Jacobson 1980, 220–22).

Finally, there are generational forces. The class of "Watergate Democrats" elected in 1974 diverge significantly from their more senior party colleagues. Almost half of these Democrats were elected to seats previously held by Republicans. Although they received more campaign money from organized labor than more senior Democrats, they are significantly less supportive of this Democratic ally in their voting behavior. For representatives of these traditionally Republican districts, "votes are more important than money" (Crotty and Jacobson 1980, 223). This generation of Democrats is also more supportive of defense spending than more senior members. Members who entered Congress while the Vietnam War was still a dominant issue are less supportive of defense (Crotty and Jacobson 1980, 223–24). Thus the fragmentation of the liberal Democratic base during Carter's administration is probably due in large part to forces beyond his control.

Even controlling for ideological diversity in the parties and adopting a relatively lenient definition of unity (more than 75 percent of the faction supporting the president), unified support for the president is not extraordinary. With the exception of Kennedy's and Johnson's in the House, the president's political base frequently failed to unify in support of his policy preferences. The other side of the issue is the unity of the out party's base in opposition to the president.

Table 4.6 also shows how often the opposition party base unified in opposition to the president. Unified opposition to the president occurs even less often than unified support. Overall, the party bases unify in opposition barely over half the time (mean = 54 percent in the House and 52 percent in the Senate). These overall averages, however, fail to reflect some systematic differences across chambers and over time.

In the Senate, there is a tendency for the president's political base to unify more often than the opposition party base. Only in the 93rd Congress, in which the Watergate scandal forced Nixon to resign and elevated the nation's first unelected president to office, was the opposition base more likely to unify than the president's partisans.

In the House, the pattern is more varied. In eight of the sixteen Congresses studied, the president's base unified more often than the opposition base. All eight of these cases occurred before the 93rd Congress (1973–74). In the period since 1973, the loyal opposition base has been slightly more likely to unify against the president. The different patterns in the House and Senate emerge most clearly during the Reagan administration. Popular perceptions suggest that during Reagan's first term, conservative Republicans were highly supportive of his policy preferences, while Democrats seemed reluctant to stand unified against him. The trends in the Senate are consistent with these perceptions. In the House, however, conservative Republicans unified in support less often than liberal Democrats unified in opposition. Also note that conservative Republicans in the House provided unified support much less often than did the president's base in the Senate. The behavior of the liberal Democratic opposition is remarkably similar in both chambers.

We noted previously that liberal Democrats in the House have become

Table 4.7 Percentage of Votes on Which Cross-Pressured Factions Unified for and against the President

	HOUSE				SENATE			
PRESIDENT AND CONGRESS	Cross-Pressured Partisans Unified		Cross-Pressured Opposition Unified		Cross-Pressured Partisans Unified		Cross-Pressured Opposition Unified	
	For	Against	For	Against	For	Against	For	Against
DDE								
83rd	45	9	17	47	45	6	25	30
84th	45	6	4	49	12	23	8	41
85th	48	8	7	66	49	12	28	36
86th	36	21	19	55	55	14	16	42
Mean	43	12	12	56	44	14	20	38
JFK								
87th	19	28	32	32	22	21	21	28
88th	26	14	17	43	26	18	47	12
Mean	22	24	27	36	23	20	28	23
LBJ								
88th	24	12	26	28	15	60	76	12
89th	13	24	35	23	21	43	45	14
90th	12	46	47	20	22	37	37	19
Mean	15	32	39	23	20	46	51	15
RMN								
91st	49	25	23	35	36	29	36	36
92nd	36	8	47	17	23	36	37	27
93rd	31	26	25	31	17	42	28	36
Mean	37	21	30	28	24	37	32	33
GRF								
93rd	29	45	5	34	21	27	15	38
94th	32	30	25	25	17	35	43	27
Mean	31	33	20	27	18	33	34	30
JEC								
95th	13	37	33	14	22	18	56	12
96th	13	40	31	22	21	19	48	13
Mean	13	39	32	19	21	18	52	13

Table 4.7 (*Continued*)

PRESIDENT AND CONGRESS	HOUSE				SENATE			
	Cross-Pressured Partisans Unified		Cross-Pressured Opposition Unified		Cross-Pressured Partisans Unified		Cross-Pressured Opposition Unified	
	For	Against	For	Against	For	Against	For	Against
RWR								
97th	28	36	41	24	41	19	30	30
98th	23	35	35	33	38	12	24	23
Mean	25	35	37	29	40	16	28	27

Note: Entries are the percentage of votes on which more than 75 percent of faction members voted for and against the president's position. Number of votes is the same as in table 4.6.

more fragmented over time. Our analysis suggests that this trend does not characterize liberal Democrats in their role of loyal opposition. While liberal Democrats may be less likely to unify in support of Democratic presidents, they have become more likely to unify in opposition to Republican presidents. During the Eisenhower administration and Nixon's first term, liberal House Democrats typically unified in opposition less than 40 percent of the time. In the 93rd Congress they unified in opposition over 60 percent of the time, perhaps because of the Watergate scandal. But the greater tendency to unify against Republican presidents persisted through Ford's presidency and remained almost as high during Reagan's first term. Furthermore, the tendency for a party base to be a more cohesive opposition is not limited to liberal Democrats. Conservative Republicans in the House unified behind Republican presidents only about 45 percent of the time, but they unified in opposition to Democratic presidents about 60 percent of the time.

Thus the party bases frequently fail to unify on presidential roll calls. Even when the party bases do unify, they rarely provide enough votes to determine the outcome of the vote. The cross-pressured factions, therefore, occupy a swing position between the two bases.

Unified Support and Opposition from Cross-Pressured Factions
Table 4.7 shows how often each of the cross-pressured factions unified in support of and opposition to the president. The table reveals the volatility of the voting behavior of the cross-pressured factions. On slightly less than half of the votes (45 percent) they are sufficiently divided that they fail to meet our definition of unity. Notice that this figure is comparable to the unity of the opposition party base and only slightly lower than the unity of the president's party base. But unlike the party bases, which unify predominantly in one di-

rection depending on the party of the president, both cross-pressured factions are about equally likely to unify in support as in opposition regardless of the party of the president. Cross-pressured members of the president's party unified in support of his position on 26 percent of conflictual votes; these same members unified in opposition on 28 percent of the votes. Members of the cross-pressured opposition provided unified support 34 percent of the time and unified opposition 27 percent of the time.

Because congressional parties have caucuses, party leaders, and whips to promote unity, we expected the cross-pressured members of the president's party to provide more unified support and less unified opposition than members of the cross-pressured opposition. Instead, we find that in about half the Congresses the cross-pressured opposition unified in support of the president more often than did his cross-pressured partisans. Furthermore, we find that cross-pressured opponents are only slightly more likely to unify in opposition than are cross-pressured members of the president's party. This finding suggests that the pull of ideology may be as strong as the push of party for cross-pressured members.

The behavior of cross-pressured Democrats and cross-pressured Republicans is similar, although conservative Democrats unify in opposition to the president more often than do liberal Republicans. We see that liberal Republicans in both chambers are more likely to unify in support of both Democratic and Republican presidents than to unify in opposition. Conservative Democrats, in contrast, are considerably more likely to unify in opposition to presidents of both parties than to unify in support. Indeed, during the Eisenhower administration, conservative Democrats in the House behaved more like a loyal opposition than did the opposition party base of liberal Democrats—conservative Democrats unified against Eisenhower 56 percent of the time, but liberal Democrats unified against him only 37 percent of the time. This behavior is consistent with the view that Eisenhower took relatively moderate positions that appealed less to conservatives. Similarly, conservative Democrats in the Senate unified against Johnson 60 percent of the time in the 88th Congress, while conservative Republicans unified in opposition only 27 percent of the time. This behavior may reflect Johnson's success in moving stalled civil rights legislation to the floor in the wake of the Kennedy assassination. Recall that there were an unusually large number of Senate votes on the 1964 Civil Rights Act passed in the 88th Congress.

This analysis of unified support and opposition from the four party factions provides an indication of how much congressional party factions differ from parliamentary parties. Even controlling for ideological diversity of congressional parties, we find that the behavior of relatively homogeneous ideological groupings falls short of disciplined party behavior in parliamentary

Table 4.8 Percentage of Important Votes on Which Party Bases Unified for or against the President

PRESIDENT AND CONGRESS	HOUSE			SENATE		
	President's Base Unified For	Opposition Base Unified Against	(N)	President's Base Unified For	Opposition Base Unified Against	(N)
DDE	53	34	(64)	64	59	(63)
JFK	95	82	(39)	85	81	(26)
LBJ	92	67	(60)	71	43	(58)
RMN	57	63	(54)	78	74	(69)
GRF	68	74	(31)	82	64	(22)
JEC	61	68	(62)	55	67	(51)
RWR	68	72	(79)	72	76	(72)

Note: Entries are the percentage of important votes on which more than 75 percent of faction members voted for or against the president's position.

democracies. This lack of unity means that on many votes the outcome may be in doubt because there are votes to be won and lost from each of the factions predisposed to support or oppose the president.

The analysis of unity of the two cross-pressured factions contributes further to our understanding of the volatility that surrounds winning and losing on the floor of Congress. The support or opposition of the cross-pressured members cannot be taken for granted, because these actors frequently fail to unify. And even if they vote as a bloc, it might be for or against the president. Overall, the odds in Congress favor majority party presidents because partisan and ideological predispositions do exert a powerful influence on the behavior of the members. Nonetheless, the effects of majority control are not nearly as predictable as they are in parliamentary parties.

Thus, across conflictual presidential roll calls, the conflict is not always partisan. In the next section we analyze our subset of important votes to see if the party factions unify more consistently.

Unified Support and Opposition on Important Votes

Table 4.8 shows how often the party bases unified for and against the president on important votes. The president's base usually unifies in support of his position more often on important votes than on all votes. Only Carter in the Senate received less support from his base on important roll calls (compare with table 4.6). The behavior of the Republican party base changes dramatically—compared to behavior on all conflictual roll calls, on important votes conservative Republicans unified in support of the president an average of 18 percent more often in the House and 14 percent more often in the Senate. Even during the Ford presidency, when conservative Republicans frequently failed to rally on conflictual issues, their behavior on important votes was more loyal. On important votes, conservative Republicans unified in support of Ford 68 percent of the time in the House and 82 percent of the time in the Senate. Liberal Democrats are only slightly more likely to unify behind the president on the important votes; the increase is 3 percent in the House and 7 percent in the Senate.

The opposition party bases are also more likely to unify in opposition to the president on important votes. Whereas the Democratic and Republican party bases unified in opposition only about half the time on all issues, they unified in opposition about two-thirds of the time on important issues. Notice that conservative Republicans unified against Kennedy on over 80 percent of important roll calls, a level of unity much closer to that of opposition parties in disciplined party systems.

The table also allows us to see whether the president's base unified more or less often than the opposition party base. In the House, the same pattern that we observed for all votes is true for the subset of important votes. For Eisenower, Kennedy, and Johnson the president's party base unified in support more often than the opposition base unified against. Indeed, liberal House Democrats' unity on important votes during the Kennedy and Johnson administrations is remarkable. For each president from Nixon through Reagan the pattern is reversed—the opposition party base was more likely to unify. In the Senate, the tendency for the president's party base to unify more often than the opposition base persisted through the Ford administration. For Carter and Reagan, the opposition party base unified on a greater percentage of important votes. Thus, on the subset of important votes, the behavior of the party bases is more consistently partisan.

The behavior of the cross-pressured factions does not change as much on important issues. Table 4.9 shows how often conservative Democrats and liberal Republicans unified for and against presidents of both parties. Comparing these averages to those for all votes in table 4.7, we see that the behavior of conservative Democrats changes the most. As supporters of the president's position, these cross-pressured Democrats are much less likely to unify behind Democratic presidents on important issues and slightly more likely to unify in support of Republican presidents.

As opponents to the president, conservative Democrats are more likely to

Table 4.9 Percentage of Important Votes on Which Cross-Pressured Factions Unified for and against the President

	HOUSE				SENATE			
	Cross-Pressured Partisans Unified		Cross-Pressured Opposition Unified		Cross-Pressured Partisans Unified		Cross-Pressured Opposition Unified	
PRESIDENT	For	Against	For	Against	For	Against	For	Against
DDE	58	5	13	59	35	18	24	33
JFK	8	28	21	41	8	35	15	12
LBJ	3	47	35	23	14	53	53	16
RMN	26	15	28	26	16	32	45	9
GRF	19	26	26	13	23	32	41	14
JEC	15	42	31	18	16	14	29	16
RWR	28	25	41	8	28	21	19	28

Note: Entries are the average percentage of votes on which more than 75 percent of faction members voted for or against the president's position. Number of votes is the same as in table 4.8.

unify against Democratic presidents and less likely to unify against Republican presidents on important votes than on all issues. For Kennedy the pattern is particularly striking. In the House, Kennedy received unified support from conservative Democrats on only 8 percent of the important votes, but this faction unified in opposition on 28 percent of the important roll calls. In addition, liberal Republicans were twice as likely to unify in opposition as in support. In the Senate, Kennedy also found that conservative Democrats were considerably more likely to unify in opposition, while liberal Republicans were about as likely to unify in support as in opposition.

In summary, while the bases are more partisan on important votes, there continues to be considerable uncertainty because of the unpredictable behavior of the cross-pressured factions. Instead of becoming more consistent partisans on important votes, cross-pressured members, especially conservative Democrats, seem to be pulled more by ideology.

Now that we have a feel for how frequently the party factions unify in support and opposition, we need to consider the implications of party unity for presidential success.

UNITY AND SUCCESS

Thus far we have described the aggregate behavior of the party factions in each presidential administration. Analyzing aggregate levels of unity, however, does not tell us much about the relationships between unity and the probability of presidential success on a vote. In this section we construct a statistical model which allows us to estimate the conditional probabilities of success under different conditions of unity across the party factions.

Normally we would regress presidential success on roll calls as a function of the unity of the various party factions. But because the dependent variable in this analysis is dichotomous—the president's preference either passes or fails—Ordinary Least Squares (OLS) regression is not appropriate. Several techniques are available to estimate models with a dichotomous dependent variable. The one used here is multivariate probit analysis.[14]

Because we are interested in estimating the probabilities of success under various conditions of faction unity, the independent variables indicating the behavior of the party factions are also measured as dichotomies—the faction was either unified (more than 75 percent voting together) or not unified. The probit models analyze unified support from the president's base and the two cross-pressured factions, and unified opposition from the opposition base and the two cross-pressured factions.[15] We constructed the models to provide separate estimates for majority and minority presidents because the effects of unified support or opposition from the various factions may vary depending on whether the president's party controls the chamber.[16]

Some might object that this procedure fails to exploit all the information about presidential success and the behavior of the four factions on each roll call. We know the size of the president's victory or loss, and we know the percentage of each faction that supported the president's position on each roll call, so why not use the percentages?

Using the dichotomous measures may be justified on conceptual grounds. As for the dependent variable, what is important is whether the president's

14. A linear regression model with a dichotomous dependent variable violates two assumptions of OLS: (1) the error terms are not normally distributed, and (2) the errors are heteroskedastistic. If these assumptions are violated, the estimates are not efficient and classical tests of significance do not apply. If the proportion of observations scored 1 on the dependent variable is between 0.10 and 0.90, any of the alternative estimation techniques yield virtually equivalent results (Cox 1970; Naylor 1964).

15. We do not analyze unified support from the opposition party base or unified opposition from the president's base because these conditions rarely occur. Because the cross-pressured factions unify against the president about as often as they unify in support, we analyze the effects of both types of behavior. Note that including both unified support and opposition from these groups in the model does not pose estimation or interpretation problems because on a given roll call the conditions are mutually exclusive.

16. The models estimate separate slopes and intercepts for majority and minority presidents with a single probit equation. The procedure is the same as that recommended by Gerald Wright (1976) for OLS regression models. The estimates produced using Wright's method are exactly the same as estimates produced by dividing the sample into majority and minority presidents and estimating separate equations.

position prevails, not how close or lopsided the vote is. When it comes to policymaking, crossing the majority threshold is the necessary and sufficient condition. Lopsided losses may be embarrassing, but a near miss is not significantly better—the president still fails to get what he wants. Overwhelming support may be heartening, but a minimum winning coalition is just as good.[17]

As for the independent variables, we are not concerned with how marginal changes in support from the various party factions relate to success or failure. Instead, we are interested in the probability that the president's preference succeeds on the floor under different conditions of faction unity. For our purposes, it is less important to estimate the effects of increasing a factions' support from, say, 32 percent to 35 percent, than to see what happens when the behavior of the members of a faction crosses a minimum threshold of unity. Furthermore, because the two cross-pressured factions join the opposition about as often as they join the president's coalition, it is useful to analyze the different effects of unified support and opposition from cross-pressured members. Using percentage support assumes that the relationship is linear across the range of behavior—e.g., increasing support from 50 percent to 75 percent has the same impact as decreasing support from 50 percent to 25 percent. Defining the independent variables in terms of unity permits us to determine if the effects of unified support on the probability of success are greater than or less than the effects of unified opposition.

Table 4.10 reports the results of the probit analysis. Overall, the models perform well. Knowing whether the various factions are unified allows us to predict accurately the outcome of nearly 90 percent of conflictual presidential roll calls. All of the probit coefficients are statistically significant, indicating that unified behavior in any of the factions exerts a significant, independent effect on the probability that the president's position will prevail. As one would expect, unified support from any faction increases the probability of success; unified opposition decreases the probability of success.

Although probit analysis is similar to regression, probit coefficients do not have the same straightforward interpretation as regression coefficients. Probit coefficients estimate the effect of an independent variable on the probability of an event's occurrence (in this case the outcome of a presidential roll call), but the probit coefficients themselves are not probabilities. The relationship they

17. Indeed, under certain conditions minimum winning coalitions are more desirable because the benefits for each member of the winning side are maximized (Riker 1962). The expectation of an equilibrium of minimum winning coalitions assumes perfect information in a zero-sum game. Because leaders in the United States Congress rarely have perfect information, coalitions are frequently larger than minimum winning size to provide a cushion for uncertainty and errors in estimating support. Moreover, many votes in Congress are viewed as positive-sum because benefits are concentrated and visible and costs are dispersed and hidden.

Table 4.10 Probit Estimates of the Effects of Unity on Success

	HOUSE		SENATE	
BEHAVIOR OF PARTY FACTION	b	(s.e.)	b	(s.e.)
Majority Presidents				
Unified Support				
President's base	1.81	(.18)	1.86	(.11)
Cross-pressured partisans	.61	(.20)	1.17	(.15)
Cross-pressured opposition	.87	(.19)	.58	(.12)
Unified opposition				
Opposition base	−.78	(.18)	−.86	(.11)
Cross-pressured opposition	−.53	(.15)	−1.02	(.13)
Cross-pressured partisans	−1.56	(.16)	−1.35	(.12)
Intercept	.36		.52	
Minority Presidents				
Unified support				
President's base	.71	(.15)	1.35	(.22)
Cross-pressured partisans	.60	(.13)	.57	(.15)
Cross-pressured opposition	.37	(.14)	.88	(.16)
Unified opposition				
Opposition base	−1.78	(.15)	−2.56	(.24)
Cross-pressured opposition	−.97	(.13)	−.82	(.16)
Cross-pressured partisans	−.63	(.16)	−.78	(.16)
Intercept	.76		.85	
% correctly predicted	86		88	
Null prediction	62		68	

Note: Entries are probit coefficients. Standard error of the estimate in parentheses.

estimate, however, can be converted into a probability. The procedure for making this conversion is explained in appendix B. Table 4.11 reports the calculated probabilities showing the marginal impact of the unity of different party factions.

The table shows the predicted probability that the president's position wins under four sets of conditions: (1) no unity in any faction (i.e., the intercept in each model); (2) unified support from one or more factions with no unified opposition; (3) unified opposition from one or more factions with no unified support; and (4) unified support from one or more factions countered by unified opposition from one or more factions. In this analysis, we have not calculated all possible combinations of faction unity. Instead, we look at three of the most likely situations: (1) unity in a party base, (2) unity in a party base and the cross-pressured members of that party (i.e., a party coalition), and (3) unity in a party base and the cross-pressured opposition (i.e., an ideological coalition). The difference between the probability of success when no faction is unified and the probability when one or more factions unify indicates the marginal effect of unity.

As one would expect, the effects of unity vary depending on whether the president's party controls the chamber. For majority presidents, if no faction unifies for or against the president's position, the probability of winning is .64 in the House and .69 in the Senate, only slightly better than a coin toss. If the president takes a position that attracts unified support from his party base without generating unified opposition from the opposition base or a cross-pressured faction, the probability of success increases to near certainty ($p >$ .99 in both chambers). And because the probability is near certainty, adding unanswered unity from a cross-pressured faction does not help much.

Unanswered unity from the opposition base decreases the probability winning to about one in three ($p = .34$ in the House and .36 in the Senate). The change in probability compared to the base condition of no unity is of about the same magnitude as the change associated with unanswered unity from the president's political base. But unanswered unity from a party coalition (unified opposition from the opposition base and the cross-pressured opposition) or an ideological coalition (unified opposition from the opposition base and the cross-pressured faction of the president's party) reduces the probability of winning considerably. Unified opposition from an ideological coalition hurts the most, reducing the probability of winning to .02 in the House and .05 in the Senate.

Unified support countered by unified opposition is a more interesting condition. If a majority president takes a position that generates a party split, then the probability of winning increases to above .90. And the probabilities are about the same regardless of whether the party split involves only the party bases unifying against each other, or the president's party coalition (base plus the cross-pressured faction) unifying against the opposing party coalition. Opposing ideological coalitions are not as effective for majority presidents. When this condition occurs, the president wins about three out of four times, only slightly better odds than under the condition of no unity.

Thus majority presidents can increase their chances of success if they take positions that unify their partisans, especially members of their political base, who have the greatest predisposition to agree with the president. And even if

Table 4.11 Estimated Probabilities of Presidential Victory under Various Conditions of Faction Unity

BEHAVIOR OF PARTY FACTION	HOUSE			SENATE		
	$\hat{z}$	$\hat{p}$	Diff.	$\hat{z}$	$\hat{p}$	Diff.
Majority Presidents						
No unity (intercept)	.36	.64	—	.52	.69	—
Unified support						
President's base	2.17	.995	.35	2.38	.991	.30
President's base + cross-pressured partisans	2.78	.997	.36	3.55	.999	.31
President's base + cross-pressured opposition	3.04	.999	.36	2.96	.998	.31
Unified opposition						
Opposition base	−.42	.34	−.30	−.34	.36	−.33
Opposition base + cross-pressured opposition	−.95	.17	−.47	−1.36	.09	−.60
Opposition base + cross-pressured partisans	−1.98	.02	−.62	−1.69	.05	−.64
Unified support vs. unified opposition						
President's base vs. opposition base	1.39	.92	.28	1.52	.93	.25
(President's base + cross-pressured partisans) vs. (opposition base + cross-pressured opposition)	1.47	.93	.29	1.67	.95	.26
(President's base + cross-pressured opposition) vs. (opposition base + cross-pressured partisans)	.70	.76	.12	.75	.77	.08
Minority Presidents						
No unity (intercept)	.76	.77	—	.85	.80	—
Unified support						
President's base	1.47	.93	.16	2.20	.986	.19
President's base + cross-pressured partisans	2.07	.98	.21	2.77	.997	.20
President's base + cross-pressured opposition	1.84	.97	.21	3.08	.999	.20

Table 4.11 (*Continued*)

	HOUSE			SENATE		
BEHAVIOR OF PARTY FACTION	$\hat{z}$	$\hat{p}$	Diff.	$\hat{z}$	$\hat{p}$	Diff.
Unified opposition						
Opposition base	−1.02	.16	−.61	−1.71	.04	−.76
Opposition base + cross-pressured opposition	−1.99	.02	−.75	−2.53	.01	−.79
Opposition base + cross-pressured partisans	−1.65	.05	−.72	−2.49	.01	−.79
Unified support vs. unified opposition						
President's base vs. opposition base	−.31	.38	−.39	−.36	.36	−.44
(President's base + cross-pressured partisans) vs. (opposition base + cross-pressured opposition)	−.68	.24	−.53	−.61	.27	−.53
(President's base + cross-pressured opposition) vs. (opposition base + cross-pressured partisans)	−.57	.28	−.49	−.26	.40	−.40

Note: Z-scores estimated from probit equations. The estimated $\hat{p}$ is the probability that the president's position wins under the specified condition. The difference is the change from the condition of no unified behavior of any faction.

unified support from one or both factions of the president's party is countered with unified opposition from the opposition party factions, the probability of success is still better than .90. The situation for minority presidents is different.

Compared to majority presidents, minority presidents are more likely to win if no faction unifies—$p = .77$ in the House and .80 in the Senate. The only condition that increases the probability of success for a minority president is if he takes a position that unifies his supporters without generating unified opposition. In this situation, the probability of success is greater than .90, only slightly less than the estimates for majority presidents under the same condition. Similar to the situation with majority presidents, unified opposition that is not countered by unified support virtually assures defeat of a minority president's position. But unlike the situation for majority presidents, unified support countered by unified opposition also decreases a minority president's probability of success to between .24 and .38 in the House and between .27 and .40 in the Senate.

Minority presidents, therefore, may face a dilemma that does not affect majority presidents. If unified behavior in the president's base tends to generate unified opposition from the opposition base, then minority presidents will have the highest probability of victory when all factions are divided. Majority presidents, in contrast, can still improve their chances of victory by taking positions that appeal to their base even if opposition factions unify against. The next section analyzes the relationship between the behavior of the president's party base and the behavior of the other factions to identify the trade-offs. Before looking at the analysis of trade-offs, however, we need to examine some specific examples. Reagan's experience in the House in 1981 appears to differ from the generalization made above about minority presidents, and Carter appears to differ from other majority presidents.

Reagan had a string of stunning victories on the House floor in 1981—two votes on his budget that made deep cuts in domestic programs (Gramm-Latta I and Gramm-Latta II) and a major tax cut. On the first budget vote, both Republican factions and cross-pressured conservative Democrats unified in support of the president, and the liberal Democratic base unified in opposition. On the other two votes, both Republican factions unified in support, liberal Democrats unified in opposition, and cross-pressured conservative Democrats provided divided support.

Using the probit coefficients in table 4.10 to estimate probabilities of victory under the conditions observed on these votes, we find that Reagan's chances of success are .74 on Gramm-Latta I (with three factions unified against a unified Democratic base) and .62 on the other votes (with the two Republican factions unified against the Democratic base). Note that these estimates are less than .77, the probability of victory if no faction is unified. Hence, contrary to the prediction of the probit analysis, Reagan appears to have beaten the odds and won all three of these key votes by taking positions that generated both unified support and unified opposition. And if all four factions had been divided, providing average levels of support, the president would have lost all three votes.

These three votes, however, are not typical. Overall, when House Republicans were unified during Reagan's first term, the President's position prevailed 73 percent of the time, about the level predicted. Unity of both factions of the Republican party was extraordinary on the budget and tax cut votes in 1981—the President did not lose a single vote from his base on any of the three votes, and he lost only two cross-pressured Republicans on Gramm-Latta II and one on the tax cut. The strategy of unifying the factions worked in

1981 primarily because of the relatively close party split and the relative sizes of the party factions. Given the same conditions of faction unity in the 98th Congress (1983–84), with a less favorable distribution of members across the four party factions (see table 4.1), the president would have lost all three votes.

Thus Reagan's experience is consistent with the general thesis of the book: the distribution of partisan and ideological forces sets the basic parameters of presidential success or failure in Congress. While Reagan's persuasive and structuring skills may have permitted him to capitalize on the advantages he had in 1981, when the parameters changed after the midterm elections, the same skills and strategy could not prevent defeats.

Carter's experience also may appear inconsistent with the results of the probit analysis. Carter won less often than other majority presidents, despite having the advantage of large majorities in Congress with a large number of liberal Democrats. Indeed, Carter had a larger party base in the House than any other president (223 liberal Democrats in the 97th Congress and 230 in the 98th Congress) and ties with Johnson for the largest base in the Senate (44 liberal Democrats in the 95th Congress and 51 in the 98th Congress). The probit model predicts that a majority president should win more than 90 percent of the time when his base unifies.

A breakdown of Carter's success rate when his party unified reveals that Carter's experience is consistent with the prediction of the probit analysis. When liberal Democrats unified in support of Carter, he won 91 percent of the time in the House and 93 percent in the Senate. When he received unified support from both factions of his party, he won 100 percent of the time in the House and 95 percent of the time in the Senate. These observed percentages are very close to the levels predicted and in some cases are higher than Kennedy's and Johnson's. Carter won less often overall than other majority presidents because his base unified less often. In the House, Carter's base unified on 57 percent of presidential roll calls compared to 90 percent and 87 percent for Kennedy and Johnson respectively (see table 4.6). In the Senate, the difference for Carter is less. Liberal Democrats unified in support of Carter 57 percent of the time compared to 74 percent and 61 percent for Kennedy and Johnson. As a result, Carter's overall success rate in the Senate is close to that of other Democratic presidents.

In this section we examined how different conditions of unity of support or opposition from the various factions changed the conditional probability of presidential success on roll call votes. While unity in support or opposition has the expected impact on presidential success, factors which increase the probability that any one faction unifies do not necessarily have that effect on the other factions. Indeed, unified support from one faction may be associated with a decrease in support from one or more of the other factions. In the next section, therefore, we turn to the issue of trade-offs with an examination of how the level of support from the president's party base is related to levels of support from the other factions.

TRADE-OFFS

Table 4.12 reports a regression analysis showing the effects of support from the president's party base on support from the other three factions. A negative regression coefficient indicates that there is a trade-off in support from the factions—i.e., increased support from the president's base is associated with less support from the other faction. A positive regression coefficient indicates that there is no trade-off, and the president can increase support from both factions.

The regression analysis indicates that increasing support from the president's base tends to increase support from both cross-pressured factions and decrease support from the opposition party base. Except for minority presidents in the House, the pattern and magnitude of relationships are similar in the House and Senate and for majority and minority presidents. In general, a 1 percent increase in support from the president's party base is associated with about a one-half to two-thirds percent increase in support from his cross-pressured partisans, about a three-fourths percent increase in support from the cross-pressured opposition, and slightly more than a one-half percent decrease in support from the opposition party base. For minority presidents in the House, a 1 percent increase in support from the president's base is associated with a 1 percent increase in support from the cross-pressured opposition, an eight-tenths of a percent increase in support from his cross-pressured partisans, and slightly more than a three-fourths percent decrease in support from the opposition party base.

Although positions that appeal to members of the president's party base also tend to attract support from the cross-pressured factions, both cross-pressured factions are unlikely to unify in support of the president's position. As support from one cross-pressured faction increases, support from the other cross-pressured faction tends to decrease. This finding suggests that generating unified support from more than two party factions is difficult. Coalitions are likely to be either partisan or ideological, but both cross-pressured factions are not likely to join in a coalition with either party base.

These results indicate that presidential support across the party factions is not positive-sum. If the president takes a position that increases the unity of his party base, there is a strong likelihood that it will generate opposition from the opposition party base. In light of the findings about the effects of party unity, the presence of these trade-offs generally does not pose a problem for majority presidents. If a majority president has unified support from his party

Table 4.12 Trade-offs in Support

	HOUSE			SENATE		
	Cross-Pressured Partisans	Cross-Pressured Opposition	Opposition Base	Cross-Pressured Partisans	Cross-Pressured Opposition	Opposition Base
Majority Presidents						
President's base	.68	.77	−.57	.58	.73	−.57
	(.03)	(.03)	(.03)	(.03)	(.03)	(.02)
Opposition base	.78	.85	—	.45	.58	—
	(.03)	(.03)		(.03)	(.02)	
Cross-pressured opposition	−.61	—	.57	−.47	—	.48
	(.03)		(.02)	(.02)		(.02)
Cross-pressured partisans	—	−.55	.47	—	−.40	.31
		(.03)	(.02)		(.02)	(.02)
Intercept	1.82	−6.03	20.73	21.13	8.58	30.87
Minority Presidents						
President's base	.82	1.03	−.78	.54	.75	−.50
	(.03)	(.03)	(.03)	(.04)	(.03)	(.03)
Opposition base	.81	.62	—	.74	.40	—
	(.02)	(.03)		(.03)	(.04)	
Cross-pressured opposition	−.39	—	.39	−.24	—	.25
	(.02)		(.02)	(.03)		(.03)
Cross-pressured partisans	—	−.59	.77	—	−.32	.61
		(.03)	(.02)		(.03)	(.02)
Intercept	−9.18	−10.15	25.20	2.26	−3.10	22.14
R^2	.58	.56	.63	.34	.43	.40

Note: Entries are unstandardized regression coefficients. Standard error of the estimate in parentheses.

base, then the probability of victory is high regardless of what the opposition party does. For a minority president, however, these results present a different picture. Minority presidents do face the dilemma noted in the previous section. The only condition in which a minority president's probability of victory is greater than under the condition of no unity is if he attracts unified support without generating unified opposition. But unified support from the president's party base tends to be associated with unified opposition from the opposition party base.

SUMMARY AND CONCLUSIONS

The findings presented in this chapter provide general support for our decision to place party and ideology at the center of the explanation of presidential-congressional relations. Members of Congress do provide levels of support for the president that are broadly consistent with their partisan and ideological predispositions. Facing a Congress composed of a more favorably predisposed cast of actors does increase the chances of presidential success.

The party linkage, however, is relatively weak. The literature frequently argues that ideological diversity in American parties is the major roadblock to more responsible parties. The analysis in this chapter shows that the lack of unity is only partly the result of ideological diversity. Even using a relatively relaxed standard of unity (75 percent voting together), members of the more ideologically homogeneous party bases unify far less often than in parliamentary systems with responsible parties. Overall, the president's party base provided unified support on about 60 percent of presidential roll calls. Only under Kennedy and Johnson in the House did behavior of the president's party base approach a responsible party standard. And the opposition party base was even less disciplined, unifying against the president on only slightly more than half the roll calls.

Nonetheless, reducing ideological diversity in the parties would increase cohesion. And on the subset of important presidential roll calls, the behavior of party bases is more disciplined—the president's party base provides unified support on an average of more than 70 percent of important votes, and the opposition party base unifies against the president about two-thirds of the time.

For majority presidents, unity in the party base is a key ingredient of success. When a majority president's base is unified, the chances of victory approach certainty. If the base is split, the probability of victory drops considerably. And the base is frequently split. In parliamentary systems, partisan control of the legislature virtually assures victories; in the United States, having more members in Congress who are predisposed to support the president is an advantage, but one insufficient to guarantee victories.

If party control is divided, the president's chances of victory generally decrease if the party factions unify. And divided control was the condition for more than half the period of this study. Thus party unity in a presidential system results in something of a paradox. Under a majority president, actions that strengthen the party linkage also strengthen the linkage between the president and Congress. Under a minority president, in contrast, actions that strengthen the party linkage tend to increase tensions between the executive and legislative branches.

The behavior of the party factions does not occur in a vacuum. Congressional leaders exert a major influence on members' behavior. Therefore, in the following chapter, we turn out attention to the behavior of party and committee leaders and the effects of leaders' cues on congressional decisions to support the president's policy preferences.

CHAPTER 5

CONGRESSIONAL LEADERSHIP
AND PRESIDENTIAL SUCCESS

The institutional structure of Congress imposes constraints on members' behavior. Few institutions of Congress exert as much influence on members' behavior as congressional leaders. Congressional leaders, therefore, are pivotal actors in interactions between the president and Congress. Indeed, as members of Congress with long tenure, congressional leaders are likely to have more influence on how Congress responds to presidential preferences than anything the president can do personally. Presidents sometimes acknowledge their dependence on congressional leaders. At a White House bill signing ceremony, President Lyndon Johnson handed one of the pens he had used to Speaker of the House John McCormack (D–Massachusetts), and quipped: "I have found out that if I get along with the Speaker, you get these signing ceremonies more often. I think that the Speaker works on the basis that a bill a day keeps the President away" (quoted in Adler 1966, 237).

The Speaker of the House is among the most important congressional leaders. The centralization of power in the hands of the Speaker reached its apex between 1890 and 1910. Speakers' domination of the House of Representatives during this period has led some refer to this period as "the House under Czar Rule" (Cooper and Brady 1981, 411). The last of the czars was Speaker Joseph G. Cannon (R–Illinois), who served from 1903 to 1910. Although Cannon's powers differed little from those of his immediate predecessors, his exercise of the prerogatives of the chair to achieve his own goals bordered on the dictatorial. A staunch conservative, Cannon used his power to stifle many of President Theodore Roosevelt's progressive policies (Davidson and Oleszek 1985, 174). An observer of Cannon's domination of the House quipped that "when a constituent asked his Representative for a copy of the House's rules and regulations, the member sent him a picture of Speaker Cannon" (MacNeil 1963, 79).

An example of Cannon's congenial but autocratic style occurred once when Democrats discovered that most of the Republicans were absent from the House floor. Democrats called for a quick vote on a bill they favored, hoping to pass it while they had a majority on the floor. House rules provided for calling the roll twice. But Cannon thwarted the Democrats' victory by quietly asking the clerk to call the roll a third time in violation of House rules. The Democratic minority angrily demanded that the Speaker justify his arbitrary action. Cannon answered calmly and candidly: "The Chair will inform the gentlemen. . . . The Chair is hoping a few more Republicans will come in." The Democrats laughed at Cannon's candor, and his lieutenants rounded up enough Republican votes to defeat the bill (MacNeil 1963, 78).

The House rebelled against "Cannonism" in 1910–11 and stripped the Speaker of the tools to enforce autocratic rule. The revolt "permanently altered the Speaker's personal control over the House, but it did not destroy totally . . . the Speaker's influence over decisions of the House" (MacNeil 1963, 80). Instead, the reforms forced the Speaker to exercise the powers of the chair more fairly, and they enhanced the power of committee chairs chosen on the basis of seniority. With the protection of an automatic seniority system, some committee chairs ran their committees like personal fiefdoms, often frustrating the goals of party leaders and presidents. Reforms in the mid-1970s altered the seniority system and forced committee leaders to be more responsive. But just as strong Speakers before and after Cannon exercised influence through personal friendship, persuasion, and savvy knowledge of House rules, committee leaders in the contemporary Congress continue to wield considerable influence using the same techniques.

This chapter, therefore, will analyze the influence of congressional leaders on presidential-congressional relations. We explore the support that presidents receive from party and committee leaders in Congress and the impact that leaders' support has on the behavior of the various party factions.

AN OVERVIEW OF CONGRESSIONAL LEADERSHIP

Congressional leadership is not monolithic. The structure of Congress establishes two sets of leaders in each chamber: (1) party leaders elected by a majority of the members of each party caucus, and (2) committee chairs and ranking minority members chosen on the basis of committee seniority. The two types of leaders—elected and seniority—perform different institutional roles.

While leaders continue to pursue political goals based on personal or constituency preferences, their institutional positions systematically affect their behavior, including how they are likely to respond to the president's policy preferences. Furthermore, the efficacy of leaders' efforts to influence the outcome of presidential roll calls is likely to be affected by whether they lead the majority or minority party and whether elected and seniority leaders within each party are united in support or opposition.

Elected Party Leaders

Because they are elected, party leaders are likely to come from their party's ideological mainstream, and they must be responsive to members' needs. Members of Congress expect the party leaders to perform several important functions, including (1) organizing and running the chamber in a way that allows individual members to meet their goals, (2) being articulate communicators and defenders of the party's positions, and (3) building coalitions on legislation of importance to party members (Sinclair 1983). The expectations hold for both majority and minority party leaders, although minority leaders' influence over scheduling is limited by their minority status.

In their efforts to promote programs of the national party, the president's party leaders typically assume the role of administration lieutenants in Congress. For example, during his first term, President Reagan received enthusiastic support from his party leaders in Congress. House Minority Leader Robert Michel (R–Illinois) said, "I'm a servant of the president. I like being a good soldier" (quoted in Ripley 1983, 225). Senate Majority Leader Howard Baker (R–Tennessee) expressed a similar view of his role: "I'm the president's spear carrier in the Senate" (quoted in Oleszek 1984, 30); "I intend to try to help Ronald Reagan [carry out] the commitments he made during the campaign" (quoted in Sundquist 1981, 402).

Party leaders from the president's party, however, are not always so strongly committed to supporting the administration. Leaders in Congress are constrained by institutional interest and loyalty. They may be the administration's lieutenants, but they are leading an undisciplined army that makes its own demands on them. The tensions that may exist between the congressional party leadership and the White House arise because one or more of the demands that party leaders in Congress need to meet are inconsistent with presidential needs. For example, leaders' need to schedule legislation for floor consideration in a fashion that is consistent with the time demands of party members may be in conflict with the scheduling needs of the president.

Because Congress is a coequal branch, congressional leaders often view themselves as peers rather than servants of the president. Speaker Sam Rayburn (D–Texas) was once asked how many presidents he had served under. Rayburn replied, "I haven't served under any, but I've served *with* several, and I've seen 'em come and go" (quoted in Holley 1987, 18, emphasis in original). Similarly, during the Carter administration, Senate Majority Leader Robert Byrd (D–West Virginia) made it clear that his primary loyalty lay with the Senate: "He [Carter] urges certain actions and says he hopes he'll have our support. But he can't force it. The president is expected to make his proposals, and we have a responsibility to him and the country to weigh them and act on them if, in the judgment of the Senate, we should" (quoted in Edwards 1984, 188). Byrd's separation from the White House did not go unnoticed. A Carter staffer once said of Byrd, "God, is he independent. He ain't our man—he's the Senate's man" (quoted in Edwards 1984, 187).[1] Thus, whereas Michel and Baker saw themselves as closely linked to the policy goals of the president, Rayburn and Byrd were clearly more conscious of being at the opposite end of Pennsylvania Avenue and sought a degree of independence from the president.

Opposition party leaders may choose from a variety of roles, ranging from constructive opposition (the party proposes alternative programs and seeks to win concessions from the president) to obstructionism (the party seeks to defeat the president's policy preferences without proposing any alternatives). Which role the opposition plays is influenced by whether it is the majority or minority party.

The majority party shares with the president the responsibility for governing, and it must participate in building majority coalitions in Congress. As a result, a majority opposition is constrained to propose and pass its own programs over the president's objection, or try to reach a compromise with the president if there are not enough votes to override a veto. In 1974, for example, the large Democratic majorities in Congress passed numerous programs over President Ford's vetoes. During the 100th Congress (1987–88), in contrast, the Democrats experienced more difficulty sharing the responsibility to govern. Reagan was frequently uncompromising on key budget issues, but the Democrats did not have the votes to override a presidential veto. In 1987, Republicans in the House refused to support the President's budget or to participate in negotiations over the Democratic alternative, saying that the Democrats were the majority party and had to take responsibility. Frustrated Democrats complained that the Republicans were behaving irresponsibly.

A minority opposition party has more leeway to choose from the full range of roles. The choice depends on such variables as the closeness of the party division in the chamber and how aggressive and partisan the president is (Jones 1970). For instance, Eisenhower had cordial relations with the Democratic minority in the 83rd Congress. After Democrats won back control of Congress in the 1954 elections, Speaker Sam Rayburn (D–Texas) explained why relations had been friendly when the Democrats were the minority and would likely continue so now that they would be the majority: "In the past about 85 percent of the time Eisenhower's programs were just an extension of Democratic principles. . . . We're not going to hate Eisenhower bad enough for us to change our principles" (quoted in Congressional Quarterly 1965, 29). In addition, Republican control of the 83rd Congress was narrow, and

1. The separation, however, should not be exaggerated. Although relations between Byrd and Carter were strained at first, by the second session of the 95th Congress (1978), the majority leader had a more comfortable working relationship with the White House, especially on important legislative issues (Ornstein, Peabody, and Rohde 1985, 23).

Eisenhower had a modest program. Conditions were different in the 89th Congress. Republicans were so hopelessly outnumbered after the Democratic landslide in 1964 that they were largely powerless to prevent or even delay Johnson's ambitious program. When Republican ranks grew in the 90th Congress, they were able to limit Johnson's success.

Thus party leaders are likely to exercise considerable influence over presidential-congressional relations. As noted above, however, party leaders' support of or opposition to the president is constrained by institutional forces in Congress. Standing committees are among the most important congressional institutions, and committee actions constrain party leaders. Ripley (1983, 232) reports that party leaders usually adopt the position of their party delegation on the relevant committee and work to obtain passage of that position. Leaders of the majority and minority parties on each standing committee have, with few exceptions, acquired their office through the operation of an automatic seniority rule.

Committee Leaders

Because seniority automatically elevates the member to a leadership position, committee leaders often come from the cross-pressured faction of their party, and they are relatively insulated from pressure to support the positions of party majorities. Richard Bolling (D–Missouri) cites a committee chairman in the 1920s who told his colleagues, "You can go to hell; it makes no difference what a majority of you decide; if it meets with my disapproval it shall not be done; I am the committee" (quoted in Bolling 1965, 39). Although this example represents an extreme case, leaders chosen on the basis of seniority can operate independently of the party leadership in deciding whether to support or oppose positions of the national party. Relative to elected party leaders, therefore, committee leaders from the president's party are less likely to support his preferences, and opposition committee leaders are more likely to support him.

Conflict between party and committee leaders makes party unity less likely. While it is reasonable to expect that on most pieces of legislation the party leadership and ranking party member on the relevant committee will take the same position, these instances of agreement typically result from shared preferences or compromise.

Reforms in the mid-1970s made committee leaders more accountable and responsive to the party majorities. Both Republicans and Democrats adopted reforms between 1971 and 1973 that made committee leaders subject to election by secret ballot. The defeat of three senior House committee chairs in 1975 demonstrated that the majority would use its power to hold unresponsive committee chairs accountable.

The weakening of the seniority system is a mixed blessing for the president. On the one hand, committee leaders must be more responsive to the preferences of the party mainstream. But on the other hand, the president can no longer negotiate with a small number of powerful committee leaders. The president now must deal with a much larger group of representatives. And reforms adopted during this same period that strengthened subcommittees widened the circle of relevant congressional actors even more.

LEADER INFLUENCE IN CONGRESS

A primary function of congressional leaders is to build winning coalitions. Leaders' efforts to influence members to join party coalitions, however, is constrained by a second function—the need to "maintain peace in the family" (Sinclair 1983, 1). Using the available resources in a heavy-handed way might produce success in the short run but would exacerbate intraparty conflict in the long run. Such an outcome could make future coalition building more difficult and perhaps even threaten the leader's tenure in office. Sinclair (1983) argues that rather than using their powers to reward or punish members based on their votes, party leaders use their resources to allow as many party members as possible to meet their individual goals. By so doing, leaders hope to build up a feeling of obligation on the part of members who receive some favor from the leadership, thereby increasing the likelihood of future support. The need to maintain cordial relations within the party increases the leadership's difficulty in building winning coalitions.

Influence before the Floor Vote

Whether leaders succeed in their efforts to build winning coalitions while keeping peace in the family depends in large part on what they do before the floor vote. Much of party leaders' influence derives from their ability to read the mood of Congress and the skill with which they use the formal powers available to them—discretion over assignment of legislation to a standing committee, scheduling debate and floor votes at the best time, and influence over the conditions under which legislation is considered on the floor (e.g., rules proposed by the Rules Committee in the House and arranging unanimous consent agreements in the Senate).

The power of committee leaders, especially the committee chair, is obviously strongest while the legislation is still in the committee. Prior to the reforms of the mid-1970s, committee chairs could on some occasions single-handedly prevent proposed legislation from reaching the floor. Emanuel Celler (D–New York), chair of the House Judiciary Committee from 1955–73, was once asked how he stood on a bill in his committee. He replied, "I don't stand on it. I am sitting on it. It rests four-square under my fanny and will never see the light of day" (quoted in Udall 1988, 229). While reforms in the mid-1970s increased the power of subcommittees at the expense of full committee chairs and ranking minority members, the influence of full committee leaders has not "wholly evaporated" (Hall 1987, 113). Legislation that reaches the floor bears the imprint of committee activities during hearings and mark-up. And committee recommendations are accepted on the floor about 90 percent of the time (Dyson and Soule 1970), usually without amendment (Ripley 1983, 200).

One must be careful, however, not to exaggerate committee chairs' power to single-handedly deny the majority an opportunity to express its will on proposed legislation. Most bills that die in committee without even a hearing probably have little support. And Fenno (1973) finds that the strategic premise of some committees is to report legislation that will pass. Thus a major reason why committees are successful on the floor is that they often anticipate floor reactions.

Wilbur Mills (D–Arkansas), chair of the powerful House Ways and Means Committee from 1958 to 1975, is the classic example of a committee chair who supposedly held the fate of major presidential programs in his hands. Mills was an especially important player during the Kennedy administration because Ways and Means had jurisdiction over most of Kennedy's major legislative proposals. Mills supported the administration on tax reform, foreign trade, and increasing the debt ceiling, and the bills all passed. Mills opposed Kennedy on Medicare, among the administration's highest priorities, and it remained stalled in committee until 1965 (MacNeil 1963, 265; Manley 1970).

But even in the Medicare case, Mills may have correctly read the mood of the House. Mills was a cautious man who did not like to lose.[2] Although Democrats had a large majority in the 87th Congress, many were conservatives who opposed Medicare. Furthermore, Republicans were solidly opposed, and the American Medical Association engaged in intense lobbying against the proposal. Given such unfavorable conditions, it was not clear that Medicare could pass on the House floor. After the Johnson landslide in 1964 brought many more liberal Democrats to the House, the chances of building a majority coalition in support of Medicare improved. The swollen Democratic ranks in the House also changed the party ratio on Ways and Means, and the new Democratic committee seats were filled with Medicare supporters. Faced with a situation in which a majority of both the committee and the House favored Medicare, Mills changed his position, and the bill passed by an over-

2. Mills lost in his first vote as chair of Ways and Means in 1958. This major embarrassment caused him to be more cautious in the future (MacNeil 1963, 334). Note that Ways and Means is the committee in Fenno's study most strongly committed to the strategic premise of writing bills that would pass (Fenno 1973, 55). After that initial embarrassment, Mills rarely lost a floor vote.

whelming margin (313–115). Yet the closeness of the vote on a watered-down Republican substitute suggests that the program could not have passed earlier if Mills had permitted it to come to the floor. Mills's recalcitrance, therefore, may have saved himself and Kennedy from a major defeat on the House floor (Congressional Quarterly 1969, 752–65). Thus we see that leaders are important as barometers of congressional responses even if they do not, or cannot, determine the success of presidential positions in Congress.

Influence on Floor Votes

While leaders' actions prior to the floor vote often determine whether a bill will pass or fail, their actions on roll call votes are important also. Party leaders frequently have commitments from a few members willing to support the leadership if their votes will change the outcome. A dramatic example occurred October 29, 1987, when Speaker Jim Wright (D–Texas) used tactics parallel to those of "Czar" Cannon in the case discussed at the beginning of the chapter to hand President Reagan and House Republicans a one-vote defeat on the budget reconciliation bill.

Republicans won the first round by defeating the rule 203–217 with the help of conservative Democrats who were uneasy about welfare reform provisions included in the bill. Wright countered with an unusual parliamentary tactic to bring the bill back up almost immediately. The Rules Committee met quickly and produced a second rule removing the welfare provisions and some other disputed provisions. The House is required to wait a day after committee action before taking up a rule, so Wright ended the legislative session for the day and within minutes started a new legislative day. The new rule was adopted 238–182, with all but thirteen Democrats voting against all but one Republican. But the drama did not end there. The vote on final passage appeared to be a loss for the Speaker. When the fifteen minutes normally allowed for voting had expired, the vote was 205–206. Wright delayed announcing the outcome until Jim Chapman, a second-term Democrat from Wright's home state, rushed back to the floor and changed his vote and the outcome. When Wright declared the bill passed, Republicans were furious and "booed the Speaker with rare ferocity" (Wehr 1987, 2653–55, quotation at 2653).

Committee chairs also exercise considerable influence on roll call votes. Chairs are often the floor managers of committee bills.[3] Under House rules, chairs are expected to support the committee's recommendation and resist

---

3. In the Senate, the majority leader is often the floor manager of routine floor business. And since the 93rd Congress, most House bills have been managed on the floor by subcommittee chairs (Deering and Smith 1985, 196–97). But even when they are not floor managers, chairs of the parent committees continue to exert influence because of the knowledge of and expertise in the subject they have acquired over a period of time.

changes from the floor, or allow another committee member to manage a bill they cannot support (Congressional Quarterly 1976, 343).[4] Wilbur Mills's skillful performance in 1962 managing a bill to increase taxes is credited with persuading the House to pass it. The timing was not conducive to passing a tax increase—the vote occurred in March, just eight months before the election. Mills's performance was so impressive that a leading opponent of the bill took the floor to praise Mills as the "most capable" chairman of Ways and Means he had ever seen (MacNeil 1963, 326). Although examples of party leaders and committee chairs turning defeat into victory on the floor are rare, they nonetheless demonstrate that leaders' actions are important at the floor vote stage as well as earlier.

As noted in chapter 2, determining the influence of congressional leaders on the voting behavior of the rank and file is problematical. We can observe whether leaders and followers vote together on roll calls, but we cannot observe the causal process that leads to the agreement. Agreement may result from several causal processes, including (1) leaders' using their powers to persuade members to vote with the party, (2) members using leaders' positions as voting cues, (3) leaders and members voting together because they share the same values, and (4) leaders' anticipating and responding to the preferences of the members. Furthermore, because all four causal processes operate simultaneously, with each one accounting for some of the agreement on any given vote, it is not possible to determine the mix of causes.

Nonetheless, analyzing the extent to which leaders and followers vote together contributes to understanding presidential success in Congress regardless of the process that produces the agreement. If members vote with leaders because of bargaining or cue-taking, then support from leaders would produce some additional votes for the president's position. But even if agreement results from shared values or from leaders' being influenced by the rank and file, the analysis of leader-follower agreement is useful. If there is an association between the votes of leaders and followers in Congress, then knowing whether party and committee leaders support the president's position indicates likely levels of support from factions in Congress. In short, leaders may be viewed as *barometers* that can be used to test the climate in Congress.

Effectiveness of Leaders

The effectiveness of congressional leaders on presidential roll calls is affected by several variables. The literature often focuses on personal qualities of leaders—their ability to read the mood of Congress correctly, their personal style,

---

4. Disagreement between the chair and the committee does not occur often. One study found that committee chairs agreed with committee majorities 87 percent of the time in the House and 80 percent of the time in the Senate (Fleisher and Bond 1983a).

and their parliamentary skills. Although personal qualities are no doubt important, the literature fails to provide guidelines for reliable measurement of this type of variable. Moreover, the impact of such variables is very much dependent upon the perceptions of other congressional actors, and perceptions can change dramatically from one issue to another as contextual conditions change.

Two variables likely to influence effectiveness of leaders in general, however, are readily observable: (1) whether they are leaders in the majority or minority party, and (2) whether party and committee leaders in each party are unified or whether the committee chair and ranking minority member agree on a united committee position.

The analysis in the previous chapter reveals that majority or minority status systematically affects support that presidents receive from the different party factions. Majority presidents have the advantage of being able to bargain within their own party. Minority presidents, in contrast, have no choice but to seek support from members of the opposition. While we are not able to observe presidential negotiations with congressional leaders across the entire sample of presidential roll calls, we should be able to observe the effects of such negotiations in patterns of leader support. Because minority presidents have a greater need to make concessions to the opposition party than do majority presidents, minority presidents should receive greater support from party and committee leaders of the opposition, and opposition leader support should exert a greater effect on the success of the positions of minority presidents.

Unity among leaders is also important. If both party and committee leaders are unified, they provide reinforcing cues for the rank and file as well as a consistent reading of the likely congressional response for the president. Unity of both leaders in a party is likely to have the greatest effect on members of the party bases. Unity of both committee leaders against the president's party leader is likely to decrease party unity. Committee unity may have greater effect on cross-pressured members. In the previous chapter, we found that minority presidents are less likely to receive unified support from their party base. We speculated that this might result from minority presidents' being opposed by committee leaders more often. We will look at this possibility below.

In the following section we look at presidential support from four leaders in each chamber—the majority and minority floor leaders, and the chair and ranking committee members of the committee that considered the bill.[5] We will determine whether elected leaders are more supportive than seniority leaders and whether the differences discovered have changed since the re-

5. We are not able to analyze the behavior of the Speaker of the House because he rarely votes.

Table 5.1 Party and Committee Leader Support for the President

	HOUSE				SENATE			
	PRESIDENT'S		OPPOSITION		PRESIDENT'S		OPPOSITION	
PRESIDENT	Party Leader	Com-mittee Leader	Party Leader	Com-mittee Leader	Party Leader	Com-mittee Leader	Party Leader	Com-mittee Leader
DDE	80	69	57	50	90	81	43	51
(DDE— 83rd)*	(89)	(79)	(53)	(50)	(87)	(86)	(46)	(45)
JFK	93	87	35	39	87	63	32	38
LBJ	92	87	35	43	77	57	57	55
RMN	87	81	45	52	67	64	19	46
GRF	85	83	31	52	66	74	27	49
JEC	77	74	33	46	72	66	49	56
RWR	81	71	39	47	88	71	33	44
Majority presidents	86	81	35	44	80	65	46	50
Minority presidents	83	75	43	50	76	72	29	49

Note: Entries are the percentage of votes on which each leader voted in agreement with the president's position.
*Support for Eisenhower in the Republican-controlled 83rd Congress.

forms to the seniority system in 1975. In addition, we will look to see if there are different patterns for majority and minority presidents and whether the behavior of leaders differs on important issues. Finally, we look at support from combinations of leaders to analyze the effects of leader unity.

SUPPORT FROM PARTY AND COMMITTEE LEADERS

Individual Leaders' Support on Conflictual Votes

Table 5.1 reports the percentage of votes on which party and committee leaders from the president's and the opposition party supported the president's position on roll call votes. Party and committee leaders generally behave as expected. The president's party leader is generally more supportive than the committee leader of his party; the opposition party leader is generally less supportive than the committee leader of the opposition party. While opposition leaders are less likely to support the president than are leaders of his party, the opposition leaders perform the role of loyal opposition less consistently than leaders of the president's party perform the role of his lieutenants.

Behavior of the leaders, however, does not vary greatly for majority and minority presidents. In the House, minority presidents receive slightly less support from their own party and committee leaders and slightly more support from the opposition party's leaders than do majority presidents. This difference suggests that minority presidents are more likely to make concessions to the opposition. In the more individualistic Senate, the expected difference between majority and minority presidents does not show up. Minority presidents receive considerably less support from the opposition floor leader, while support from the opposition committee leaders is essentially the same for both majority and minority presidents.

There is variation in support across administrations, and a few cases do not conform to the general pattern. The perception that Eisenhower maintained cordial relations with Democratic leaders is supported by our analysis. Democratic party and committee leaders supported Eisenhower's position about as often as they opposed him. In fact, the Democratic floor leader in the House supported Eisenhower's position more often than did the Democratic committee leaders. Democrats' support for Eisenhower is not much different in the Republican-controlled 83rd Congress. Republican party and committee leaders in the House, however, were 9 to 10 percent more supportive when Republicans controlled the House. The behavior of Senate Republican leaders is not much different in the 83rd Senate.

Leaders' support for Carter is also consistent with popular perceptions. Carter received support from leaders of his party less often than other majority presidents. In the House, both the Democratic floor leader and committee chairs were much less supportive of Carter. In the Senate, majority leader support for Carter was only slightly less than for Johnson, but Senate committee chairs supported Carter more often than they supported either Kennedy or Johnson.

Committee chair support for Johnson in the Senate was unusually low. Indeed, Republican party and committee leaders supported Johnson about as often as did his committee chairs in the Senate. But in the House, Kennedy and Johnson received support from the Democratic floor leader more than 90 percent of the time, and they received support from committee chairs 87 percent of the time. The only other president to receive such consistent support from his party and committee leaders was Eisenhower in the Senate. In the House, however, the Republican floor leader's support for Eisenhower was lower than for other minority presidents.

The behavior of Senate Republican leaders toward Ford is unusual. Ranking committee members supported Ford's position nearly three-fourths of the time, while his elected floor leader supported him only two-thirds of the time. House leaders' support for Ford is more typical.

The quotations from Reagan's party leaders cited above lead one to expect unusually high support. In the Senate, the Republican floor leader (Howard Baker) supported Reagan 8 percent more often than the average for majority presidents. But in the House, Reagan's floor leader (Bob Michel) was less supportive than average.

The behavior of seniority leaders on roll call votes did not become more partisan after the reforms and the defeat of Democratic committee chairs in the mid-1970s. As noted above, Democratic committee chairs in the House supported Carter less often than they supported Kennedy and Johnson. Reagan received less support from Democratic committee leaders in both chambers than did other Republican presidents, but support is only about 3 percent below the average for other Republican presidents. Republican committee leaders were also less supportive of Reagan's positions. Thus the reforms may have made committee leaders more responsive to the rank and file in terms of how they exercise the formal powers of leadership (scheduling hearings, reporting bills to the floor, etc.), but committee leaders did not become noticeably more partisan in their roll call voting behavior on presidential roll calls.

Thus the behavior of congressional leaders is generally consistent with expectations. With few exceptions, elected party leaders are more likely to support the position of the national party mainstream than are seniority leaders. The previous chapter revealed that the behavior of the party bases was more partisan on the subset of important votes. If the issues are more intensely partisan in this subset, then elected party leaders' behavior should become more partisan, but seniority leaders might be insulated from these increased partisan pressures.

Individual Leaders' Support on Important Votes

Table 5.2 shows how often leaders supported the president on important votes. The behavior of elected party leaders changes the most on important votes relative to behavior in the entire sample. On important roll calls, the president's party leader is more likely to support him and the opposition party leader is less likely to support him. In general, elected party leaders in the House are about 5.2 percent more partisan on important votes, and elected party leaders in the Senate are 9.5 percent more partisan.

In several cases, the differences are striking. In the House, every president received the support of his floor leader on at least 80 percent of important votes, and five presidents got their floor leader's support more than 90 percent of the time. Notice that while Reagan's floor leader in the House supported him less often than average overall, on important votes he agreed with Reagan's position more often than average (91 percent). And Kennedy received the sup-

Table 5.2 Party and Committee Leader Support for the President on Important Votes

	HOUSE				SENATE			
	PRESIDENT'S		OPPOSITION		PRESIDENT'S		OPPOSITION	
PRESIDENT	Party Leader	Committee Leader	Party Leader	Committee Leader	Party Leader	Committee Leader	Party Leader	Committee Leader
DDE	80	62	55	59	89	79	30	50
(DDE— 83rd)*	(85)	(77)	(46)	(69)	(67)	(70)	(40)	(30)
JFK	100	90	17	23	100	58	17	20
LBJ	91	95	26	44	88	42	44	45
RMN	94	76	38	58	79	71	9	56
GRF	97	90	20	48	70	83	23	25
JEC	81	67	34	42	75	62	33	38
RWR	91	84	34	41	96	69	31	35
Majority presidents	90	84	29	41	88	60	34	36
Minority presidents	89	76	38	50	83	77	18	51

Note: Entries are the percentage of important votes on which the leader voted in agreement with the president's position.
*Support for Eisenhower in the Republican-controlled 83rd Congress.

port of his party leader in both the House and Senate on every important vote. In the Senate, party leader support tends to increase more on important votes, but it is still generally lower than that of House party leaders. Only Kennedy and Reagan received support from their Senate floor leader on more than 90 percent of important votes, but support for Eisenhower and Johnson was also close to the 90 percent mark.

Committee leaders' behavior changes less on the subset of important votes. House committee leaders are an average of 1.8 percent more partisan, and Senate leaders are 3 percent more partisan. But the magnitude and direction of the changes vary considerably. For example, Johnson received support from House committee chairs on 95 percent of important votes, 8 percent more often than on all votes. Senate committee chairs, however, supported him on only 42 percent of important roll calls, much less often than overall.

The analysis thus far reveals that presidents frequently have the support of party and committee leaders. This analysis, however, does not reveal how often both elected and seniority leaders of each party take the same position and how often committee chairs and ranking minority members agree on presidential roll calls.

Support from Pairs of Leaders

On a meaningful percentage of votes, each leader fails to support the president's position. If party and committee leaders oppose the president on the same votes, then the percentage of votes with mixed cues is less than if the two types of leaders oppose the president on different votes. For example, suppose the president's party and committee leader each oppose him on 15 percent of roll calls. If these key cue-givers oppose the president on the same 15 percent of the votes, then he has unified leader support 85 percent of the time. If the two leaders oppose him on different votes, then the president has unified leader support on only 70 percent of roll calls. When party and committee leaders take opposing positions on a roll call, it is possible that the president's committee leader is aligned with the committee leader of the opposition party, thereby presenting a united committee cue. Hence we turn our attention to discovering how often party and committee leaders of both parties present reenforcing cues and how often both committee leaders take the same position.

Table 5.3 shows the percentage of votes on which the president received support from both, one, or neither of his party's leaders. Ripley (1983, 242–43) reports that party leaders usually work with the senior members of the reporting committee to pass the committee's recommendations. The results of our analysis of presidential roll calls support this observation. On a large percentage of votes, party and committee leaders of the president's party take the same position, usually in support of the president. When party and committee leaders take opposing positions, the president is more likely to have support from his party leader.

Party and committee leaders in the House take the same position more often than leaders in the Senate. More than 70 percent of the time both of the president's leaders support his position on the floor. Although majority presidents are more likely to receive unified support from both leaders, there is considerable variation across both majority and minority presidents. Eisenhower, Carter, and Reagan received both of their leaders' support about two-thirds of the time; Nixon and Ford received united leader support a little more than three-fourths of the time; and Kennedy and Johnson received support from both leaders more than 85 percent of the time.

In the Senate, the president's congressional leaders are less likely to unify in support of and are more likely to unify in opposition to his position. Across administrations, unified leader support varies from a low of about half for John-

Table 5.3 Frequency of Unified and Divided Cues from Party and Committee Leaders of the President's Party

	HOUSE				SENATE			
PRESIDENT	Both	Party Leader	Committee Leader	Neither	Both	Party Leader	Committee Leader	Neither
DDE	64	17	6	14	76	13	4	7
JFK	87	5	0	7	63	24	1	13
LBJ	86	6	2	5	50	24	7	19
RMN	76	10	4	9	53	15	11	22
GRF	79	8	4	8	61	6	13	20
JEC	65	13	9	13	55	18	12	16
RWR	66	17	5	12	69	18	2	11
Majority presidents	78	9	4	9	59	20	6	15
	(80)	(10)	(4)	(6)	(55)	(31)	(4)	(10)
Minority presidents	70	14	5	11	63	14	9	15
	(72)	(18)	(4)	(6)	(71)	(13)	(5)	(11)

Note: Entries are the percentage of votes on which neither, one, or both leaders of the president's party voted in agreement with his position. Support on important votes in parentheses.

son, Nixon, and Carter to a high of slightly over three-fourths for Eisenhower. Presidents generally receive unified leader support less often in the Senate. Kennedy and Johnson, the presidents who attracted support from both leaders most often in the House, were the least successful at attracting support from both Senate leaders. Only Eisenhower and Reagan received unified support from their congressional leaders more often in the Senate.

The pattern on important votes is not greatly different. On important issues, the president is slightly more likely to have the united support of his congressional leaders and less likely to have both opposed. The single exception is for majority presidents in the Senate, where the president's party and committee leaders are less likely to unite in support on important votes.

Table 5.4 presents the same analysis for opposition party and committee leaders. Leaders of the opposition party are less cohesive in their behavior than are leaders of the president's party. Whereas the president's party and committee leaders in the House took the same position about 84 percent of the time, opposition House leaders agreed on about three-fourths of presidential

Table 5.4 Frequency of Unified and Divided Cues from Party and Committee Leaders of the Opposition Party

	HOUSE				SENATE			
PRESIDENT	Both	Party Leader	Com-mittee Leader	Neither	Both	Party Leader	Com-mittee Leader	Neither
DDE	41	18	10	32	33	11	18	38
JFK	21	15	17	48	22	8	14	56
LBJ	28	8	16	49	38	10	17	35
RMN	40	7	12	41	11	8	35	46
GRF	28	3	23	47	17	11	34	38
JEC	25	8	22	46	36	13	20	31
RWR	37	3	12	48	19	12	25	44
Majority presidents	27	9	18	47	31	12	19	39
	(21)	(9)	(19)	(51)	(21)	(10)	(14)	(55)
Minority presidents	37	8	13	42	22	8	28	42
	(36)	(7)	(14)	(43)	(14)	(6)	(37)	(43)

Note: Entries are the percentage of votes on which neither, one, or both leaders of the opposition party voted in agreement with the president's position. Support on important votes in parentheses.

roll calls. In the Senate, the president's leaders agreed about three-fourths of the time, while opposition Senate leaders agreed about two-thirds of the time. And, while agreement between the president's party and committee leaders is overwhelmingly in support of the president, opposition leaders unify against the president a little more than 40 percent of the time and in support of his position about 30 percent of the time.

Behavior on important votes is only a little more consistent with the role of loyal opposition in a responsible party system. Opposition leaders unite in opposition to majority presidents slightly more than half the time. But under minority presidents, opposition leaders are no more likely to unify against the president on important votes than overall.

Table 5.5 analyzes the behavior of the committee chair and ranking minority member of the committee reporting the bill to determine how often committee leaders agreed on presidential roll calls. The ranking Democratic and Republican committee members agree about half the time in the House

Table 5.5 Frequency of Unified and Divided Cues from Committee Leaders

	HOUSE				SENATE			
PRESIDENT	Both	President's Leader	Opposition Leader*	Neither	Both	President's Leader	Opposition Leader	Neither
DDE	35	33	14	17	44	37	6	13
JFK	35	52	3	10	32	32	6	30
LBJ	41	46	2	11	36	22	19	23
RMN	48	32	4	16	42	21	4	33
GRF	45	37	7	11	44	28	5	23
JEC	36	38	10	16	47	20	8	24
RWR	42	29	6	23	35	36	10	19
Majority presidents	38	43	6	13	38	28	11	23
	(36)	(49)	(6)	(12)	(23)	(37)	(14)	(27)
Minority presidents	43	32	7	18	43	28	5	23
	(40)	(37)	(11)	(13)	(42)	(33)	(9)	(16)

Note: Entries are the percentage of votes on which neither, one, or both committee leaders voted in agreement with the president's position. Support on important votes in parentheses.

and about two-thirds of the time in the Senate. When the two committee leaders take the same position, they support the president more often than they oppose him. On important votes, the chair and ranking minority member are less likely to take the same position.

Earlier we speculated that members may be less unified under minority presidents because minority presidents may have committee support less often than majority presidents. We see that both committee leaders agree with minority presidents about 5 percent more often than they agree with majority presidents. In the Senate, both majority and minority presidents receive support from neither leader a little less than one-fourth of the time, but in the House, minority presidents are opposed by both leaders more often. When committee leaders are split, the president is much more likely to have the support of the committee leader of his party, which means that majority presidents have the support of the committee chair much more often than do minority presidents. Minority presidents have support from the committee chair (either alone or in combination with the ranking member) only about half the time in each chamber; majority presidents have support from the chair on 81 percent of House roll calls and two-thirds of Senate roll calls.

Thus this analysis basically confirms our expectations about leaders' behavior. Party and committee leaders of each party in the United States Congress are often split on presidential roll calls. Earlier we speculated that the lack of leader unity might affect support from members of the various party factions. In the next section, we turn our attention to the issue of the effects of leader support.

EFFECTS OF LEADER SUPPORT

In the analysis of relationships between leaders' positions on presidential roll calls and the behavior of the various party factions, we should remember that our observation of leader behavior occurs at the same time as our observation of rank and file behavior. Because we have not observed the interactions, we cannot determine which of the four processes discussed above caused agreement between leaders and followers. But as we argued above, even under the weakest causal process—leaders viewed as barometers of likely member responses—it is useful to analyze agreement. The relationships reveal which leaders are likely to be the most relevant predictors on presidential roll calls.

Table 5.6 shows the results of a multiple regression of presidential support from each party faction on support from party and committee leaders. Following the practice in the previous chapter, we report separate estimates for majority and minority presidents. The regression coefficients estimate the change in the percentage of support from the faction if the leader supports the president's preference.[6]

The behavior of the party bases is more predictable than is the behavior of cross-pressured factions. In the House, between 45 and 55 percent of the variance in support from the two bases is explained by leaders' positions, while the models of support from the cross-pressured factions explain less than 20 percent. In the Senate, the difference between the models is less, but the models of the party bases explain more variance than the models of the cross-pressured factions. These results are consistent with our argument that the interaction of members' party and ideology creates predispositions to support or oppose the president, and that leaders' positions may be viewed as barometers

---

6. These models estimate the relationship for each leader individually. This specification assumes that the effect of support from two or more leaders is linear and additive. We estimated models with interaction terms of various combinations of leaders. The more complex models did not perform significantly better than the simple linear models; the increase in explained variance averaged less than 2 percent. Moreover, using the parameters of the linear models to predict support from each faction under different combinations of leader support produces reasonable predictions. No combination, for example, produces an estimate of support greater than 100 percent. Therefore, we rely on the more parsimonious linear models.

of likely member responses. From this perspective, it is not surprising that congressional leaders' positions are less accurate barometers and less effective cues for cross-pressured members than for members of the party bases.

The party bases tend to be most responsive to the party leaders and next most responsive to the party's committee leader. Support from the opposition party floor leader tends to reduce support from a party base, and support from the opposition committee leader is generally insignificant. The pattern of relationships is similar in both chambers for both the president's party base and the opposition party base and for both majority and minority presidents. There is, however, some variance in the general pattern.

Support from members of the president's party base increases by more than 30 percent if he has the support of his party's floor leader. The single exception to this pattern is under minority presidents in the Senate, when support from the president's base increases only 24 percent if he gets the support of his party leader. Support from the president's committee leader increases base support by more than 13 percent, except in the Senate under majority presidents, when support from the president's committee leader adds less than 8 percent.

Members of the opposition party base also increase support for the president if he has the support of the opposition floor leader. If a minority president takes a position that is supported by the opposition party leader (i.e., the majority leader), then support from the opposition party base increases by more than 40 percent in the House and 37 percent in the Senate. Majority presidents, in contrast, benefit less from support from the opposition party leader, gaining only about 27 percent more from the opposition base. But notice that taking positions that appeal to the opposition floor leader tends to reduce support from the president's own party base. And the decline in support from the president's partisans is nearly twice as great for minority presidents (10 to 11 percent) as it is for majority presidents (about 5.5 percent).

The pattern of relationships for the cross-pressured factions is more erratic. Under majority presidents in the House, members of both cross-pressured factions are about equally responsive to cues of their own party and committee leaders, and positions of party and committee leaders of the other party are insignificant. In the Senate under majority presidents, cross-pressured members of the president's party are much more responsive to support from the committee chair ($b = 27.5\%$) than to support from their party leader ($b = 12.1\%$). Members of the cross-pressured opposition are most responsive to their own party leader ($b = 20\%$), while the increase associated with support from the committee leader is about half as much ($b = 11.5\%$). But notice that support from the president's own party leader also increases support from the cross-pressured opposition by more than 11 percent.

Under minority presidents, the cross-pressured factions are even less con-

Table 5.6 Relationships between Leader Support and Support from the Party Factions

	House				Senate			
	President's Base	Cross-Pressured Partisans	Cross-Pressured Opposition	Opposition Base	President's Base	Cross-Pressured Partisans	Cross-Pressured Opposition	Opposition Base
Majority Presidents								
President's party leader	32.48 (2.77)	14.16 (3.93)	8.58 (5.26)	−6.10 (2.69)	36.04 (1.70)	12.12 (2.11)	11.44 (2.43)	−8.46 (1.73)
President's committee leader	18.15 (2.36)	11.98 (3.37)	−1.14 (3.65)	−4.28 (2.30)	7.92 (1.45)	27.52 (1.80)	−4.04 (2.06)	.18 (1.47)
Opposition party leader	−5.54 (1.82)	6.20 (2.59)	14.19 (2.80)	27.58 (1.77)	−5.48 (1.36)	1.76 (1.69)	19.86 (1.94)	26.51 (1.38)
Opposition committee leader	.26 (1.76)	−.02 (2.51)	17.88 (2.72)	13.79 (1.72)	−2.14 (1.37)	1.18 (1.71)	11.51 (1.96)	12.78 (1.34)
Intercept	40.11	18.56	34.21	18.62	44.13	23.62	40.12	21.02

Minority Presidents

President's party leader	36.48 (2.19)	12.31 (3.10)	18.76 (3.36)	-4.42 (2.13)	23.55 (2.02)	24.39 (2.60)	.97 (2.99)	2.52 (2.13)
President's committee leader	13.33 (1.93)	10.44 (2.74)	3.06 (2.97)	-6.28 (1.88)	18.53 (2.03)	13.91 (2.52)	3.23 (2.90)	-1.05 (2.06)
Opposition party leader	-10.86 (1.84)	25.47 (2.62)	-5.94 (2.83)	40.69 (1.79)	-9.94 (1.81)	22.20 (2.25)	-9.37 (2.59)	37.17 (1.84)
Opposition committee leader	-1.12 (1.88)	1.84 (2.67)	20.81 (2.90)	10.07 (1.83)	-.11 (1.79)	.66 (2.22)	28.80 (2.56)	13.20 (1.82)
Intercept	31.63	26.34	22.66	19.87	44.16	16.06	32.08	10.52
R^2	.45	.19	.16	.55	.37	.29	.21	.42

Entries are unstandardized regression coefficients. Standard error of the estimate in parentheses.

sistent in the pattern of cue-taking. Cross-pressured members of the president's party in the House are about equally responsive to support from their party's floor ($b = 12.3$ %) and committee leaders ($b = 10.4\%$). But the increase associated with support from the opposition floor leader ($b = 25.5\%$) is greater than the combined effect of the party and committee leaders of their own party. The president's cross-pressured partisans in the Senate also respond to support from the opposition party leader ($b = 22.2\%$), but they are most responsive to their own party leader ($b = 24.4\%$). Indeed, they are more responsive to the party leader than are members of the president's base. Members of the cross-pressured opposition are most responsive to support from their committee leaders in both the House ($b = 20.2\%$) and the Senate ($b = 28.8\%$). But support from their party leader tends to reduce support about 6 percent in the House and 9 percent in the Senate. And in the House, support from the president's party leader is associated with about 19 percent more support from members of the cross-pressured opposition.

Thus floor positions of party and committee leaders are related to the behavior of the party factions. For both majority and minority presidents, the party bases tend to be most responsive to support from congressional leaders of the same party; presidential support from opposition leaders is generally insignificant or negative. Cross-pressured members tend to respond to support from leaders of the opposite party as well as to support from their own party, and minority presidents may tend to attract more support from cross-pressured members if they have support from opposition leaders.

Leader Support and Unity of the Party Factions

The analysis in the previous chapter revealed that unity of the various factions is important to understanding presidential-congressional relations. The coefficients in table 5.6 can be used to estimate which conditions of leader support and opposition are likely to result in unified support or opposition from the various party factions.

In the previous chapter we defined unity as 75 percent of members voting together. The estimates from the regression analysis reveal that if the president has the support of both leaders of his party, then he will usually receive unified support from his party base. The predicted level of support from the base when both leaders support the president exceeds the 75 percent threshold in both chambers and for both majority and minority presidents. If the president has support from his party leader but is opposed by his party's committee leader, then predicted support from the president's base exceeds the 75 percent threshold only in the Senate for majority presidents (predicted support of 80 percent). In the House under majority presidents, predicted support with only the party leader's support falls just short of being unified (73 percent). If minority presidents have support from only their party leader, the model predicts that the president will receive less than unified support from his base (about 68 percent in both chambers).

Thus this analysis of leaders helps us understand why the president often fails to receive unified support from his base and why the frequency of unified support is less for minority presidents. The analysis in the previous chapter revealed that the party base of majority presidents unified on an average of 78 percent of House votes and 65 percent of Senate votes. The base of minority presidents unified about 42 percent of the time in the House and 58 percent of the time in the Senate. Majority presidents are likely to get unified support from their base if they have their party leader's support, and majority presidents get their party leader's support on an average of 86 percent of House votes and 80 percent of Senate votes (see table 5.1). Minority presidents are likely to get unified base support only if they have the support of both the party and committee leaders, but minority presidents receive support from both leaders on only 70 percent of House votes and 63 percent of Senate votes (see table 5.3).

The analysis in the previous chapter also revealed that the opposition party base is less likely to unify against the president than the president's base is to unify in support. Overall, the opposition party bases unified barely over half the time (mean = 54 percent in the House and 52 percent in the Senate). The behavior was not greatly different for majority and minority presidents. Using the estimates in table 5.6 to predict the conditions under which the opposition base will unify against the president's position (i.e., support less than 25 percent), we discover that unified opposition is likely if the president is supported by his own party leader and opposed by both the party and committee leaders of the opposition party. But both opposition party leaders oppose the president only about 40 percent of the time (see table 5.4). If the president gets the support of either opposition leader, then unified opposition is less likely. The predictions with support from the opposition committee leader alone are right at the 25 percent mark, but support from the opposition party leader alone increases support from the opposition base to around 40 percent for majority presidents and 50 percent for minority presidents. And note that minority presidents have the support of the opposition party leader (either alone or with some other leader) 43 percent of the time in the House and 29 percent in the Senate (see table 5.1).

Members of the cross-pressured factions seldom unify either for or against the president's position. The estimates from table 5.6 indicate that unified support or opposition from the cross-pressured factions tends to occur when both party leaders and the president's committee leader take the same position. It is rare for all three leaders to support or oppose the president, and in some cases the maximum prediction from a cross-pressured faction falls short of the 75 percent threshold.

Now that we have a picture of the relationships between leader support and support from the various party factions, we turn our attention to the relationship between leader support and presidential success or defeat. Although we could use the coefficients from the regression analysis of leader effects on each faction to estimate presidential wins and losses on roll calls, the mechanics of estimating wins from the regression equations is complex because of the large number of coefficients that must be interpreted simultaneously. To simplify the interpretation, therefore, we estimate a reduced form of the model.

Leader Support and Presidential Success

Table 5.7 reports the results of a probit analysis estimating the effects of support from each of the four leaders (support = 1) on presidential success/ defeat. Following our usual practice, we estimate separate models for majority and minority presidents. The models correctly predict 80 percent of the cases. All of the coefficients are positive, indicating that support from any of the four leaders tends to increase the chances that the president's position will prevail on the floor. As one would expect, however, support from some leaders is more important than others, and several coefficients are not statistically insignificant.

For majority presidents, support from the president's floor leader has the strongest effect on success in both the House and Senate. The coefficients for the president's committee leader and the opposition floor leader are both significant and of similar magnitude, although the effects are not as strong as the effect of support from the majority leader. The opposition committee leader has a much weaker effect; the coefficients are small in comparison to those for other leaders, and neither is statistically significant (although the one in the House just misses the .05 level). Thus for majority presidents, support from the majority leader and committee chairs is most important, and support from the minority floor leader helps about as much as much as committee chair support. The ranking minority committee member's position on the floor has little effect.

The same leaders exert similar effects on the success of minority presidents. Support from the opposition party leader (i.e., the majority leader) has the greatest impact on floor success, followed by support from the opposition committee leader (i.e., the committee chair) and the president's floor leader. Support from the president's committee leader is weak, and the coefficient in the House is not statistically significant. Minority presidents, therefore, tend to have the greatest chances of success if they take positions that gain the support of party and committee leaders of the other (majority) party. Although parties in the United States Congress are weak and undisciplined, majority

Table 5.7 Probit Estimates of the Effects of Leader Support on Presidential Success

	HOUSE		SENATE	
	b	(s.e.)	*b*	(s.e.)
Majority Presidents				
President's party leader	1.81	(.19)	1.29	(.11)
President's committee leader	.79	(.16)	.75	(.10)
Opposition party leader	.75	(.16)	.69	(.11)
Opposition committee leader	.27	(.14)	.13	(.10)
Intercept	−1.23		−1.94	
Minority Presidents				
President's party leader	.74	(.17)	.80	(.15)
President's committee leader	.10	(.14)	.28	(.14)
Opposition party leader	1.28	(.13)	1.13	(.13)
Opposition committee leader	.74	(.13)	.91	(.11)
Intercept	−1.53		−1.61	
% correctly predicted	80		82	
Null prediction	64		67	

Note: Entries are probit coefficients. Standard error of the estimate in parentheses.

control is important. As a result, minority presidents are more likely to win if they compromise and avoid taking positions that provoke partisan coalitions.

Table 5.8 reports the probability of success given support from different combinations of leaders.[7] As one would expect, if the president receives support from none of the four leaders, his preference has little chance of passing on the floor. For majority presidents, the probabilities are .11 in the House and .17 in the Senate. For minority presidents, the probabilities are even less—$p = .06$ in the House and .05 in the Senate. If the president has the support of all four leaders, then the chances of success increase to better than

7. These probabilities are estimated from the probit equations in table 5.7. See appendix B for a discussion of the procedure for converting probit estimates into probabilities.

Table 5.8 Estimated Probabilities of Presidential Victory under Various Conditions of Leader Support

	HOUSE		SENATE	
	$\hat{z}$	$\hat{p}$	$\hat{z}$	$\hat{p}$
Majority Presidents				
No leader support (intercept)	−1.23	.11	−.94	.17
President's party leader	−.05	.48	.34	.63
President's committee leader	−.44	.33	−.19	.42
President's party and committee leaders	.74	.77	1.10	.86
President's party leader and both committee leaders	1.01	.84	1.23	.89
All four leaders	1.76	.96	1.82	.97
Minority Presidents				
No leader support (intercept)	−.53	.06	−1.61	.05
President's party leader	−.79	.21	−.81	.21
President's committee leader	−.14	.08	1.33	.09
President's party and committee leaders	−.69	.25	−.53	.30
President's party leader and both committee leaders	.05	.52	.38	.65
Opposition party leader	−.25	.40	−.48	.32
Opposition party and committee leaders	.48	.68	.43	.67
All four leaders	1.33	.91	1.51	.93

Note: Z-scores estimated from probit equations. The estimated $\hat{p}$ is the probability that the president's position wins under the specified condition.

.90 for both majority and minority presidents. It is rare, however, for all four leaders to vote together, either in support of or in opposition to the president. The president usually has the support of at least one leader of his party, and he is usually opposed by at least one leader of the opposition.

Under typical conditions of various leaders supporting and opposing the president, the probabilities of success vary considerably for majority and minority presidents. If a majority president has the support of only his party leader (assuming both committee leaders and the opposition floor leader oppose), the probability of success is .48 in the House and .63 in the Senate. Support from the committee chair alone does not help as much as ($p = .33$ in the House and .42 in the Senate). Minority presidents, in contrast, are helped far less by support from their party and committee leaders alone. The probability of a minority president's position winning with the support of only the ranking minority member remains less than one in ten in both chambers, and support from the minority floor leader alone increases the chances to only one in five.

When a majority president gets support from both the party and committee leaders of his party (assuming both opposition leaders oppose), then the chances of success are better than three out of four ($p = .77$ in the House and .86 in the Senate). And if he picks up both committee leaders with his party leader, then the probabilities of success are .84 in the House and .89 in the Senate. For a minority president, the chances of success when his party and committee leaders support him remain low—$p = .25$ in the House and .30 in the Senate. Getting the support from both committee leaders and his party leader increases a minority president's chances of success to only .52 in the House and .65 in the Senate—about the levels predicted for a majority president with only his party leader, and much lower than the predicted probability for majority presidents under the same conditions of leader support. Minority presidents generally benefit more from opposition leader support than do majority presidents. If a minority president has the support of both opposition leaders (assuming opposition from both of his party leaders), then the chances of victory are about two out of three in both chambers, better than when he has the support of his own party leader and unified committee leader support.

SUMMARY AND CONCLUSIONS

Thus congressional leaders are important actors influencing relations between the president and Congress. In the previous chapter, we found that the party bases often fail to unify. The analysis of the behavior of congressional leaders in this chapter helps us understand why the party link is relatively weak.

Leaders of the president's party generally support his positions, while leaders of the opposition are more likely to oppose. But the role leaders play in the United States Congress differs considerably from the role of leaders in responsible party legislatures. Congressional leaders have great leeway to decide what their role should be with respect to the president.

The quotations earlier in the chapter from two recent Senate majority leaders—Senators Baker and Byrd—illustrate two views of the proper role of congressional leaders. The Baker model suggests that the leader of the president's party should assume the role of administration lieutenant in Congress and work to see that the president's preferences prevail there. The Byrd model suggests that congressional leaders should remember that they lead a separate, coequal branch of government and that their primary responsibility is to help Congress exercise independent collective judgment on presidential preferences. The behavior of these two leaders is generally consistent with their rhetoric. On important presidential roll calls Baker supported the president's preference 96 percent of the time, while Byrd agreed with the president only 75 percent of the time.

Despite the rhetoric, however, congressional leaders fall short of the responsible party model. On a significant number of roll calls, the president's party leader fails to support him. And on the other side of the aisle, the behavior of the opposition party leader is less consistent with the role of leaders in responsible party legislatures. Even on important votes, the opposition party leader supports the president about 30 percent of the time.

Furthermore, while support from party leaders increases the chances that the president's position will prevail, probabilities remain considerably less than certain. Elected party leaders share influence with committee leaders chosen by a relatively automatic seniority system. Although committee leaders agree with party majorities on most issues, they are less supportive of party positions than are elected party leaders. On presidential votes, committee leaders of the president's party are less supportive, and opposition committee leaders are more supportive. Reforms in the mid-1970s may have made committee leaders more susceptible to party pressures, but their behavior on presidential roll calls did not become noticeably more partisan.

Conflict between congressional leaders decreases the chances that the bases will be unified: the president's party base is likely to unify in support only if he has the support of both leaders, and the opposition party base is likely to unify against only if both leaders oppose the president's position. Both of the president's congressional leaders support his position only about 74 percent of the time in the House and 61 percent of the time in the Senate, and they both oppose him about 10 percent of the time in the House and 15 percent of the time in the Senate. Opposition party leaders are even less likely to present reenforcing cues. Party and committee leaders of the opposition unify against the president only a little over 40 percent of the time, and they unify in support about 31 percent of the time.

Hence lack of unity among leaders is common. And note that we analyzed the behavior of only two leaders in each party. Leadership is much more extensive than the elected floor leader and ranking party member on committees. In addition to these leaders, there are extensive whip organizations, leaders of party caucuses, subcommittee chairs, etc. Analyzing the behavior of a wider set of leaders would probably reveal more conflict than we observed here.

The lack of unity among congressional leaders helps us understand the relatively low levels of unity in Congress. The behavior of congressional leaders, however, also reflects constraints imposed on them by the expectations of the rank and file and by their own personal and constituency preferences. In addition to these constraints, policy context may also condition the behavior of leaders and followers in Congress. One policy context thought to influence presidential-congressional relations is whether the issue involves domestic policy or foreign policy. The following chapter looks at the debate over whether the president is more successful on foreign policy, and if so why.

CHAPTER 6

POLICY CONTEXT: THE TWO PRESIDENCIES THESIS

On August 2, 1964, President Johnson informed Congress and the American people that United States destroyers had been attacked by North Vietnamese patrol boats in the Gulf of Tonkin. Johnson asked Congress for support similar to that granted to his predecessors to deal with previous international crises (Sundquist 1981).

Congress responded to the President's request, granting him authority to take all necessary steps, including the use of armed force, to deal with the crisis in Southeast Asia. Senator J. William Fulbright (D–Arkansas), author of the resolution and chairman of the Senate Foreign Relations Committee, pushed the resolution through the committee after only brief testimony from the Secretaries of State and Defense. On August 7, the Tonkin Gulf resolution sailed through the House without dissent and passed the Senate with only two votes against (Sundquist 1981). It is clear from the congressional debate that the President was to decide when to use force and how much force to use.

Two years after the Tonkin Gulf resolution, Aaron Wildavsky (1966) published his classic article, "The Two Presidencies." He argued that the president has greater success in dealing with Congress on foreign and defense matters than on domestic issues. The broad-based congressional support for the president observed on the Tonkin Gulf resolution is certainly consistent with the two presidencies thesis. Like his predecessors, Johnson had to bargain and compromise with Congress as his domestic programs slowly worked their way through the legislative obstacle course. On this national security issue, in contrast, Johnson used his information advantage and position as commander in chief to dominate Congress.

THE TWO PRESIDENCIES DEBATE

Research Questions

Since the publication of Wildavsky's article, students of presidential-congressional relations have debated whether the president is more successful on foreign and defense policy than on domestic policy. The primary issue raised by the two presidencies thesis is whether the president wins more often on foreign policy than on domestic policy. If we discover that the president does indeed win more often on foreign policy, several other questions arise: (1) Has the tendency for greater success on foreign policy changed over time? (2) Does it occur to the same extent in both the House and Senate? (3) What are the sources of additional support that lead to more victories on foreign policy? That is, does the president receive more support from members of both parties on foreign policy, or does the additional support come only from members of his party or from members of the opposition?

Previous Studies of the Two Presidencies Thesis
Previous studies have used a variety of measures—box scores, key votes, individual presidential support scores—to test the two presidencies thesis empirically. Although the measures used are all appropriate indicators of presidential success, none is able to address all of the questions posed above.

The earliest empirical tests of the two presidencies thesis used box scores to compare presidential success in the two policy areas (Wildavsky 1966; LeLoup and Shull 1979). Analysis of box scores provided empirical support for the two presidencies thesis (Wildavsky 1966), although the differences decreased in the period after the Vietnam War (Peppers 1975; LeLoup and Shull 1979).

Analyzing box scores can reveal whether the president wins more often on foreign policy than on domestic policy and whether the differences change over time. But because of the problems and limitations with box scores discussed in chapter 3, this approach cannot reveal the sources of support and opposition in the two policy areas, and it does not tell us the causes of presidential defeats or in which chamber the losses occur.

Furthermore, basing an analysis on box scores assumes that the only relevant aspect of presidential-congressional relations is the fate of legislation initiated by the president. Although the president may set much of the legislative agenda (especially in foreign policy), a great deal of important legislation originates in Congress. Presidents often care about these congressional initiatives and seek to influence their outcome.

A recent example is the conflict between President Reagan and the 99th Congress (1985–86) over the issue of imposing economic sanctions against South Africa. Reagan strongly opposed sanctions, arguing that his policy of "constructive engagement" was a more effective strategy to encourage the end of apartheid. But despite the president's strong opposition, Congress passed a bill imposing sanctions and mustered the votes to override the president's veto. The passage of this congressionally initiated legislation "marked the most serious defeat Reagan . . . suffered on a foreign issue and one of the most stunning blows of his presidency" (Felton 1986, 2338). A measure that fails to take into account presidential victories and defeats on congressional initiatives is incomplete and may produce misleading results.

Sigelman (1979, 1198) criticized the use of box scores because they include a large number of "noncontroversial and largely inconsequential" presidential initiatives. He analyzed Congressional Quarterly's key votes to solve this problem and found little difference in presidential success on key domestic and foreign policy roll calls.

Analysis of key votes can answer most of the questions raised by the two presidencies thesis. We can determine whether the president wins more foreign policy votes, and we can identify any changes that might have occured over time. Furthermore, we can identify which types of individuals supported and opposed the president on each vote to determine the source of any additional presidential victories on foreign policy issues. Sigelman (1979), for example, analyzed support for the president from members of his party and from the opposition.[1]

Although analyzing presidential victories on CQ's key votes overcomes many of the problems with box scores, some important limitations remain. A major limitation of CQ's key votes is the small number. Each year CQ selects between five and twenty key votes in each chamber. The president does not express a position on all key votes, which reduces the number of usable cases, and in some years the number of foreign policy votes selected is very small. In 1973, for example, Nixon expressed a position on only three key foreign policy votes in the House and three in the Senate. Because these numbers are too small to permit meaningful comparisons within each chamber, House and Senate votes must be aggregated. And aggregating both chambers produces fewer than twenty key foreign policy votes in many Congresses. Thus relying

---

1. This analysis, however, is less useful than it might have been because Sigelman does not report average levels of support from each party on key foreign and domestic roll calls. Instead, he reports the proportion of votes on which the president received a majority (or an extraordinary majority or one-third-plus-one, depending on the decision rule) from each party. Calculating levels of partisan support in this way distorts differences between the two policy areas and may produce misleading results. In 1973–74, for example, Nixon received majority support from the opposition party on 35 percent of key domestic votes and on none of the foreign policy votes. The average levels of support from Democrats on these votes was 41 percent on domestic votes compared to 33 percent on foreign policy votes. Thus in this case Sigelman's method of comparison produces difference between foreign and domestic policy five times larger than the difference produced when we compare average levels of support (35 percent higher on domestic policy with Sigelman's method versus 7 percent higher on domestic policy when we compare averages). And the distortion in this case works against finding support for the two presidencies. Although both methods reveal that Democrats were more supportive of Nixon on domestic policy in 1973–74, it is mathematically possible for the president to receive higher average levels of support from a given party on foreign policy but still receive support from a majority of the party members on a much larger percentage of domestic policy votes.

on CQ's key votes not only precludes analyzing differences that might occur across chambers, the number of cases is still small enough to produce distortions in the success rates even after aggregating votes in both chambers across the two years of a Congress.

While Sigelman (1979, 1199) is correct that we should base our analysis on major foreign and domestic issues, the key votes selected by CQ are not the only important votes that occur in a given year. In our efforts to avoid "characterizing executive-legislative relations on the basis of a series of essentially trivial roll calls" (Sigelman 1979, 1199), we must be careful not to restrict the data base so much that it distorts results and precludes addressing important issues.

A second limitation is that CQ's key votes probably are not representative cases of presidential-congressional interactions on important issues. Although key votes are one set of roll calls judged to be important by one set of informed political observers, they are not selected to be a representative sample of nontrivial issues. Instead, they are limited to an arbitrary number each year, regardless of how many important votes occur. Because the number of important issues varies each year, we need to find a way to identify a larger, more representative sample of votes on these issues.

As an alternative to the use of box scores or key votes to test the two presidencies thesis, Edwards (1986) used individual presidential support scores to compare differences in individual members' support for the president on foreign and domestic votes. His analysis revealed that presidents of both parties tend to receive higher support from members of the opposition and less support from their partisans on foreign policy issues (Edwards 1986, table 7).

Analysis of presidential support scores can reveal whether the president receives more support from individual members on foreign policy than on domestic policy, the source of any additional support, and whether the differences vary over time (Edwards 1986, 253). Moreover, there is a sufficient number of cases to analyze the House and Senate separately and to observe changes over time within administrations. This approach, however, cannot address the primary issue raised by the two presidencies thesis: Does the president *win* more often on foreign policy than on domestic policy?

As noted in chapter 3, presidential support scores measure a different type of success than either box scores or key votes. Whereas box scores and success rates on key votes measure some aspect of the president's programmatic success, presidential support scores indicate the president's relative success in attracting votes from individuals in Congress over some specified period (usually a calendar year). Attracting support from individual members is certainly an important ingredient of presidential-congressional relations. But because policymaking in Congress results from collective decisions, analyzing support from individuals tells us little about the president's success at achieving the ultimate goal—winning votes. The president may receive higher levels of support from certain types of individuals in the different policy areas, but the additional support may fail to change the collective results. The additional support may be insufficient to increase the number of victories, or it may occur on votes the president would have won anyway without the extra votes.

Thus, based on the results of previous tests, it is still not entirely clear whether the two presidencies phenomenon ever existed, and if it did exist, whether it has changed over time. Furthermore, if the evidence ultimately reveals that the president has greater success on foreign policy, only Edwards's analysis addresses the issue of the sources of additional support that lead to more foreign policy victories. But even Edwards's analysis is incomplete on the issue of the sources of support because he fails to look at the four party factions in Congress. The two presidencies thesis is silent on whether the additional support on foreign policy comes from members of both parties, mainly from members of the president's party, or mainly from the opposition party. And the theory does not predict whether members of the party bases or cross-pressured members should change the most across the two policy areas.

In this chapter, therefore, we test the two presidencies thesis with our set of conflictual presidential roll calls. We determine first if the president wins more often on foreign policy than on domestic policy. Then we seek to identify sources of any additional support from members of the party factions and congressional leaders. Finally, we analyze our subset of important votes to determine if behavior differs on more important issues.

FOREIGN AND DOMESTIC POLICY SUCCESS ON CONFLICTUAL ROLL CALLS

Table 6.1 presents presidential success rates on conflictual foreign and domestic roll calls for each Congress. The overall averages across all Congresses appear to support the two presidencies thesis. Presidential success is 12.5 percent higher on foreign policy than on domestic policy in the House and 15 percent higher in the Senate.

Some have argued that the president's advantage has decreased over time, in large part as a result of increased congressional assertiveness on foreign policy issues after Vietnam (LeLoup and Shull 1979). Our analysis, however, reveals no such change over time.

Table 6.2 compares presidential success on foreign and domestic policy for the 83rd through 88th Congresses (1953–64) and for the 89th through 98th Congresses (1965–84). Dividing the time period after the 88th Congress is appropriate because it was in 1965 that controversy over the Vietnam War

Table 6.1 Presidential Success on Conflictual Foreign and Domestic Policy Roll Calls in the House and Senate, 83rd–98th Congresses

PRESIDENT AND CONGRESS	HOUSE					SENATE				
	Foreign		Domestic			Foreign		Domestic		
	%	(N)	%	(N)	Diff.	%	(N)	%	(N)	Diff.
DDE										
83rd	93	(14)	70	(33)	23	86	(28)	73	(71)	13
84th	92	(12)	34	(35)	58	85	(26)	53	(53)	32
85th	63	(19)	54	(67)	9	85	(33)	63	(81)	22
86th	80	(15)	47	(68)	33	66	(38)	37	(123)	29
Total	80	(60)	51	(203)	31*	79	(125)	54	(328)	25*
JFK										
87th	96	(24)	72	(69)	24	85	(47)	76	(152)	9
88th	67	(12)	87	(30)	−20	78	(27)	88	(47)	−10
Total	86	(36)	77	(99)	9	82	(74)	78	(199)	4
LBJ										
88th	60	(20)	94	(31)	−34	87	(23)	92	(154)	−5
89th	84	(25)	87	(121)	−3	70	(46)	77	(166)	−7
90th	67	(24)	66	(119)	1	69	(61)	63	(169)	6
Total	71	(69)	79	(271)	−8	72	(130)	76	(419)	−4
RMN										
91st	83	(12)	64	(59)	19	90	(21)	51	(86)	39
92nd	93	(27)	69	(48)	24	65	(48)	41	(49)	24
93rd	44	(36)	44	(111)	0	64	(45)	30	(178)	34
Total	68	(75)	55	(218)	13*	69	(114)	38	(293)	31*
GRF										
93rd	47	(15)	39	(23)	8	46	(28)	30	(20)	16
94th	60	(25)	36	(99)	24	73	(30)	47	(72)	26*
Total	55	(40)	37	(122)	18*	60	(58)	43	(92)	17*
JEC										
95th	70	(57)	62	(97)	8	92	(79)	64	(106)	28
96th	71	(94)	67	(117)	4	71	(68)	71	(143)	0
Total	71	(151)	64	(214)	7	82	(147)	68	(249)	14*
RWR										
97th	57	(37)	54	(84)	3	76	(63)	82	(115)	−6
98th	69	(74)	25	(103)	44	90	(77)	70	(50)	20
Total	65	(111)	38	(187)	27*	84	(140)	78	(165)	6

Note: Entries are the percentage of votes on which the president's position won. Number of votes in parentheses.

*$p < .05$ (significance test performed for each presidential administration).

Table 6.2 Presidential Success on Conflictual Foreign and Domestic Policy Roll Calls before and after the Vietnam War

TIME PERIOD	HOUSE					SENATE				
	Foreign		Domestic			Foreign		Domestic		
	%	(N)	%	(N)	Diff.	%	(N)	%	(N)	Diff.
1953–64	78	(116)	62	(333)	16*	81	(222)	70	(681)	11*
1965–84	68	(426)	57	(981)	11*	75	(566)	60	(1134)	15*

Note: Entries are the percentage of votes on which the president's position won. Number of votes in parentheses.
*$p < .05$.

began to break down the consensus on national security and foreign policy that had existed previously.[2] We see that the president's advantage on foreign policy declined only slightly in the House and increased in the Senate. Although the difference between foreign and domestic is still present, in absolute terms the president succeeds less often on foreign policy in the recent period.

A closer inspection of the results in table 6.1 suggests that the two presidencies phenomenon is largely a function of the party of the president rather than something that has diminished over time—Republican administrations are characterized by two presidencies; Democratic administrations are not.

Table 6.3 compares foreign and domestic policy success for Republican and Democratic presidents. We see that Republican presidents have a 22 percent advantage on foreign policy roll calls in the House and a 24 percent advantage in the Senate. Democratic presidents, in contrast, win the same percentage of foreign and domestic policy roll calls in the House, and they have only a 4 percent advantage on foreign policy in the Senate.

Note that both Democratic and Republican presidents have similar success rates on foreign policy votes. On domestic issues, however, Democratic presidents win about as often as on foreign policy, while Republican presidents have much less success on domestic issues. Thus it is low success on domestic issues rather than unusually high success on foreign policy that generates the difference for Republican presidents.

Republicans were the minority in Congress for most of the time period of this study, and lack of party control may have driven down the domestic policy success of Republican presidents. But the difference between foreign and domestic policy success rates is present even when Republicans controlled

2. This is also the dividing line used in previous studies (LeLoup and Shull 1979).

**Table 6.3 Success of Republican and Democratic Presidents
on Conflictual Foreign and Domestic Policy Roll Calls**

PARTY OF PRESIDENT	HOUSE					SENATE				
	Foreign		Domestic			Foreign		Domestic		
	%	(N)	%	(N)	Diff.	%	(N)	%	(N)	Diff.
Republican	68	(286)	46	(730)	22*	76	(437)	52	(878)	24*
Democrat	73	(256)	73	(584)	0	79	(351)	75	(937)	4*

Note: Entries are the percentage of votes on which the president's position won. Number of votes in parentheses.
$*p < .05$.

Congress. During periods of Republican control (83rd Congress and 97th and 98th Senates), Republican presidents did about as well on domestic policy as Democratic presidents. Nonetheless, even with increased success rates on domestic policy with majority status, Republican presidents still did better on foreign policy. Eisenhower's success in the Republican-controlled 83rd Congress was 23 percent higher on foreign policy than on domestic policy in the House and 13 percent higher in the Senate. Reagan had Republican majorities in the 97th and 98th Senates. Although his foreign policy success rate was 6 percent lower than his domestic policy success rate in the 97th Senate, he had a 20 percent advantage on foreign policy in the 98th Senate (see table 6.1).

Furthermore, the overall partisan averages are not disguising major differences from one Congress to another. There were ten Congresses with a Republican president. During these Republican administrations, the president's foreign policy success rate was more than 10 percent higher than his domestic policy success rate seven out of ten times in the House and nine out of ten times in the Senate. There were six Congresses with a Democratic president. During these Democratic administrations, the president's foreign policy success rate was more than 10 percent higher than his domestic policy success rate only once in each chamber.

Finally, the partisan differences in the two presidencies phenomenon persist over time. Assessing changes over time within party must be done cautiously. Eisenhower was the only Republican president in the study who served before 1965, and Kennedy's term and Johnson's first year in office are the only observations of Democratic presidents in the early period. Nonetheless, there is little evidence of a decline in the two presidencies phenomenon over time. The only decline over time occurred for Republicans in the House. Eisenhower enjoyed a thirty-one-point advantage in foreign policy in the House compared to the substantially reduced nineteen-point advantage for later Republican presidents. In the Senate, however, Eisenhower's twenty-five point foreign policy advantage is only slightly more than his Republican successors' twenty-three-point advantage. Again, looking at the absolute levels of success on foreign policy, Nixon, Ford, and Reagan all were less successful in the House on foreign policy votes than was Eisenhower. For Democratic presidents, the trend over time is reversed. Before the 89th Congress, Democratic presidents had a ten-point disadvantage on foreign policy votes in the House and a one-point disadvantage in the Senate. After the 89th Congress, Democrats won slightly more often on foreign policy roll calls (1 percent higher in the House and 8 percent higher in the Senate).

Thus analysis of success rates on conflictual roll calls reveals that only Republican administrations are characterized by two presidencies. This partisan difference is relatively stable over time, and it appears to a similar extent in both the House and Senate. What is the source of additional support that leads to more victories on foreign policy for Republican presidents? Do members of both parties tend to support the president more on foreign policy issues, or does support increase on foreign issues only from the opposition party or from the president's party?

Sources of Additional Support

Edwards (1986, table 7) presents evidence that presidents of both parties tend to receive higher support from the opposition and less support from their partisans on foreign policy issues. The findings of our analysis suggest that additional support from members of the opposition party helps Republicans more than it helps Democrats. We will look at support from the four party factions to see if different types of members behave differently toward Republican and Democratic presidents in the two policy areas.

Table 6.4 shows support for the president on foreign and domestic roll calls from the four party factions. The most consistent source of additional support for Republican presidents on foreign policy issues is the opposition political base, that is, liberal Democrats. All four Republican presidents received significantly more support from liberal Democrats on foreign policy votes in both the House and Senate. The average difference between the two policy areas is twelve points higher for foreign policy in the House and thirteen points higher in the Senate. Notice, however, that while liberal Democrats support Republican presidents more on foreign policy than on domestic policy, the actual level of support from liberal Democrats is generally lower than support from the other party factions. Only Eisenhower received support from more than half of liberal Democrats on foreign policy votes.

Support for Republican presidents from the other party factions is not consistently higher on foreign policy. Conservative Democrats in the House average fourteen points higher support for Republican presidents, but in the Senate the average is only 5 percent higher. Support from the two Republican factions does not differ greatly across the policy categories.

There are different patterns for each Republican president. Ford received significantly greater support on foreign policy from all four factions in the Senate, but in the House only liberal Democrats supported him more on foreign policy. The pattern for Reagan is just the reverse—more support from all four factions in the House, but in the Senate only liberal Democrats supported him more. Nixon received more support on foreign policy from cross-pressured Democrats in both chambers and from his base of conservative Republicans in the Senate. Eisenhower did better among liberal Republicans in the Senate.

Democratic presidents do not receive consistently greater support on foreign policy from any faction. But when there is a significant difference, it is usually greater support from members of the opposition party, primarily cross-pressured liberal Republicans. Liberal Republicans are the only faction to support Democratic presidents significantly more often on foreign policy. Looking at differences for individual presidents, we see that Carter did significantly better only among liberal Republicans in both chambers. Kennedy attracted greater support from both factions of the Republican party in both the House and Senate. Johnson received more support on foreign policy from conservative Republicans and conservative Democrats in the Senate, but in the House he did not attract significantly more support from any party faction.

Thus, like Edwards, we find that the primary source of greater foreign policy success is the opposition party. Members of the president's party are generally not more supportive on foreign policy than on domestic policy, and in several cases the president's partisans are considerably more supportive on domestic policy.[3]

Why do Republican presidents attract more support on foreign policy from liberal Democrats? One possible reason is the behavior of the president. While we cannot observe presidential activities and politicking on individual votes, we can determine if presidents systematically take different types of positions on foreign and domestic issues. If Republican presidents are more supportive of liberal positions on foreign policy than on domestic policy, then we would expect increased support from liberals in Congress.

3. We should note that in some cases it is difficult to find greater support on foreign policy from a particular faction because of ceiling effects. Kennedy and Johnson, for example, received support from over 90 percent of liberal Democrats in the House on domestic policy. It is difficult to observe significantly greater support on foreign policy when support on domestic policy is so near the maximum. Because levels of support from the opposition party factions are typically much lower, it is easier to find large differences, but the actual level remains low.

Table 6.4 Support for the President on Conflictual Foreign and Domestic Roll Calls from the Four Party Factions

PRESIDENT AND FACTION	House			Senate		
	Foreign % (N)	Domestic % (N)	Diff.	Foreign % (N)	Domestic % (N)	Diff.
Republican Presidents						
DDE						
Conservative Republicans	56 (60)	65 (203)	−9	67 (124)	79 (328)	−12
Liberal Republicans	66	64	2	77	61	16*
Conservative Democrats	28	31	−3	35	45	−10
Liberal Democrats	62	40	22*	58	27	37*
RMN						
Conservative Republicans	70 (75)	66 (218)	4	78 (114)	68 (293)	10*
Liberal Republicans	57	55	2	46	43	3
Conservative Democrats	59	49	10*	62	45	17*
Liberal Democrats	44	32	12*	30	24	6*
GRF						
Conservative Republicans	56 (40)	66 (122)	−10	78 (58)	69 (92)	9*
Liberal Republicans	55	46	9	50	39	11*
Conservative Democrats	44	49	−5	64	44	20*
Liberal Democrats	39	25	14*	31	22	9*
RWR						
Conservative Republicans	78 (111)	60 (187)	18*	77 (140)	79 (165)	−2
Liberal Republicans	54	40	14*	60	63	−3
Conservative Democrats	73	41	32*	52	53	−1
Liberal Democrats	33	22	11*	30	23	7*

All Republicans

Faction						
Conservative Republicans	68 (286)	64 (730)	4*	74 (436)	74 (878)	0
Liberal Republicans	57	52	3*	60	53	7*
Conservative Democrats	56	42	14*	52	47	5*
Liberal Democrats	43	31	12*	38	25	13*

Democratic Presidents

JFK

Faction						
Liberal Democrats	90 (36)	90 (99)	0	77 (74)	83 (199)	−6
Conservative Democrats	48	53	−5	50	53	3
Liberal Republicans	63	39	24*	64	48	16*
Conservative Republicans	32	19	13*	35	24	11*

LBJ

Faction						
Liberal Democrats	87 (69)	86 (271)	1	65 (130)	76 (489)	−11
Conservative Democrats	39	42	−3	45	39	6*
Liberal Republicans	60	56	4	73	71	2
Conservative Republicans	21	24	−3	49	40	9*

JEC

Faction						
Liberal Democrats	70 (151)	69 (214)	1	76 (147)	70 (489)	6
Conservative Democrats	33	42	−9	49	53	−4
Liberal Republicans	62	52	10*	76	65	11*
Conservative Republicans	28	27	1	24	33	−9

All Democrats

Faction						
Liberal Democrats	78 (256)	81 (583)	−3	72 (351)	76 (937)	−4
Conservative Democrats	37	44	−7	47	46	1
Liberal Republicans	62	52	10*	72	65	7*
Conservative Republicans	27	24	3	36	35	1

Note: Entries are the average percentage of the members of each party faction that voted in agreement with the president's position. Number of votes in parentheses.

*$p < .05$.

Table 6.5 President's Liberalism on Foreign and Domestic Policy

	LIBERALISM SCORE					
	Overall		Foreign Policy		Domestic Policy	
PRESIDENT	%	(N)	%	(N)	%	(N)
DDE	46	(164)	89	(47)	32	(117)
JFK	93	(106)	84	(19)	93	(87)
LBJ	91	(245)	90	(52)	91	(193)
RMN	25	(174)	30	(53)	23	(121)
GRF	14	(56)	9	(21)	17	(35)
JEC	82	(130)	81	(47)	83	(83)
RWR	12	(143)	4	(69)	19	(74)

Note: Entries are the percentage of ACA/ADA votes on which the president expressed a "liberal" position. A liberal position is disagreement with ACA or agreement with ADA. Number of votes in parentheses.

Presidential Ideology on Foreign and Domestic Issues

Table 6.5 reports liberalism scores for each president on foreign and domestic issues.[4] We see that presidents generally have similar ideology scores in the two policy areas. Among Democratic presidents, Johnson and Carter have virtually identical ideology scores on both foreign and domestic issues, and Kennedy is only slightly less liberal on foreign policy than on domestic policy.

Among Republican presidents, Eisenhower was much more liberal on foreign policy than on domestic policy, presidential behavior that could attract more support from liberal Democrats on foreign policy. Eisenhower's behavior, however, is not typical. Nixon was only seven points more liberal on foreign policy issues, and Ford and Reagan were less liberal on foreign policy, yet all three still received significantly more foreign policy support from liberal Democrats in both chambers. Thus more liberal positions on foreign policy issues provide only a partial explanation of why Republican presidents attract greater support from liberal Democrats on foreign policy votes.

Another possible explanation for increased presidential support on foreign policy is support from party and committee leaders in Congress. As noted above, congressional leaders serve as voting cues on floor votes (Kingdon

4. These scores are based on ACA and ADA votes on which the president expressed a position. A liberal position is defined as disagreement with the ACA position or agreement with the ADA position. Note that these votes are not used to calculate ideologies of members of Congress.

1981; Matthews and Stimson 1975). If Democratic leaders in Congress are more supportive of Republican presidents on foreign policy votes, then members of the Democratic party base might be encouraged to increase their support on foreign issues.

Support from Congressional Leaders

Table 6.6 shows how often the party leaders and the Republican and Democratic leaders of the committee reporting the bill voted in agreement with the president's position. Republican presidents tend to receive more support on foreign policy votes from party and committee leaders in both parties. The most dramatic increase in support occurs among Democratic leaders. Democratic leaders of committees reporting foreign and defense bills voted with Republican presidents nearly three-fourths of the time in the House and nearly two-thirds of the time in the Senate. On domestic policy votes, Democratic committee leaders voted with Republican presidents only forty percent of the time in each chamber, resulting in a thirty-four-point difference in the House and a twenty-three-point difference in the Senate. The Democratic floor leader in both the House and Senate also voted in agreement with Republican presidents more often on foreign policy, but the differences between the policy areas are not as great as the differences for Democratic committee leaders. The differences in support from Republican leaders across the policy areas are typically much less than the difference for their Democratic counterparts.

Democratic presidents tend to receive greater support on foreign policy only from Republican party and committee leaders. Although Democratic presidents receive more support on foreign policy from Democratic committee leaders in the Senate, the difference does not result from unusually high support on foreign policy. Instead, support from Senate committee chairs on domestic policy is unusually low. Kennedy, Johnson, and Carter received support from chairs of committees reporting domestic legislation only about half the time. Relatively normal levels of committee chair support on foreign policy and unusually low support on domestic policy result in a large difference between domestic and foreign policy.

Hence leader support may explain why the two presidencies phenomenon is limited to Republican presidents. Both Democratic and Republican presidents receive more support on foreign policy from the opposition leadership. Republican presidents also tend to attract more support from party and committee and leaders of their party. Consequently, there are more likely to be reinforcing bipartisan cues on foreign policy under Republican presidents. The increase in support for Republican president on foreign policy occurs mainly among Democrats because of the large increase in support on foreign policy from Democratic leaders.

Table 6.6 Support for the President from Congressional Leaders on Conflictual Foreign and Domestic Roll Calls

| | HOUSE | | | | | SENATE | | | | |
| | Foreign | | Domestic | | | Foreign | | Domestic | | |
PRESIDENT AND LEADER	%	(N)	%	(N)	Diff.	%	(N)	%	(N)	Diff.
Republican Presidents										
DDE										
Democratic party leader	81	(54)	49	(170)	32*	76	(124)	30	(316)	46*
Democratic committee leaders	69	(55)	44	(163)	25*	70	(120)	43	(307)	33*
Republican party leader	94	(53)	76	(175)	18*	87	(109)	91	(320)	-4
Republican committee leaders	78	(54)	66	(169)	12	86	(110)	79	(302)	7*
RMN										
Democratic party leader	60	(65)	39	(190)	21*	13	(112)	21	(270)	-8
Democratic committee leaders	83	(63)	41	(176)	42*	67	(101)	37	(244)	30*
Republican party leader	91	(66)	86	(194)	5	91	(112)	57	(285)	34*
Republican committee leaders	93	(68)	76	(176)	17*	73	(108)	60	(257)	13*
GRF										
Democratic party leader	37	(38)	29	(110)	8	28	(53)	26	(78)	2
Democratic committee leaders	80	(35)	40	(89)	40*	70	(44)	37	(76)	33*
Republican party leader	87	(38)	84	(103)	3	85	(55)	53	(86)	32*
Republican committee leaders	79	(34)	84	(88)	-5	87	(53)	65	(74)	22*
RWR										
Democratic party leader	57	(108)	27	(169)	30*	43	(139)	24	(161)	19*
Democratic committee leaders	70	(103)	34	(171)	36*	50	(116)	40	(145)	10
Republican party leader	91	(109)	75	(176)	16*	90	(135)	87	(160)	3
Republican committee leaders	81	(104)	65	(168)	16*	62	(116)	79	(150)	-17

	%	(N)	%	(N)	diff	%	(N)	%	(N)	diff
All Republicans										
Democratic party leader	60	(265)	37	(639)	23*	43	(428)	25	(825)	18*
Democratic committee leaders	74	(256)	40	(599)	34*	63	(381)	40	(772)	23*
Republican party leader	91	(266)	80	(648)	11*	89	(411)	75	(851)	14*
Republican committee leaders	83	(260)	72	(601)	11*	75	(387)	71	(785)	4
Democratic Presidents										
JFK										
Democratic party leader	91	(34)	93	(90)	-2	92	(74)	84	(180)	8
Democratic committee leaders	84	(32)	89	(79)	-5	90	(69)	53	(169)	37*
Republican party leader	63	(32)	25	(85)	38*	57	(68)	22	(172)	35*
Republican committee leaders	55	(33)	32	(76)	23*	74	(70)	23	(166)	51*
LBJ										
Democratic party leader	93	(58)	92	(227)	1	75	(127)	77	(462)	-2
Democratic committee leaders	91	(58)	86	(232)	5	73	(114)	52	(326)	21*
Republican party leader	43	(63)	33	(239)	10	63	(126)	55	(442)	8
Republican committee leaders	47	(59)	42	(232)	5	69	(125)	50	(343)	19*
JEC										
Democratic party leader	84	(127)	72	(170)	12*	73	(145)	71	(235)	2
Democratic committee leaders	72	(134)	74	(159)	-2	83	(122)	56	(201)	27*
Republican party leader	39	(123)	28	(162)	11*	62	(121)	40	(190)	22*
Republican committee leaders	51	(135)	41	(155)	10*	70	(129)	47	(209)	23*
All Democrats										
Democratic party leader	88	(219)	85	(487)	3	78	(346)	77	(877)	1
Democratic committee leaders	79	(224)	82	(470)	-3	81	(305)	53	(696)	28*
Republican party leader	44	(218)	30	(486)	14*	61	(315)	44	(804)	17*
Republican committee leaders	51	(227)	40	(463)	11*	70	(324)	43	(718)	27*

Note: Entries are the percentage of votes on which the leader voted in agreement with the president's position. Number of votes in parentheses.
$*p < .05$.

Table 6.7 Success of Republican and Democratic Presidents on Important Foreign and Domestic Policy Roll Calls

PARTY OF PRESIDENT	HOUSE					SENATE				
	Foreign		Domestic			Foreign		Domestic		
	%	(N)	%	(N)	Diff.	%	(N)	%	(N)	Diff.
Republican	56	(62)	61	(166)	−5	72	(81)	62	(145)	10*
Democrat	73	(40)	73	(121)	0	68	(34)	69	(101)	−1

Note: Entries are the percentage of votes on which the president's position won. Number of votes in parentheses.
*$p < .05$.

ANALYSIS OF IMPORTANT VOTES

The analysis thus far has used all conflictual roll calls. In this section we analyze our subset of more important votes to determine if behavior on important issues differs from behavior on all conflictual issues.

Table 6.7 shows success on important foreign and domestic votes for Republican and Democratic presidents. On important votes, the two presidencies phenomenon for Republican presidents disappears in the House and diminishes considerably in the Senate. And as we found in the analysis in the larger sample, for Democratic presidents there is no difference in success on foreign and domestic policy in the subset of important votes.

Comparing success rates on important votes with success on all conflictual votes reveals why the foreign policy advantage of Republican presidents disappears. Compared to success on all conflictual roll calls, Republican presidents are less likely to win important foreign policy votes and more likely to win important domestic policy votes. In the House, the shifts are large in both policy areas—success on important foreign policy votes is twelve points lower; success on important domestic policy votes is fifteen points higher. In the Senate, success on important foreign policy roll calls is only four points lower, while success on important domestic roll calls is ten points higher. Hence, because of these shifts in success rates on important votes, the foreign policy advantage for Republican presidents disappears in the House and declines in the Senate.[5] We will look at levels of support from the party factions on important votes to determine why success rates differ.

5. We also looked at differences in success on important votes before and after 1965. The trends over time are different in each chamber. In the House, there was an eight-point advantage on important foreign policy votes before 1965 and a five-point disadvantage in the recent period. In the Senate, the president won 4 percent less on foreign policy before 1965, but after 1965 he won 8 percent more often. None of the differences is statistically significant at the .05 level.

Table 6.8 Support for the President from the Four Party Factions on Important Foreign and Domestic Roll Calls

	HOUSE					SENATE				
	Foreign		Domestic			Foreign		Domestic		
	%	(N)	%	(N)	Diff.	%	(N)	%	(N)	Diff.
Republican Presidents										
Conservative										
Republicans	72	(62)	74	(166)	−2	79	(81)	82	(145)	−3
Liberal Republicans	52		58		−6	50		51		−1
Conservative										
Democrats	58		48		10*	55		52		3
Liberal Democrats	32		29		3	27		20		7*
Democratic Presidents										
Liberal Democrats	77	(40)	83	(121)	−6	66	(34)	81	(101)	−15
Conservative										
Democrats	34		38		−4	51		39		12*
Liberal Republicans	58		50		8	57		66		−9
Conservative										
Republicans	25		18		7	31		27		

Note: Entries are the average percentage of the members of each party faction that voted in agreement with the president's position. Number of votes in parentheses.
*$p < .05$.

Table 6.8 reports levels of support from the party factions on important votes. In the analysis of all conflictual votes, we found that liberal Democrats were much more supportive of Republican presidents on foreign policy than on domestic policy. On important roll calls, the behavior of liberal Democrats becomes more partisan on foreign policy—support from liberal Democrats on foreign policy votes is eleven points lower in both chambers than in the entire sample (compare table 6.4). Liberal Democrats' support of Republican presidents on domestic issues is similar on both important votes and all conflictual votes. Consequently, on important issues, Republican presidents do not receive much more support from the opposition party base on foreign policy than on domestic policy.

Table 6.9 shows that the behavior of congressional leaders on important issues is similar to the behavior observed in the entire sample. Republican presidents continue to receive more support from Democratic party and com-

Table 6.9 Support for the President from Congressional Leaders on Important Foreign and Domestic Roll Calls

	HOUSE					SENATE				
	Foreign		Domestic			Foreign		Domestic		
	%	(N)	%	(N)	Diff.	%	(N)	%	(N)	Diff.
Republican Presidents										
Democratic party leaders	48	(58)	35	(161)	13*	35	(81)	17	(142)	18*
Democratic committee leaders	63	(56)	45	(130)	18*	61	(67)	35	(120)	25*
Republican party leaders	95	(62)	87	(159)	8*	91	(78)	84	(142)	7
Republican committee leaders	85	(55)	73	(128)	12*	72	(71)	75	(122)	−3
Democratic Presidents										
Democratic party leaders	97	(38)	86	(111)	11*	79	(34)	86	(96)	−7
Democratic committee leaders	81	(36)	86	(98)	−5	70	(27)	46	(69)	24*
Republican party leaders	46	(39)	20	(107)	26*	48	(231)	30	(90)	18*
Republican committee leaders	50	(36)	34	(96)	16*	71	(28)	24	(72)	47*

Note: Entries are the average percentage of votes on which the leader voted in agreement with the president's position. Number of votes in parentheses.
*$p < .05$.

mittee leaders on foreign policy, although the difference in the House is less than in the entire sample because of lower leader support on important foreign policy votes. Democratic presidents also continue to receive more support on foreign policy from Republican party and committee leaders, and in some cases the difference between foreign and domestic policy increases. The increased difference between the policy categories on important issues, however, is not the result of more support on foreign policy. Instead, Republican leaders tend to support Democratic presidents' positions less often on important domestic roll calls, thereby enhancing the difference between domestic and foreign policy.

CONCLUSIONS

The original theory of two presidencies sought to explain why the president is able "to control defense and foreign policies and so completely overwhelm those who might wish to thwart him" (Wildavsky 1966, 7). Wildavsky's argument clearly refers to presidential success on "major" issues. He observes that during the "modern era" (which began with FDR in the 1930s), "in the realm of foreign policy there has not been a single *major issue* on which presidents . . . have failed" (emphasis added).

Although we find some support for the two presidencies thesis, the findings of our analysis, taken together, tend to dispute the original theory.[6] Republican presidents tend to win significantly more often on conflictual foreign policy roll calls than on domestic policy, primarily because of increased support from liberal Democrats on foreign policy. For Democratic presidents, however, there is little or no difference in success rates in the two policy areas. And on important roll calls, the advantage that Republican presidents enjoy on foreign policy disappears in the House and declines considerably in the Senate. The differences in Republican success across the two policy areas are reduced on important roll calls because support from liberal Democrats declines in the foreign policy area. Thus, contrary to the original conceptualization, the two presidencies phenomenon does not appear on a subset of more important issues. Instead, the difference shows up on votes that could be characterized as involving normal decision making (i.e., conflictual roll calls), and then it is limited to Republican presidents.

These findings present two troubling questions: (1) Why do Republican presidents receive additional opposition party support on conflictual foreign policy votes while Democratic presidents do not? (2) Why does the difference show up on all conflictual votes but not on important issues? Although we cannot provide definitive answers to these questions, following are possible explanations.

One possible reason for the partisan differences on conflictual roll calls is shared responsibility for governing. In the American system of "separate institutions sharing powers" (Neustadt 1960, 33), the president and Congress share responsibility for governing. Because the president is the most visible actor, he is the one who is most likely to be held accountable by the voters for any failures. Members of Congress, in contrast, are insulated by incumbency advantages and are less likely to be held accountable individually for a failure

---

6. One should remember, however, that much foreign policy does not require legislation and does not show up on roll calls. The president can still count on congressional support when he takes military action in response to a threat. For example, when Reagan ordered the invasion of Grenada in 1983 and the bombing of Lybia in 1986, he received overwhelming support from members of both parties in Congress.

to govern (Fiorina 1984). But collectively Congress must share the responsibility for governing, and that collective responsibility falls more heavily on the majority party than on the minority.

Thus the president and the majority party in Congress bear the greatest responsibility to maintain the operations of government. Although maintaining governmental operations is important in the domestic sphere, the stakes are higher on foreign and national security policy, largely for the reasons advanced in the original two presidencies argument. In the American system, the presidency and Congress are frequently controlled by different parties. When there is divided party control, the responsibility to share in governance may constrain members of a majority opposition to cooperate with the president more on foreign and defense policy in order to maintain the nation's security. While members of the minority party do not want to undermine the nation's security, there are legitimate political conflicts over foreign and defense policy. Because they have less responsibility for governing, members of an opposition minority in Congress have greater leeway to pursue their own political preferences on foreign policy as well as on domestic policy.

During the period of our study, divided party control always involved a Republican president facing Democratic majorities in Congress. We found that Democrats were more supportive of Republican presidents on foreign policy than on domestic policy, and the most consistent increase in support came from the opposition party base of liberal Democrats. Democratic presidents interacted with Democratic majorities in Congress, and conservative Republicans, who had less responsibility for governance as members of the minority, provided little additional support on foreign policy. Liberal Republicans were more supportive of Democratic presidents on foreign policy, perhaps because of ideological proximity. But there are relatively few cross-pressured liberal Republicans, and their additional support was typically insufficient to result in more success on foreign policy for Democratic presidents.

While the findings of our analysis are generally consistent with this "responsibility for governance" explanation, there are some nonconforming examples. Democrats were the minority party in the 83rd Congress (1953–54) during the Eisenhower administration and in the 97th and 98th Senates (1980–84) during the Reagan administration, yet Eisenhower and Reagan still received greater support from liberal Democrats.

In the case of Eisenhower, liberal Democrats may have supported his foreign policy preferences because of ideological proximity on foreign policy. Recall that Eisenhower was more liberal on foreign policy than on domestic policy. Compared to other Republicans, Eisenhower received less foreign policy support from conservative Democrats and more support from liberal Republicans.

The Reagan case is more difficult to explain. Reagan's positions on foreign policy issues were more conservative than his positions on domestic policy, yet he still received 13 percent more support on foreign policy from liberal Democrats in the Senate. In this case, however, Republican control of Congress was incomplete. Because the Democrats controlled the House, the Democratic minority in the Senate may have felt a greater responsibility for governing than would normally be the case for a minority party. Moreover, Democrats had controlled the Senate for nearly thirty years, and they viewed their new minority status as temporary.

Thus the responsibility to share in governance may explain why liberal Democrats are more supportive of Republican presidents on conflictual foreign policy roll calls, but why do they become less supportive on more important foreign policy roll calls? The answer may lie in the types of cues and pressures on the subset of important issues.

The set of all conflictual votes involves the maintenance of the foreign policy and defense establishment—the foreign aid bill, State Department authorizations, votes for continuing operation of the military, etc. While these issues involve controversy, most are not highly visible and salient to members' constituents. Therefore, members are less likely to receive constituency pressure that conflicts with cues from party and committee leaders. And recall that congressional leaders are more supportive of presidents on foreign policy.

The subset of important votes involves the most salient and conflictual aspects of foreign and defense policy. These issues are more visible and more likely to be salient to members' constituencies. While congressional leaders support the president about as often on important foreign policy votes as on more normal foreign policy votes, members of Congress are more likely to have information and constituency interests on visible, important roll calls that conflict with the bipartisan cues from the leadership. As a result, behavior on important foreign policy roll calls is similar to behavior on important domestic policy roll calls.

Another possible explanation for these results lies in the "foreign policy consensus" that characterized elite opinion following World War II. Holsti and Rosenau (1984, 222), for example, argue that

> the two decades following the end of WW II were marked by a substantial foreign policy agreement that supported internationalism over isolationism, containment rather than efforts to roll back the Soviet Empire to its 1939 frontiers; the first peacetime alliances in American history; participation in a wide range of international organizations; liberalization of trade; and foreign aid on an unprecedented scale.

If elites in and out of government shared such a set of beliefs during the post–World War II period, the Vietnam War diminished it substantially. Holsti and Rosenau's analysis of elite attitudes during 1976 and again during 1980 show that the foreign policy consensus was severely shaken. Our data on presidential success on foreign policy votes supports the view that presidents won more often on foreign policy votes prior to 1965. In terms both of winning roll call votes and the level of support received from liberal Democrats, Eisenhower did much better than his Republican successors. Thus, if there was a foreign policy consensus prior to Vietnam, it boosted President Eisenhower's totals on foreign policy votes. But if the consensus ended because of American involvement in Southeast Asia, why do Republican presidents continue to succeed more often on foreign policy votes than on domestic votes, and why does their success disappear on important votes?

One possible answer to the first question is that Vietnam did not completely destroy the foreign policy consensus. Parts of it continued to be supported by large segments of elites both in and out of government. For example, the majority of members of both parties remained committed to internationalism, maintaining our alliances with other countries (especially NATO), continued participation in and leadership of international organizations, and the responsibility to aid in the development of Third World nations. John Reilly's 1986 survey of leaders both in and out of government found that there were a number of foreign policy issues on which a sufficient number of leaders held the same position, so that it would not be incorrect to suggest that a consensus existed (Reilly 1988).[7] When foreign policy votes dealing with such issues arose, Republican presidents could expect to receive more support from liberal Democrats and hence to win more often.

But Vietnam did have its effects on the foreign policy beliefs of national leaders. After the Vietnam experience, the Democratic majority in Congress began to question major aspects of United States foreign policy, including (1) the role of the United States in supplying funds to anti-communist movements in the Third World; (2) the amount of military buildup necessary for the country to maintain an adequate national defense; (3) the use of the American military in certain world hot spots; (4) the proper role of the United States in the international world economy; and (5) the role of the United States in identifying and dealing with human rights violations in other countries. Reilly (1988) found that although there was elite consensus on some issues, there were foreign policy issues on which American elites were seriously divided. For example, leaders were divided on such issues as supplying military and

7. For example, 99 percent of leaders believed that it was best for the United States to take an active part in world affairs; 93 percent supported sending United States troops if the Soviets invaded Europe; 93 percent favored using aid for foreign economic development and technical assistance; 78 percent favored foreign military aid.

economic aid to rebels fighting against communist supported governments, whether tariffs were necessary, whether protecting Americans' jobs was very important, and whether the Vietnam War was wrong or immoral. Issues such as these are more visible and are more likely to be identified as important votes.

During the Reagan years, for example, important votes deal with (1) United States aid to Central America, (2) weapons procurement on such items as the MX missile and chemical munitions, (3) nuclear freeze, (4) intelligence agencies, and (5) trade policy. Republican presidents during this period do better on foreign policy issues than on domestic issues when the foreign policy legislation falls under the more limited "consensus." But given how much more limited that consensus is today, there are a greater number of visible bills that are contested in the Congress. Thus there are two presidencies, but the phenomenon is limited and conditional.

In the following chapters we turn to the analysis of presidency-centered explanations of success.

CHAPTER 7

PRESIDENTIAL POPULARITY
AND PRESIDENTIAL SUCCESS

The preceding chapters have demonstrated that the partisan and ideological predispositions of members of Congress set the broad parameters of presidential success. The partisan and ideological links, however, are relatively weak. As a result, presidents facing a Congress with a favorable partisan and ideological mix are not assured success, and presidents with an unfavorable mix may overcome the disadvantages. Because presidential success varies widely within the broad parameters set by party and ideology, previous authors have argued that we must look for some other sources of linkage (Neustadt 1960). In a system with weak parties, there is a natural tendency to focus on the impact that individuals have on policy outcomes. This leads to an analysis that centers on the president as a prime determinant of the relationship between the branches.

In analyzing the impact of the president, previous works have paid particular attention to two characteristics of the president: (1) how popular he is with the public and (2) how skilled is he in the give and take of legislative politics. This chapter analyzes the effects of presidential popularity on the relationship between the president and Congress. In the next chapter, we will turn our attention to the effects of legislative skills.

A classic example of the apparent influence of presidential popularity is President Reagan's stunning budget victory in the Democratic-controlled House in 1981. At the Democratic caucus before the key vote on the Gramm-Latta substitute which Reagan supported strongly, Speaker Thomas P. O'Neill (D–Massachusetts) pleaded with Democrats not to vote for the massive cuts that the president wanted. Acknowledging Reagan's popularity, he urged Democrats to support their party: "The opinions of the man in the street change faster than anything in this world. Today, he does not know what is in this program, and he is influenced by a President with charisma and class. . . . But a year from now he will be saying 'You shouldn't have voted that way'" (quoted in Kernell 1986, 117).

The Speaker's argument changed only one vote. The president's budget passed 253 to 176 with support from sixty-five Democrats. Representative

Toby Moffett (D–Connecticut) explained why more than one-fourth of Democrats deserted their party: "They say they're voting for it because they're afraid" (quoted in Kernell 1986, 117).

The words of O'Neill and Moffett illustrate the problem of determining the effects of presidential popularity as a source of linkage between the president and Congress. Moffett's assessment of the budget vote is no doubt accurate. This example demonstrates that a popular president can sometimes use public support as a club to make some members afraid to oppose him. Such cases, however, are rare and are not representative of presidential-congressional relations in general.

O'Neill's analysis is sound too. While some members ignored his argument on the budget vote, the perspective expressed by the Speaker is more reflective of the typical situation. Members of Congress know that presidential popularity is highly fluid and that when they run for reelection very few constituents will know or care how often they support the president. Consequently, on most votes members follow their partisan and ideological predispositions; the president's public approval cannot move them very far from those predispositions. Even on the budget vote, when the president's popularity was supposedly pressuring members to deviate from their basic predispositions, forty-four of the sixty-five Democratic votes were from conservatives who had ideologies closer to the Republican mainstream than to their own party. Furthermore, the level of support from Democrats on the budget vote was not unusual; presidents typically attract support from more than one-fourth of the opposition party. It was Republican support that was extraordinary on the budget vote—the president did not lose a single Republican vote.

This chapter explores the relationship between presidential popularity and success in Congress. The first section is a brief overview of presidential popularity that describes trends in public approval over the time period of the study and discusses the competing perspectives of the effects of presidential popularity on presidential success in Congress. Next we present the results of two types of analysis designed to test the competing theoretical perspectives. The first test replicates the usual approach in previous research, looking at the effects of the level of presidential popularity on wins and losses and on support from members of Congress. The second test analyzes the effects of presidential popularity as a context.

AN OVERVIEW OF PRESIDENTIAL POPULARITY

Trends in Presidential Popularity

Figure 7.1 shows the trends in overall and partisan public approval of the seven presidents in our study.[1] As others have discovered, every president ex-

1. The measure of public approval is the Gallup poll question "Do you approve or disap-

Figure 7.1 Trends in Overall and Partisan Approval of the President

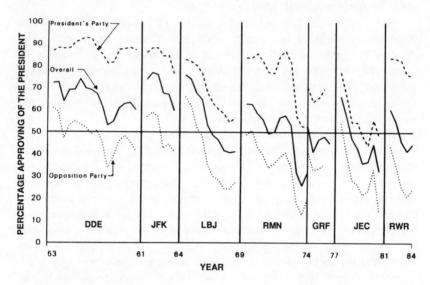

Source: Gallup poll (various years).

perienced considerable variation in popularity over the course of his term
(Mueller 1970; Stimson 1976; Kernell 1978). Public approval tends to be high
at the beginning of the president's term and to decline in subsequent years.
Johnson and Carter experienced relatively steady declines over the course of
their terms. Public approval of Eisenhower, Nixon, and Reagan, in contrast,
rebounded to start-of-term levels in their third and fourth years as they ap-
proached the reelection campaign. It is no surprise that incumbent presidents
whose popularity rebounded after the initial decline were successful in their
reelection bids. Those who failed to turn the trend around were denied a second term—Johnson was forced to withdraw, and Carter was defeated for reelection after a strong challenge for renomination within his own party. Ford
was defeated for reelection even though his popularity increased after a sharp
decline in the early months of his administration, but his approval rating at the
time of the election was less than 50 percent. Kennedy's popularity declined
from levels greater than 75 percent to about 63 percent at the time of his death.

Although the tendency for a president's popularity to start out high and

prove of the way [the incumbent] is handling his job as president?" (Gallup, 1953–84) This is the
measure used in most empirical studies of the effects of presidential popularity in Congress.

decline over the course of his term persists across the entire period of our study, there is a systematic shift in public evaluations of presidents who served after Johnson. Presidents who served between 1953 and 1968 began their terms with greater public approval and were more popular in general than were presidents who served after 1969. The average start-of-term approval for the early period (1953–68) was 75 percent with a standard deviation of 3.1 percent; in the recent period (1969–84), average start-of-term approval fell more than fifteen points to 59.7 percent and the standard deviation increased to 8.6 percent.[2] The overall mean for the early period was 62.3 percent compared to a mean of 48.1 percent for the period after 1969.[3] Thus, at the peaks of their popularity, public approval of recent presidents (Nixon, Ford, Carter, and Reagan) is about at the average for earlier presidents (Eisenhower, Kennedy, and Johnson). And perceptions seem to reflect this shift in the trends. For instance, Reagan, the "great communicator," was perceived as highly popular during much of his first term, yet the high points of his public approval are less than the mean for the presidents who served before 1969.

Trends in partisan approval tend to mimic the overall trends. The president is always much more popular among his party identifiers than among the opposition, but the trends for both parties tend to ebb and flow together over time.

Hypothesized Effects of Public Approval
As we observed above, there is some confusion concerning the nature of the relationship between public approval of the president and support for his preferences in Congress. The Moffett quotation at the beginning of this chapter suggests that presidential popularity has a strong, direct effect on congressional behavior—that is, as the president's popularity increases, so does his success in Congress. And political scientists present systematic quantitative evidence in support of this perspective. For example, Edwards (1980) finds strong correlations between presidential popularity and support in Congress. He argues that his "research provides evidence that members of Congress *do* respond to . . . the president's current popularity among their supporters" (110, emphasis in original), and that presidential popularity "must be added

---

2. Start-of-term popularity is defined as the mean approval during each president's first six months in office. One might suspect that including unelected presidents distorts the means. Public sympathy following the assassination of President Kennedy may have artificially inflated Johnson's popularity during his first six months in office. Using the first six months of 1965 reduces the average for the early period to 71.4 percent. Public reaction to the Watergate scandal and the circumstances under which Ford became president may have artificially deflated his popularity. Excluding Ford from the calculations for the recent period increases the mean to 63.8 percent. Thus, while the difference between the two periods is less if we exclude the unelected presidents, it is still present.

3. The standard deviations for the two periods are about the same—11.3 percent and 10.9 percent.

to the list of variables that have been found useful in explaining roll call behavior" (109). Rivers and Rose (1985, 195) say that their "analyses show that
presidential influence in Congress rises and falls with the president's public
prestige." Similarly, Ostrom and Simon (1985, 350) conclude "that the 'public' and 'legislative' presidencies are linked via the reciprocal relationship between approval and success."

In chapter 2, we discussed some problems with these studies that purport
to show strong, direct effects of public approval. Moreover, there are theoretical reasons to believe that the effects of presidential popularity are more limited and indirect. While presidential popularity may exert some influence at
the margins, it is not likely to alter greatly the behavior of individuals already
in Congress. Neustadt (1960, 87) notes that while Washingtonians, including
members of Congress, gauge the president's popularity, "rarely is there any
one-to-one relationship between appraisals of his popularity in general and responses in particular." Instead, public prestige "is a factor operating mostly
in the background as a conditioner, not the determinant of what Washingtonians will do about a President's request." The effects of popularity, therefore, are likely to be indirect and marginal: "The prevalent impression of a
President's public standing tends to set the tone and to define the limits of what
Washingtonians do for him, or do to him." There is systematic quantitative
evidence to support this perspective (Bond and Fleisher, 1980, 1984; Bond,
Fleisher, and Northrup 1988).[4]

There is also some disagreement about the appropriate way to conceptu-
alize and measure presidential popularity. Most empirical studies use the Gallup approval question and relate the actual percentage of the public approving
of the president to some measure of support or success in Congress (Edwards
1980; Bond and Fleisher 1980, 1984; Bond, Fleisher, and Northrup 1988;
Rivers and Rose 1985; Ostrom and Simon 1985). Neustadt (1960, 89) argues,
however, that the president's public prestige is defined by the perceptions of
Washingtonians rather than being something that is measured directly in public opinion polls: "Like reputation, prestige as a matter to be judged, not
'known'" (Neustadt 1960, 93).

Washingtonians judge the president's public prestige in a variety of ways,
including looking at public opinion polls (89), and Neustadt himself utilizes
the Gallup poll to gauge variation in the president's public prestige (96). But
according to Neustadt, the percentage approving at any given point in time
does not capture Washingtonians' perceptions of the president's public prestige. He argues that "in looking at these figures [i.e., Gallup polls], one can
and probably should ignore the variations month by month; what cannot be

4. Edwards has adopted this perspective in his recent book (Edwards 1989, chap. 6).

ignored is [a] sharp shirt of range" (96) that tends to stabilize for many months thereafter. Examples of such shifts of range were seen when Truman's approval shifted from the forties to the twenties in 1950 and when Eisenhower's approval shifted from the sixties to the fifties in 1958 (Neustadt 1960, 96). Thus, in addition to analyzing the effects of the level of public approval, we need to construct an indicator of presidential popularity as a contextual variable that captures large shifts in the range of approval.

THE EFFECTS OF THE LEVEL OF POPULARITY ON SUCCESS

In this section, we look at the relationship between the actual level of public approval of the president and different indicators of success. We begin with an analysis of wins and losses on roll call votes. Next we analyze support from the different party factions. Finally, we analyze the effects of the level of public approval in a multivariate model.

Winning and Losing Roll Call Votes

Table 7.1 reports correlations (Pearson's r) between presidential success on roll call votes (win/lose) and the percentage of the public approving of the president's job performance at the time of the vote.[5] Across all votes, the correlations are positive but weak ($r = .09$ in the House and $.13$ in the Senate), indicating that the president's position is not much more likely to win when he is popular than when he is unpopular.[6]

Although the relationship is weak across all votes, the effects of public opinion might vary across different types of votes. One might suppose, for

---

5. Presidential popularity is based on answers to the Gallup poll question given in note 1 above (Gallup, 1953–84). The Gallup poll asked this question between ten and twenty-six times in each of the years of the study, providing nearly monthly indicators of presidential popularity. Only 32 of the 384 months between 1953 and 1984 are missing. Most of the missing months are in presidential election years, when Gallup suspended polling between the party conventions and the election. We used the most recent poll taken before the date of the vote. In most cases, the poll used is from the preceding month, but in months with multiple votes, votes late in the month are matched with a poll taken earlier in the month. We did not include votes if there was no sampling of public opinion within the previous six weeks.

6. We are aware of the limitations of correlation analysis. Although correlation analysis is limited, it is adequate for our purpose in this section—to show the absence of a relationship. More complex methods appropriate for these data, such as probit analysis, reveal the same weak relationships. Because the interpretation of probit coefficients is not straightforward (see appendix B), we decided to rely on easily interpretable correlation coefficients for this bivariate analysis. More complex methods are used in subsequent analyses when they are required. Relationships that are statistically significant at the .05 level or better are indicated for readers who might be interested. But because of the large sample size, significant tests are useful mainly as a criterion for rejecting weak relationships. For statistically significant relationships, we rely on the size of the coefficient for our interpretation.

Table 7.1 Correlations between Overall Presidential Popularity and Success on Roll Call Votes, 1953–84

	HOUSE	SENATE
Conflictual votes	.09*	.13*
Important votes	.08	−.03
Other votes	.09*	.15*
Foreign/defense votes	.12*	.06*
Domestic votes	.09*	.16*

Note: Entries are Pearson's r.
*$p < .05$.

example, that the president's public standing would be most influential on highly visible important votes, such as the budget vote discussed above. But on the subset of more important votes, the relationship between presidential popularity and success is weaker than in the whole sample. In the House, the correlation is .08, virtually the same as for less important votes. In the Senate, the correlation on important votes is near zero and negative ($−.03$). Furthermore, the type of policy (foreign/domestic) does not systematically change the weak relationships found in the whole sample. Presidential popularity has a slightly stronger relationship on foreign policy issues in the House and on domestic policy in the Senate, but the correlations remain small.

Thus our analysis suggests that the president's popularity with the public is only marginally related to success on floor votes in Congress. The analysis, however, is based on roll calls occurring over a thirty-two year period. This long time span might be disguising systematic differences across presidents who faced different partisan and ideological mixes in Congress. Moreover, recall that the average level of presidential popularity is lower for presidents who served after 1969; high popularity for Nixon, Ford, Carter, and Reagan is only about average for Eisenhower, Kennedy, and Johnson. Table 7.2 reports correlations between popularity and success for each presidential administration and for majority and minority presidents. This analysis controls for the different ranges in public approval and the particular circumstances facing each president. We see that Johnson is the only occupant of the White House whose success in Congress is even moderately related to his popularity ($r = .21$ in the House and .32 in the Senate). The relationships for all other presidents are quite weak and in some cases negative. Although the correlations for majority presidents are higher than for minority presidents, this difference results from the stronger relationships during the Johnson presidency. The cor-

Table 7.2 Correlations between Overall Presidential Popularity and Success on Roll Call Votes for Each Administration

PRESIDENT	HOUSE		SENATE	
	Conflictual Votes	Important Votes	Conflictual Votes	Important Votes
DDE	.04	−.19	.08	−.08
JFK	.00	−.19	−.04	.03
LBJ	.21*	.30*	.32*	.10
RMN	.10*	.19	.09*	−.16
GRF	−.06	−.03	−.09	−.02
JEC	−.03	−.08	.00	−.06
RWR	.10*	.26*	.02	.11
Majority presidents	.12*	.05	.14*	.04
Minority presidents	.05	.09	.07*	−.14

Note: Entries are Pearson's r.
*$p < .05$.

relations for other majority presidents (Kennedy, Carter, and Reagan in the Senate) are near zero, and two are negative.[7]

Support from Party Factions

Although public approval of the president's job performance does not systematically increase the chances of victory on floor votes, the behavior of certain members of Congress might vary in response to variation in presidential popularity. Specifically, we speculated that while members of the party bases are likely to be influenced very little by the president's public approval, members of the cross-pressured factions might be more responsive because the president's standing with the public would reinforce one of the conflicting cross-pressures. And Edwards's (1980, 92–98) research suggests that members of Congress are much more responsive to the president's popularity among their party identifiers in the public than to the president's overall popularity. Hence in this section we analyze the effects of overall and partisan popularity on support from the different party factions. Table 7.3 reports the correlations between the percentage of each party faction supporting the president's preference

7. The correlations for Eisenhower in the Republican-controlled 83rd Congress are −.08 in the House and .29 in the Senate.

Table 7.3 Correlations between Percentage of Support from the Party Factions and Presidential Popularity with the Public at Large and Partisans

PRESIDENTIAL POPULARITY	HOUSE				SENATE			
	President's Base	Cross-Pressured Partisans	Cross-Pressured Opposition	Opposition Base	President's Base	Cross-Pressured Partisans	Cross-Pressured Opposition	Opposition Base
All Presidents								
Overall	.08*	.18*	−.14*	.05*	.14*	.06*	−.05*	.09*
President's party	−.03	.22*	−.17*	.09*	.11*	.13*	−.20*	.02
Opposition party	.05*	.19*	−.14*	.08*	.13*	.03*	−.02	.12*
Majority Presidents								
Overall	.23*	.24*	−.10*	−.02	.19*	−.02	−.01	.06
President's party	.23*	.24*	−.11*	.00	.18*	.09*	−.13*	.00
Opposition party	.19*	.23*	−.09*	.01	.17*	−.05*	.03	.11*
Minority Presidents								
Overall	−.10*	.13*	−.20*	.14*	.03	.22*	−.18*	.13*
President's party	−.05	.08*	−.17*	.07*	.00	.21*	−.21*	.12*
Opposition party	−.11*	.17*	−.21*	.16*	.02	.23*	−.17*	.15*

Note: Entries are Pearson's r.
*p < .05.

on each roll call and the president's popularity with the public at large and with partisan groupings at the time of the vote.

The analysis of differences in the relationships for the party bases and the cross-pressured factions leads to the same conclusion as the analysis of success—the effects of presidential popularity are limited for all party factions. Members of the cross-pressured factions are not consistently more responsive to variation in presidential popularity than are members of the party bases.

When they are in the minority, cross-pressured members of the president's party are more responsive to variation in presidential popularity than are members of his party base. The correlations between overall popularity and support from the base are $-.10$ in the House and $.03$ in the Senate. The correlations for cross-pressured partisans are slightly higher ($r = .13$ in the House and $.22$ in the Senate). When the president's party is in the majority, however, the expected difference does not appear. In the House, the correlations are virtually identical for both the party base ($r = .23$) and cross-pressured members ($r = .24$). In the Senate, popularity is more strongly associated with support from the president's party base ($r = .19$) than from cross-pressured partisans ($r = -.02$).

For the opposition party factions, the effects of presidential popularity vary considerably, but not in the expected way. Under minority presidents, the relationship between overall popularity and support from the opposition party base is positive but weak ($r = .14$ in the House and $.13$ in the Senate). The relationship for members of the cross-pressured opposition is slightly stronger but negative ($r = -.20$ in the House and $-.18$ in the Senate), indicating that the president tends to receive less support from these members when he is popular. Under majority presidents, we also find negative relationships. In the House, the relationship for members of the cross-pressured opposition is $-.10$; the correlation for the opposition party base is not significant. In the Senate, neither correlation is significantly different from zero.

The negative relationships between presidential popularity and congressional support are counterintuitive. Previous research suggested that members of the opposition party might be less supportive of the president when he is popular for two reasons. First, a popular president might be less compromising with the opposition party, which would lead to more partisan voting. Second, members of the opposition party are not likely to receive credit at election time for helping the president. Because their opponents will benefit from the president's popularity, members of the opposition might be inclined to follow their basic partisan predisposition and try to make the president look bad (Bond and Fleisher 1980). Although this reasoning might explain the negative correlations for members of the opposition in general, it does not explain why members of the opposition party base respond positively while members of the cross-pressured opposition respond negatively. In fact, the proposed explanations for a negative relationship would seem to apply more to members of the opposition party base than to members of the cross-pressured opposition.

Perhaps the more interesting result is the failure to find a stronger relationship with partisan popularity. The most important insight of Edwards's (1980) research is that members of Congress are less responsive to the president's popularity with the public overall than to his popularity with their partisan supporters—that is, Democrats in Congress are most responsive to the president's popularity among Democratic voters; Republicans are most responsive to his popularity among Republican voters. And he presents empirical support for this argument. The correlations between presidential support scores and overall public approval are moderate ($r = .50$ in the House and $.40$ in the Senate), whereas the correlations with partisan approval are much stronger, ranging from $.75$ to $.88$ (Edwards 1980, 93–94).

Our analysis of levels of support from the four party factions indicates that members of Congress are no more responsive to the president's popularity with the relevant partisans in the public than to his popularity with the public overall (see table 7.3). Although there are a few instances in which support from a party faction is related slightly more strongly to the president's popularity with the relevant partisans in the public, partisan popularity generally performs less well than the president's overall popularity. Indeed, under minority presidents, support from cross-pressured members of the president's party correlates most strongly with his popularity among voters of the other party. The differences in correlations, however, are trivial.

How can we reconcile the discrepancy between these results and Edwards's (1980) findings of strong correlations between partisan popularity and partisan support in Congress? One might suppose that the different research designs account for the different results. Our analysis is based on different units of analysis and spans a longer time period. Edwards analyzed variation in presidential support scores across individual members for the period 1953 to 1976. Our study analyzes variation in support from groupings of individuals across roll call votes for the period 1953 to 1984. The difference in time periods is not the reason for the different results. We estimated relationships for each administration and found the same pattern of weak correlations for every president. And it is hard to imagine why the different units of analysis would produce such radically different results. If individuals in Congress vary their support for the president in response to variation in his public approval, then the relationship should show up using our research design, which permits a more accurate matching of congressional behavior with presidential popularity at the time the behavior occurs.[8]

8. See chapter 3 for the critique of the practice of using individual presidential support scores in analyses of the effects of presidential popularity.

A closer inspection of Edwards's (1980) research design reveals that the high correlations between partisan popularity and partisan support are spurious. The spurious correlations result from the decision to correlate Democratic (or Republican) presidential approval with Democratic (or Republican) presidential support scores across presidents of different parties. Consider the trends in both variables over time. Over the twenty-four-year period of Edwards's study, the mean yearly presidential approval among Democrats in the public is generally high if the president is a Democrat and generally low if he is a Republican. And the average Democratic presidential support score tends to be high under Democratic presidents and low under Republican presidents. The trends for Republican public approval and Republican support in Congress are similar, but the peaks and valleys are shifted—both variables tend to be high under Republican presidents and low under Democratic presidents. Hence Edwards's research design ensures that high values on both variables will occur together and that low values will occur together—that is, the variables are spuriously correlated because the party of the president determines when each is high and low.

A simple and effective way to avoid spurious correlations in this analysis is to measure the party variables as president's party/opposition party rather than Democrat/Republican.[9] An analysis of the relationship between presidential popularity and individual presidential support scores using a research design that corrects the spurious correlation problem reveals that partisan popularity performs no better than overall popularity (Bond, Fleisher, and Northrup 1988). Because same party and opposition party public approval are strongly correlated with overall approval ($r = .81$ and $.94$ respectively) as well as with each other ($r = .71$), we should not be surprised to find that the different measures of presidential popularity have similar relationships to support in Congress.[10] Thus, although partisan and overall popularity are different conceptually, they do not differ much empirically. Consequently, we rely on overall presidential popularity in subsequent analyses.

The analysis thus far has reported only simple bivariate correlations. Al-

9. Edwards (1980, 97–98) reports partial correlations controlling for the president's party, and he calculates correlations separately for Democratic and Republican years. These controls correct the spurious correlation problem. The results, however, are less consistent. Some of the correlations remain high, but some are reduced considerably and some turn negative.

10. Edwards (1980, 93) reports a correlation of $-.48$ between Democratic and Republican approval of the president, arguing that Democrats and Republicans in Congress are responding to different sets of opinion. But this negative correlation is misleading because it results from each party's evaluation changing in opposite directions from generally high to generally low depending on the party of the president. Holding the president's party constant, Democratic and Republican approval of the president covary over time. Approval among members of the president's party is higher than approval among members of the opposition, but the trends tend to move together. Hence there are strong positive correlations.

though we found a consistent pattern of weak correlations, it is possible that some other variable is suppressing the hypothesized relationship between presidential popularity and support in Congress. Before we accept the conclusion that the current level of public approval has only a marginal effect on members of Congress, we should examine the effects of presidential popularity in a multivariate model.

Multivariate Relationships

The analysis in chapter 5 revealed that the behavior of the party factions is related to the positions of party and committee leaders (see table 5.6). Table 7.4 reports estimates of the model of the effects of leader support on the behavior of the party factions with popularity added.[11] Controlling for leader support does not change the findings of previous analyses. The regression coefficients for the leader variables are similar to those in the basic model without presidential popularity. The coefficients for popularity reveal that, ceteris paribus, the president's public approval at the time of the vote has only a marginal influence on support from members of Congress.

In the models of the party bases, the coefficients for presidential popularity are near zero in both chambers and not statistically significant. Although the coefficients for popularity are stronger in the models of the cross-pressured factions, the substantive effects remain limited. Cross-pressured members of the president's party are slightly more supportive if he is popular with the public. A 10 percent increase in popularity is associated with about a 4 percent increase in support from cross-pressured partisans in the House ($b = .39$) and less than a 1 percent increase in the Senate ($b = .08$).[12] But the increases in support from cross-pressured partisans are offset by equal or greater losses of support from members of the cross-pressured opposition. A 10 percent increase in public approval is associated with 4 percent less support from the cross-pressured opposition in the House ($b = -.41$) and 3 percent less in the Senate ($b = -.31$). And note that a 10 percent change in public approval of the president is relatively large. The average six-month change in popularity over the period of our study (1953–84) was -2.7 percent; in more than three-fourths of the months the six-month change in popularity was less than $+/-$ 10 percent. Thus relatively large changes in public approval are associated with relatively small changes in support from the cross-pressured factions, and because the two cross-pressured factions respond in opposite ways, the overall effects are even more limited.

---

11. Since the previous analysis suggests that the effects of public approval on the behavior of party factions are similar under majority and minority presidents, the model does not estimate separate slopes for presidential popularity.

12. The coefficient for cross-pressured partisans in the Senate is not significant at the .05 level, but it is larger than its standard error.

This multivariate analysis suggests that other variables are not disguising the relationship between presidential popularity and congressional support. The analysis thus far has tested the effects of the actual level of public approval at the time the vote occurs. Perhaps presidential popularity is better viewed as a context.

PRESIDENTIAL POPULARITY AS A CONTEXT

Neustadt argues that popularity "may not decide the outcome in a given case but can affect the likelihoods in every case . . ." (1960, 93). If popularity affects the probabilities in every case, then across a large number of votes we should see a pattern of more victories when the president is popular. But the effects are not likely to be observed unless there is "shift of range" (96)—that is, the president's approval must have increased or decreased significantly. And the effects of large increases and decreases are not equal: "Popularity may not produce a Washington response. But public disapproval heartens Washington's resistance" (90).

Table 7.5 reports the results of a probit model of the effects of the contexts of presidential popularity and partisan control on presidential success (win/lose). The context of popularity is measured by four dummy variables to indicate the current condition of public approval (high or low) and the direction of change over the preceding six months (increasing or decreasing). Defining the point at which current popularity becomes high or low and whether approval has significantly changed is somewhat arbitrary. Because the nature of public evaluations of the president changed after 1969, using the same standards for the entire time period is inappropriate. Therefore, we use the mean and standard deviation of current popularity and of six-month changes in popularity for each period. The popularity variables are constructed as follows:

1. High popularity equals 1 if the percent public approval at the time of the vote is more than one standard deviation above the mean for the period and zero otherwise;
2. low popularity equals 1 if approval is more than one standard deviation below the mean for the period and zero otherwise;
3. increasing popularity equals 1 if the six-month change is more than one standard deviation above the mean for the period and zero otherwise; and
4. decreasing popularity equals 1 if the six-month change is more than one standard deviation below the mean for the period and zero otherwise.[13]

13. For the early period (1953–68) the mean level of public approval was 62.3 percent with a standard deviation of 11.3; for the recent period (1969–84) the mean was 48.1 with a standard deviation of 10.9. The mean and standard deviation for the six-month change in popularity are −2.2 percent +/− 6.3 in the early period and −3.1 percent +/− 10.9 in the recent period.

Table 7.4 Effects of Leader Support and Presidential Popularity on Support from the Party Factions

	HOUSE				SENATE			
	President's Base	Cross-Pressured Partisans	Cross-Pressured Opposition	Opposition Base	President's Base	Cross-Pressured Partisans	Cross-Pressured Opposition	Opposition Base
Presidential popularity	.04	.39	−.41	.06	.04	.08	−.31	.03
	(.04)	(.06)	(.06)	(.04)	(.04)	(.05)	(.05)	(.04)
Majority Presidents								
President's party leader	32.20	11.86	10.86	−6.49	35.65	11.62	13.04	−8.88
	(2.78)	(3.87)	(4.22)	(2.70)	(1.72)	(2.13)	(2.42)	(1.75)
President's committee leader	18.01	11.03	.63	−4.46	7.94	27.45	−4.35	.13
	(2.38)	(3.31)	(3.61)	(2.31)	(1.45)	(1.80)	(2.05)	(1.48)
Opposition party leader	−5.53	6.04	14.54	27.58	−5.67	1.45	19.86	26.43
	(1.83)	(2.54)	(2.77)	(1.77)	(1.37)	(1.70)	(1.94)	(1.40)
Opposition committee leader	.43	1.14	16.95	14.01	−1.83	1.79	10.73	12.81
	(1.77)	(2.47)	(2.69)	(1.72)	(1.39)	(1.72)	(1.96)	(1.41)
Intercept	38.00	.13	53.48	15.44	42.46	19.52	56.43	19.42

Minority Presidents

President's party leader	36.51	12.48	18.27	-4.61	23.44	23.69	2.96	2.14
	(2.21)	(3.07)	(3.35)	(2.14)	(2.13)	(2.64)	(3.00)	(2.17)
President's committee leader	13.57	11.20	2.40	-6.39	18.17	14.26	3.74	-1.07
	(1.95)	(2.71)	(2.96)	(1.89)	(2.06)	(2.55)	(2.90)	(2.09)
Opposition party leader	-11.18	23.05	-4.12	40.19	10.16	21.95	-7.74	37.21
	(1.86)	(2.59)	(2.83)	(1.81)	(1.83)	(2.27)	(2.59)	(1.87)
Opposition committee leader	-.86	-.71	19.98	10.41	.17	.24	28.26	13.09
	(1.90)	(2.64)	(2.89)	(1.84)	(1.81)	(2.24)	(2.55)	(1.84)
Intercept	29.15	6.12	44.25	16.86	42.56	12.33	46.71	9.04
R^2	.46	.22	.19	.56	.37	.29	.22	.42

Note: Entries are unstandardized regression coefficients. Standard error of the estimate in parentheses.

Table 7.5 Probit Estimates of the Effects of the Context of Popularity on Presidential Success

	HOUSE		SENATE	
	Conflictual Votes	Important Votes	Conflictual Votes	Important Votes
Current popularity				
High	.25	−.01	.20	−.51
	(.13)	(.25)	(.10)	(.25)
Low	−.11	−.23	−.29	.08
	(.09)	(.21)	(.07)	(.19)
Six-month change				
Increasing	−.17	−.09	−.10	−.18
	(.10)	(.21)	(.10)	(.25)
Decreasing	−.13	−.06	−.20	−.41
	(.08)	(.20)	(.08)	(.21)
Majority control	.59	.50	.66	.24
	(.07)	(.16)	(.06)	(.15)
Intercept	.09	.21	.15	.40
% correctly predicted	64	58	68	67
Null prediction	62	65	68	67

Note: Entries are probit coefficients. Standard error of the estimate in parentheses.

Partisan control is also measured as a dummy variable (1 = majority). Thus the intercept in the model is the condition of average popularity that has been relatively stable over the preceding six months for minority presidents.

Measuring presidential popularity as a context does not change the pattern of weak relationships found above using less complex measures and methods. The models do not predict any better than chance, and the strongest variable is majority control. The coefficients for current popularity indicate that the president's position is more likely to prevail if he is highly popular and less likely to prevail if he is highly unpopular, but the coefficients are small in both chambers and not statistically significant in the House model. The effects of changes in public approval are also weak. The coefficients for increasing popularity are in the wrong direction. Although decreasing popularity has the appropriate negative sign, suggesting that public disapproval does hearten resistance as Neustadt argued, the effects are marginal.[14]

14. We also estimated the model for the subset of important votes. The effects of the various contexts are even weaker on important votes.

Table 7.6 Estimated Probabilities of Presidential Victory under Different Conditions of Popularity

CONTEXT	HOUSE			SENATE		
	$\hat{z}$	$\hat{p}$	Diff.	$\hat{z}$	$\hat{p}$	Diff.
Majority Presidents						
Average popularity— stable	.68	.75	—	.81	.79	—
High popularity— stable	.93	.82	.07	1.01	.84	.05
High popularity— decreasing	.80	.79	.04	.81	.79	.00
Low popularity— stable	.57	.72	−.03	.52	.70	−.09
Low popularity— decreasing	.44	.67	−.08	.32	.63	−.16
Minority Presidents						
Average popularity— stable (intercept)	.09	.53	—	.15	.56	—
High popularity— stable	.34	.63	.10	.35	.64	.08
High popularity— decreasing	.21	.58	.05	.15	.56	.00
Low popularity— stable	−.02	.49	−.04	−.14	.44	−.12
Low popularity— decreasing	−.15	.44	−.09	−.34	.37	−.19

Note: Z-scores estimated from probit equations. The estimated $\hat{p}$ is the probability that the president's position wins under the specified condition. The difference is the change in probability from average-stable popularity.

Table 7.6 shows the estimated probabilities of victory for majority and minority presidents under different conditions of presidential popularity. Under the condition of average, stable popularity, the probability of victory on roll call votes is about three out of four for majority presidents and about a coin toss for minority presidents. No condition of popularity changes that probability by more than .20, and in most contexts the change in probability is less than .10. Although this estimate is about half of the benefit of majority control, recall that most of the coefficients used to make the estimates are not statistically significant. If the insignificant coefficients are assumed to be zero, then the estimated changes in probabilities are nil.

CONCLUSIONS

Thus the findings are consistent and clear: the effects of the president's public approval on success in Congress are limited. Our analysis reveals that the president does not consistently win more votes nor does he consistently receive higher levels of support from the party factions when he is popular than when he is unpopular. This finding holds regardless of whether one conceptualizes presidential approval as an interval level or a contextual variable. Similarly, presidential success on roll call votes is not affected by the change in the president's popularity over the previous six months. And contrary to the major finding of Edwards's (1980) research, we find no support for the proposition that partisan groups in Congress are more responsive to the president's popularity among their party identifiers in the public than to his overall popularity. Moreover, this pattern of weak relationships is not substantially different in the House or Senate, for domestic or foreign policy issues, for important or less important votes, or (with the exception of President Johnson) for different presidential administrations. These findings, of course, do not deny that for some individuals on some votes, the president's popularity with the public is a crucial—perhaps even a deciding—consideration. The weak relationships do suggest that, as an empirical generalization, the conclusion that presidential popularity is a major cause of legislative outcomes needs to be reconsidered.

The proposition that the president's popularity systematically alters congressional support is based on a rather naive theory of democracy and representation that assumes levels of citizen knowledge and interest that rarely exist. Most members of Congress know that very few voters are likely to have information about their votes on specific roll calls or about their support for the president. Voters are, however, more likely to be aware of a representative's general voting pattern reflected by party and ideology. Incumbents seldom lose because they support a popular president too little or support an unpopular president too much; they are more likely to lose because they are too liberal or conservative for their constituencies.

The weak relationship observed in this analysis does not mean that presidential popularity is unimportant. Popularity does affect presidential-congressional relations indirectly through elections by altering the partisan and ideological composition of Congress. Several researchers (Tufte 1975; Kernell 1977) provide evidence that the outcomes in midterm congressional elections are influenced by the president's popularity, at least indirectly (Jacobson and Kernell 1983). Thus the president's public prestige may affect his success in Congress not because it alters the behavior of individuals who are already there, but because it affects the number of members of the president's party who win seats in Congress.

We now turn our attention to examining the impact of another factor linked to presidential success in Congress that has generated considerable disagreement in the literature—the president's skill as a legislative actor. Together with popularity, presidential leadership skills comprise important components of a presidency-centered explanation of presidential success in Congress.

CHAPTER 8

PRESIDENTIAL LEADERSHIP SKILL

President Reagan's string of victories in the Democratic-controlled House during his first year in office surprised most political observers and won him respect, if not admiration, even from his opponents. Hedrick Smith (1982, 274), chief Washington correspondent for the *New York Times,* expressed the prevailing view as follows:

> His accomplishment was striking not only because it came in spite of a
> Democratic majority in the House, but also because such political mastery of the legislative branch eluded the last three occupants of the
> White House. . . . [N]ot since Lyndon B. Johnson's Great Society surge
> in the mid-sixties had Washington seen a president perform so persuasively with the legislature.

This view of Reagan as a masterful legislative leader contrasts sharply with the conventional view that Carter was inept in his dealings with Congress. Michael Malbin (1983, 216) notes, for example, that "President Carter neither enjoyed this part of his job nor was he very skilled at it."

For many observers, the stark contrast between Reagan and Carter demonstrates that a competent and skillful leader can overcome the inevitable resistance in Congress and get what he wants when he wants it. But was Reagan more successful than one should expect given the circumstances in 1981? Was Carter less successful than one should expect given the conditions he faced? The issue raised by these questions reflects one of the most important and persistent debates in the study of presidential-congressional relations: Can the president, through the skillful pursuit and exercise of power, significantly affect his success rate in Congress, or is success determined largely by political and institutional forces over which the president has little control?

Although students of presidential-congressional relations agree that success in Congress is a function of both leadership skill and political conditions, they disagree over which explanation should be emphasized. One school of thought emphasizes leadership skill as the key variable explaining presidential success. Political and institutional forces determine the relative advantages and disadvantages facing the president, but his leadership skill determines whether he will be able to capitalize on the advantages and overcome the disadvantages. Evidence supporting this interpretation consists mainly of perceptions of observers involved in or close to the decision making process in a small number of cases.

Another school of thought argues that skills affect presidential success only at the margins. Presidential activity may change the outcome in a few cases, but representatives in Congress respond to their own political needs and preferences, which cannot be fundamentally altered by presidential politicking, no matter how skillfully it is done. Evidence supporting this interpretation consists of quantitative analysis of a large sample of cases.

To resolve this controversy, our analysis must recognize the contributions of each school of thought. On the one hand, the skills explanation cannot be dismissed as unsystematic and anecdotal. Too many politicians and observers close to the decision making process believe that skills play a crucial role for their effects to be merely idiosyncratic. Those who study the process from a more detached perspective have an obligation to listen to what the participants have to say and to take their explanation seriously.

On the other hand, the consistent negative findings of quantitative studies cannot be rejected as irrelevant. It is always appropriate for a science to ask if a particular case is representative and if the conclusion derived from that case can be generalized. Moreover, the debate over the relative importance of skills cannot be resolved simply by saying that skills matter some of the time on some issues. If skills are an important component of presidential-congressional relations, then they must have some effect beyond influencing the outcome of a small number of issues, regardless of how important those issues may be to the president.

This chapter seeks to shed light on this issue with an empirical test of the effects of presidential leadership skill on success in Congress. The conventional view is that skilled presidents are not just successful but "uncommonly successful in recruiting allies" (Davidson 1984, 374). To determine whether skilled presidents are uncommonly successful requires that we establish a common base line for comparison. Our approach is to estimate a base line to determine how often each president should win, and then see if those with reputations as highly skilled win more often than predicted and if those perceived as less skilled win less often than predicted. Before we discuss the appropriate base line, however, we need to review perceptions of recent presidents as skilled or unskilled.

Skilled and Unskilled Presidents

Because professional reputations are defined by perceptions, we cannot develop a precise, quantitative measure of skill. Nonetheless, every president develops a general reputation as more or less skilled. While every Washingtonian will not share the general view, there "usually is a dominant tone, a central tendency, in Washington appraisals of a President" (Neustadt 1960, 62). An examination of the literature, therefore, should permit a relatively valid and reliable placement of recent presidents into general categories based on perceptions of their leadership skill.

Much folklore about the importance of skills can be traced to Franklin Roosevelt and the unmatched success he enjoyed during his first one hundred days in office. Neustadt (1960, 161) holds Roosevelt up as the prototype to be imitated:

> No President in this century has had a sharper sense of personal power,
> a sense of what it is and where it comes from; none has had more
> hunger for it, few have had more use for it, and only one or two could
> match his faith in his own competence to use it. Perception and desire
> and self-confidence, combined, produced their own reward. No modern
> President has been more nearly master in the White House.

Others agree. James MacGregor Burns (1956, 186), for example, describes Roosevelt's reputation as an astute and masterful leader as follows:

> The classic test of greatness in the White House has been the chief
> executive's capacity to lead Congress. Weak presidents have been those
> . . . whose proposals have been bled away in the endless twistings and
> windings of the legislative process. Strong presidents have been those
> who finessed or bulldozed their programs through Congress and wrote
> them into legislative history. By this classic test Roosevelt—during his
> first years in the White House—was a strong president who dominated
> Congress with a masterly show of leadership.

The performance and success of subsequent presidents, therefore, are measured against the standard set by FDR. The seven presidents in our study fall into three groups: three are perceived as highly skilled, two fall into a middle range, and two are perceived as relatively unskilled.

Highly Skilled Presidents: Johnson, Reagan, and Ford

There is wide agreement that Johnson and Reagan are the most highly skilled leaders since FDR. Johnson is commonly referred to as a "master congressional tactician." His masterful dealings with Congress, especially during his first three years (1964–66), contributed much to the "lore about presidential legislative style." Serving as Senate majority leader gave Johnson an intimate understanding of Congress and access to the centers of power there. He was a "child of Congress" who liked interacting with its members and pulling the levers of power to get what he wanted. Like FDR's, his performance set "the standard by which other presidents would be measured, regardless of changes in political conditions" (Jones 1983, 106–7).

In the eyes of Washingtonians, Reagan measures up favorably not only to Johnson but also to Roosevelt. Reagan impressed Washingtonians with his efforts to establish good relations with Congress even before his inauguration. His early successes in the Democrat-controlled House are widely attributed to his "mastery of the legislative branch." This impressive performance is often compared to Johnson's (Smith 1982, 274; also see Malbin, 212). Despite later conflicts and setbacks, Reagan's style kept his reputation relatively untarnished into his second term.[1] Indeed, his style is described as closely resembling that of Franklin Roosevelt (Jones 1983, 126).[2]

The third president in the highly skilled group is Ford, although he probably ranks behind Johnson and Reagan. In terms of background and approach to dealing with Congress, Ford is most like Johnson. Ford served twenty-five years in the House before becoming the first vice-president chosen by Congress under provisions of the Twenty-fifth Amendment. His tenure as minority leader "schooled him in the give and take" of congressional politics and made him "sensitive to congressional realities" (Koenig 1981, 174). His techniques were very similar to Johnson's: "He was accessible, he worked closely with party leaders on Capitol Hill, he implicated members in his legislative program, he invited close contact with the legislative liaison people" (Jones 1983, 117). Eric Davis (1983, 64) notes that Ford's legislative liaison was very similar to Johnson's and that the staff worked "under the close supervision of a politically skilled and legislatively experienced president."

Mixed Assessments: Eisenhower and Kennedy

The literature is mixed and ambiguous about Eisenhower's and Kennedy's reputed skills in dealing with Congress. This lack of consensus suggests that these two presidents should be placed in a middle category behind the presidents perceived as most skilled but ahead of those perceived as unskilled.

The original view of Eisenhower was that of an inexperienced, unskilled

1. The view of Reagan's leadership may be less favorable in assessments made after the details of the Iran-Contra debacle became public through the Tower Commission report and the Congressional hearings in 1987. But it is probably accurate to say that Reagan's reputation as a skilled legislative leader remained intact through the midterm elections in 1986, although it could not prevent the loss of Republican control of the Senate.

2. Actually, the comparison is even more flattering. Jones says that Roosevelt's style resembles Reagan's rather than vice versa.

president who disdained politics and sought to keep the presidency above the inevitable conflicts. Neustadt was highly critical of Eisenhower's performance. If Roosevelt is the model of how to succeed, Eisenhower is the model of how not to succeed. And Neustadt placed the blame for Eisenhower's failure squarely on the man himself, on his insensitivity to power and on his lack of understanding of the rules of the game (Neustadt, 1960, 165–71). Sam Rayburn, Speaker of the House during much of Eisenhower's presidency, is quoted as saying of Eisenhower, "Good man. Wrong profession" (quoted in Neustadt 1960, 194).

The revisionist view, however, is more positive. In later editions of his book, Neustadt modifies his evaluation of Eisenhower's performance. Looking back after the deceptions of the Johnson and Nixon administrations, he now feels that Eisenhower's concern for his own prestige contributed to the office's advantage and is "a more impressive contribution" than he originally thought (Neustadt 1980, 169). Eisenhower institutionalized liaison operations in the White House, building upon more ad hoc beginnings in the Roosevelt and Truman administrations (Davis 1983, 60–61). And scholars now credit Eisenhower with succeeding in *his* view of the presidency, which was more limited than that of his immediate predecessors. He preferred to work through intermediaries, allowing subordinates to take the heat and criticism in order to protect the president and the office. He frequently used his supposed lack of skill for his own political advantage. For example, when his press secretary, James Hagerty, conveyed an urgent request from the State Department that he not discuss publicly the delicate matter of using nuclear weapons to defend Quemoy and Matsu, Eisenhower replied, "Don't worry, Jim, if that question comes up, I'll just confuse them." When the issue did come up at a press conference in March 1955, Eisenhower responded with vagueness and ambiguity contrived to serve his political ends (Greenstein 1982, 69).

Kennedy is generally viewed as less skilled than Johnson. Although Kennedy spent fourteen years in Congress, he was never viewed as a member of the inner club. Consequently, he never enjoyed Johnson's access to the centers of power in Congress. Moreover, Kennedy had "little taste for . . . dealing with legislators" (Cronin 1980, 169), and he is criticized for his lack of attention to legislative affairs and for coming too late to many problems (Koenig 1981, 172).

To Kennedy's credit, however, the appointment of Lawrence O'Brien to direct his Office of Congressional Relations gave him great advantages in dealing with Congress. O'Brien was a skilled political operative and is "considered the father of modern legislative liaison." Because of O'Brien's long personal relationship with Kennedy, members of Congress knew that when he spoke, he spoke for the president (Davis 1983, 62).

Unskilled Presidents: Nixon and Carter

Nixon and Carter are generally viewed as relatively unskilled presidents. Nixon had little knowledge of the workings of Congress, despite his service there. He neither trusted nor respected Congress, and he expressed his contempt publicly. For example, shortly before delivering his State of the Union message in 1971, Nixon issued a harsh criticism of Congress: "In the final month and weeks of 1970, especially in the Senate of the United States, the nation was presented with the spectacle of a legislative body that had seemingly lost the capacity to decide and the will to act" (quoted in Jones 1983, 113). The timing of the statement is telling. Jones (1983, 113) observes, "It was unusual to have the president humiliate Congress just weeks before presenting his legislative program." Nixon also seemed to lose interest in his programs and is criticized for his lack of follow-through (Edwards 1980, 139). He had no stomach for face-to-face confrontations with members of Congress. When he did negotiate with a member of Congress, his style was "the antithesis of the insistent Johnson treatment" (Evans and Novak 1971, 107).

Carter's distaste for personal politicking and his lack of understanding of Congress are widely perceived to be the cause of his problems with Congress (Malbin 1983, 216; Davidson 1984, 374, 378; Jones 1981, 238; Davis 1979, 285–94). He ran for and was elected president as a Washington outsider. His outsider approach explicitly rejected many of the proven elements of skilled interaction with Congress. As president, Carter did not consult with key members of Congress, he did not have a good sense of when to compromise, he eschewed the usual favors and services that members of Congress expected, and he failed to set priorities (Jones 1983, 122–23).

In sum, the perceived ranking of presidents' leadership skills is as follows: Johnson and Reagan are the most skilled, followed by Ford; Eisenhower and Kennedy are in a middle category; Nixon and Carter are the least skilled.

TEST OF THE SKILLS THEORY

The review of the skills theory in chapter 2 suggests that evidence from case studies may be rich and suggestive, but as a test of the theory, the case study approach is deficient. Edwards's (1986a) approach is an improvement. His approach is to measure presidential support among individual members of Congress, and then see whether presidents with reputations as skilled receive greater support from different groups of members (i.e., northern Democrats, southern Democrats, and Republicans) than do presidents with reputations as unskilled. Further, he compares support using four different measures ranging from a comprehensive measure based on all votes on which the president expresses a position to a selective measure based only on Congressional

Quarterly's key votes. The index based on key votes is noteworthy because it focuses on the types of issues that the president is likely to care the most about and "may reveal differences in support that broader indexes mask" (Edwards 1986a, 12). Thus Edwards's test anticipates a potential criticism from those who argue that the appropriate test of leadership skills is on a small number of important votes, although we do not know if the key votes selected by CQ are viewed as important by the president. This analysis reveals that presidential leadership skills are not "a predominant factor in determining presidential support in Congress on most roll call votes, despite the commonly held assumptions to the contrary" (Edwards 1986a, 40).

Although Edwards's analysis of leadership skill provides a more persuasive test, it has a limitation that suggests the need for another approach. His analysis focuses on support from individual members. It can tell us whether the president's reputation as skilled or unskilled is associated with support from individuals, but it cannot reveal the effects (if any) on programmatic success.

Influencing behavior of individual members is certainly an important ingredient of presidential-congressional relations. After all, the president's interpersonal skills are employed on individuals, not on votes. But influencing individuals is only the penultimate step in the journey toward the ultimate goal—winning the vote. Because policymaking in Congress requires collective decisions, analyzing the effects of skills on individuals is an incomplete test. Presidential activity may systematically increase support from certain types of individuals but fail to change the collective result. Or the president's activity may appear not to be related to support from various groups of members (as Edwards found) because it affects too few individuals in each group to produce significant differences, but the few votes gained from each group might be enough to win more roll calls. Thus it is appropriate and necessary to analyze the association between skills and success on votes.

Edwards (1986a, 10) argues that we "cannot use box scores or victories-on-votes figures because winning votes and passing legislation depend heavily on the party composition of Congress." While it is true that passing legislation is a function of variables other than presidential skill, that does not preclude analyzing success on votes. We know what many of these variables are, and we can control for their influence. Indeed, Edwards notes one in the passage just cited.

Base Line

Of all the linkage agents analyzed, skill is the least susceptible to the type of systematic analysis employed throughout this book. Because such empirical testing is difficult, our approach to analyzing the effects of skill is indirect. We construct a base line from the major variables that define the balance of political forces and conditions known to affect presidential success in general. Once we have defined a base line, we can compare each president's success to a common standard, rather than comparing it to the success of other presidents who operated under a different set of conditions.

Although many political forces influence the outcome of votes in Congress, the literature identifies three variables that seem to be especially important: (1) partisan control of Congress, (2) the level of public approval of the president, and (3) the "cycle of decreasing influence." The first two variables represent two types of political capital available to the president (Light 1983, chap. 1; Edwards 1980, chaps. 3 and 4; Fleisher and Bond 1983b, 745–58). The third is an inevitable and recurrent pattern resulting from the depletion of the president's political capital and the erosion of the president's time and energy over the course of his term (Light 1983, 36–37). These variables are largely beyond manipulation by the president and, as such, operate independently of skill.[3] Thus they provide a reasonable and parsimonious base line to use to evaluate the effects of presidential leadership skill.[4]

To establish a base line, we regress the president's annual percentage success on votes as a function of (1) the percentage of the president's party in the chamber, (2) the president's average popularity for the year, and (3) the total number of years the president has been in office. These models account for 45 percent of the variance in success in the House and 50 percent in the Senate.[5] The regression equations are then used to predict how successful the president should be given the effects of these political forces. The residuals indicate, for each year, whether the president won more or less often than the model predicted. Thus we are able to compare all the presidents' success to the same standard.

3. Some might view public approval as an exception. Presidents often attempt to manipulate public opinion as a strategy to influence Congress. The president's ability to improve his standing in the polls, however, is limited. A speech or a foreign trip may result in short-term gains, but presidents generally have been unable to avoid a general decline in popularity over the course of a term. And increased popularity from a single action may have little effect on congressional support on other issues. President Reagan's order to bomb Libya, for example, was very popular. Despite widespread public and congressional support for the bombing, the House still rejected the President's request for more aid to the rebels in Nicaragua, and the votes occurred the day after the Libya bombing. For these reasons, it seems reasonable to view public approval as a contextual variable largely beyond the president's control.

4. Although other variables such as constituency interest and region affect congressional voting, the effects of these variables on presidential support vary from vote to vote depending on the president's position. Since presidential positions over time do not systematically favor any particular constituency or region, it is reasonable to assume that the effects of these variables are randomly distributed in the model.

5. Success is measured as the percentage of victories on conflictual roll calls, as discussed in chapter 3. The number of years of service is included to account for the "cycle of decreasing

Empirical Expectations

We recognize that the residuals from this analysis are not a direct measure of the effects of presidential skills. The unexplained variance could be due to many factors other than the president's leadership skill. But our base line model includes the major systematic influences on presidential success identified in the literature. It seems reasonable to assume that the effects of most other unmeasured variables are randomly distributed. Given the importance attributed to skills in the literature, any unmeasured systematic influence should be less important. Thus, if skills systematically affect presidential success, then we should observe certain regular patterns in the residuals. Because unmeasured variables affect presidential support, even if we observe the expected patterns, we cannot determine how many more victories skills are worth. But the mere existence of the expected pattern will provide support for the theory, while failure to observe the expected patterns would suggest that skills have only a limited impact on presidential success.

The skills theory leads us to expect presidents with superior skills to do better in any given political situation than presidents with lesser skills. Specifically, the theory predicts:

1. Presidents with reputations as skilled (Johnson, Reagan, and to a lesser degree Ford) should win consistently more often than predicted by the variables in the base line.
2. Presidents with reputations as unskilled (Nixon and Carter) should win consistently less often than predicted by the variables in the base line.
3. Presidents in the middle category (Eisenhower and Kennedy) should have success rates close to the predicted level, and the residuals should not be consistently higher or lower.

The theory gives no indication that the skills necessary to influence Senators are different from those necessary to influence members of the House. Because leadership skill is a characteristic of a president, the degree of skill is relatively constant across chambers for a given president, and the pattern of residuals for each president should be similar in the House and Senate.

---

influence" (Light, 1983, 36–37). Public approval is the percent approving "of the way [the incumbent] is handling his job as president" from the Gallup poll. The House equation is:

SUCCESS = 5.52 + .86 PARTY + .27 POPULARITY −0.07 SERVICE + e

The Senate equation is:

SUCCESS = 34.59 + .73 PARTY + .09 POPULARITY −4.10 SERVICE + e

Party is significant in both models; years of service is significant in the Senate model; popularity is not significant in either. We left insignificant variables in both models to make predictions because theory suggests that they affect success and the coefficients are in the expected direction.

Furthermore, leadership skill for a given president is relatively constant or perhaps increasing over the course of his term. Light (1983, 37) observes a "cycle of increasing effectiveness" as the president gains experience. Presidents certainly do not become less skilled over time. Hence, controlling for the balance of political forces in the base line, the pattern of residuals for each president should be relatively constant or increasing over the course of his term.[6]

Some will object to this approach because it is not a definitive test. We agree, and our hope is that those dissatisfied with our test will devise a better one. Until that time, we believe that our approach provides a more systematic test than others (e.g., Edwards 1986a; Kellerman 1984) and that it allows us to make some inferences about the importance of skills.

Some will also object to this test on the ground that the effects of skills will be evident only sporadically on a small number of the most important votes. Therefore, we will also analyze presidential success on two subsets of conflictual roll calls. First, we will compare success rates on our subset of important votes. Second, we will look at patterns of success on votes on which the margin of victory or defeat was close (i.e., margins of 10 percent or less). Realistically, if presidential persuasion is going to make a difference, it is most likely to do so when changing the position of a small number of individuals can change the outcome on the issue at hand. One noted student of the presidency cites the common supposition that "a masterful political operator works at the margins turning close calls into narrow victories" (Rockman 1984, 203). If skills matter, then presidents with reputations as skilled (Johnson, Reagan, and Ford) should win the largest percentage of close votes, and presidents with reputations as unskilled (Nixon and Carter) should win the smallest percentage of close votes; presidents in the middle category (Eisenhower and Kennedy) should fall somewhere in between.

RESULTS

Table 8.1 contains the residuals for each year from 1953 to 1984; figure 8.1 is a graphic comparison of predicted and actual success rates. Although we can find some cases that support the skills theory, in general, perceptions of leadership skill are not associated with whether a president succeeds more or less often than predicted. The correlations between the ranking on perceived skill and the difference between actual and predicted success are .01 in the House and .24 in the Senate. While these correlations are in the right direction

---

6. Recall that we have controlled for Light's "cycle of decreasing influence" with the years of service variable in the model, as well as party losses at midterm and any decline in popularity, so greater success over time is a reasonable expectation.

(the most skilled presidents should have the largest positive residuals), they are near zero, indicating an almost complete lack of a relationship.[7]

The most striking feature evident from a visual inspection of the table and figure is the lack of any consistent pattern. Presidents reputed to be skilled do not win consistently more often than predicted; presidents reputed to be unskilled do not win consistently less often than predicted. In the few cases in which the pattern is consistent with the skills theory, it is evident in only one chamber. And even though the base line accounts for the cycle of decreasing influence, there is no general tendency for success to improve over the course of a term.

Skilled Presidents

The success rate of President Johnson, the master legislative tactician, was not extraordinary. In the House, the residuals were positive in four of the five years he served, and on average Johnson won about 5.5 percent more often than expected. This success, however, was not repeated in the Senate. Although he won more often than expected in three years, only one residual (1965) was greater than 5 percent. The negative residuals were −21.9 percent and −5.9 percent, resulting in an average Senate success rate about 3.2 percent lower than predicted. The only time that Johnson's success rate was better than expected in both chambers simultaneously was during his first two years in office (1964 and 1965). Moreover, none of his positive residuals was greater than 10 percent. Other presidents with less skill, including Nixon and Eisenhower, had positive residuals greater than 10 percent. Nixon and Eisenhower, of course, were not nearly as active as Johnson, so he won more in absolute numbers.[8] Nonetheless, these examples reveal that less skilled presidents occasionally were more successful than expected in achieving *their* agendas than Johnson was in achieving his.

Thus Johnson won more votes and passed more legislation than other presidents, an accomplishment which may attest to his agenda-setting skill, his sense of timing, and his ability to take full advantage of favorable condi-

7. Although our base line model controls for majority or minority status by including percentage of the president's party in the chamber, one could argue that the advantage of majority status involves more than merely having more partisans on the floor. Majority presidents also have their partisans in control of standing committees and scheduling. As a result, the appropriate comparisons are within the categories of majority or minority status. Even with this additional control, there is only limited support for the skills theory. For majority presidents in the House (Johnson, Eisenhower in the 83rd Congress, Kennedy, and Carter) the perceived ranking matches the empirical results well—the correlation is .84. But in the Senate, the correlation for majority presidents is a weak .22. And the correlations for minority presidents are in the wrong direction in both chambers.

8. In the House, Johnson took a position on an average of 66 conflictual votes per year compared to only 33 for Eisenhower and 50 for Nixon. In the Senate, the average number for Johnson was 122 per year compared to 57 for Eisenhower and 66 for Nixon.

Table 8.1 Difference between Actual and Predicted Presidential Success in the House and Senate

PRESIDENT AND YEAR	HOUSE	SENATE	PRESIDENT AND YEAR	HOUSE	SENATE
DDE			**RMN**		
1953	21.0	10.7	1969	2.2	−1.9
1954	−4.8	2.2	1970	14.9	−8.3
1955	−20.9	3.2	1971	24.2	6.0
1956	−10.4	0.1	1972	23.0	−12.0
1957	−14.3	13.0	1973	−15.1	−17.7
1958	6.4	18.0	1974	8.0	3.8
1959	−6.2	−23.4	Mean	9.5	−5.0
1960	10.4	0.9	**GRF**		
Mean	−2.4	3.1	1974	−13.9	−22.3
JFK			1975	−1.4	0.5
1961	0.4	−7.5	1976	−9.7	−3.9
1962	2.5	0.0	Mean	−8.3	−8.6
1963	4.6	7.7	**JEC**		
Mean	2.5	0.1	1977	−13.9	−16.7
LBJ			1978	−11.5	5.9
1964	8.5	3.4	1979	−4.4	6.0
1965	9.3	6.6	1980	−1.2	−0.2
1966	7.4	−21.9	Mean	−7.8	−1.3
1967	−4.2	1.8	**RWR**		
1968	6.4	−5.9	1981	9.6	7.8
Mean	5.5	−3.2	1982	−14.1	8.7
			1983	−4.2	17.0
			1984	−8.8	18.1
			Mean	−4.4	12.9

tions. But his unusual success rate on this ambitious agenda was limited to his first two years in office. Furthermore, Johnson's unusual success in the 89th Congress, the famous Great Society Congress which is the source of much lore about his uncommon skill, occurred mainly in the House. In the Senate, his success rate was slightly better than expected for the first session, but in the second session his success rate was nearly 22 percent less than expected.

It is noteworthy that the Senate, where he developed and perfected the "Johnson treatment" reputed to be so effective, was the first chamber to re-

Figure 8.1 Actual and Predicted Presidential Success Rates in the House and Senate

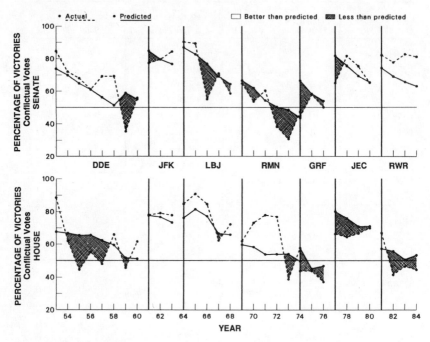

Source: Tables 3.1 and 8.1.

buke his leadership. Perhaps the hard sell treatment is effective only under conditions of broad consensus. The assassination of President Kennedy and the landslide election victory in 1964 made Johnson a consensus president. So long as the consensus held, Johnson's leadership techniques worked well. But by 1966, when the consensus began to break down in the face of the escalating war in Vietnam, growing inflation, and the approaching midterm elections, the effectiveness of techniques that had worked well before began to be questioned (Congressional Quarterly 1969, 625).

President Reagan is also perceived to be uncommonly skilled and successful in his dealings with Congress. Our analysis suggests that this perception is only partly accurate. Like Johnson, Reagan got off to a good start, winning more often than expected in both chambers during his first year. Although his unusual success in the Senate continued and even increased throughout his first term, his reputation for skilled leadership failed to maintain the same pattern in the House. Reagan's success rate in the House was considerably less than expected in each year from 1982 to 1984. The differences between actual and predicted levels of support are not trivial. Across the four years of his first term, the residuals in the Senate averaged nearly 13 percent above predicted. In the House, the four-year average is −4.38, and after the first good year his success rate averaged 9 percent below what should be expected given the effects of party, popularity, and time in office.[9]

Keep in mind that our base line model controls for the effects of majority and minority status by including percentage of the president's party in the chamber. Johnson and Reagan enjoyed majority status in the Senate, and the model predicts similar levels of support for both in that chamber. Reagan's actual level of success exceeded that prediction throughout his first term; Johnson's did not. In the House, where Republicans were in the minority, the model predicts a much lower level of success for Reagan than for Johnson. Reagan's actual success rate fell substantially below this lower prediction, while Johnson's exceeded the higher prediction. Moreover, this method does not preclude a minority president from exceeding predictions. Nixon and Reagan faced Democratic majorities in the House, and the model predicts similar success rates for both. Yet Nixon, who was reputedly less skilled than Reagan, exceeded predictions throughout his first term.

The third president perceived as highly skilled is Gerald Ford. Ford had an unusually heavy burden in dealing with Congress, assuming the presidency as he did in the wake of the Watergate scandal and forced Nixon resignation. The results of our analysis indicate that his congressional experience and reputed leadership skill were insufficient to overcome this added burden. His success rate was substantially below the base line in both chambers during his first year in office. After a bad initial year, his success rate in the Senate improved to near the predicted level, and his 1975 House success rate was only slightly below the base line. But overall Ford had a difficult time in both chambers, averaging 8.33 percent below expected in the House and 8.57 percent below expected in the Senate. Note, however, that in the House Ford's average success rate relative to the base line is not substantially different than Reagan's −9 percent average for the comparable three years (i.e., the midterm election year and two subsequent years); and Reagan is reputed as more skilled and did not have Ford's extra burden. Thus the magnitude of Ford's lack of success relative to the base line is not unique among presidents with reputations as

9. The finding that Reagan won more often than predicted in the House during his first year supports our argument that analysis of support from individuals needs to be followed up with an analysis of success on votes. In an earlier study comparing actual and predicted support from individual members of the House, we found that, on average, members of the House supported Reagan slightly less often than should be expected during his first year (Fleisher and Bond 1983b, 751). Thus, despite less than expected support from individuals, he still won more often than expected during his first year.

highly skilled, but he is the only one who failed to exceed the predicted level in either chamber.

Unskilled Presidents

Nixon and Carter, the two presidents perceived as least skilled in dealing with Congress, did not win consistently less often than should be expected. Nixon began his presidency with success rates at about the predicted level—slightly higher in the House, slightly lower in the Senate. In the Senate, his success relative to the base line deteriorated, and the pattern is generally consistent with the skills theory. Although the Senate residuals were positive in 1971 and 1974, the negative residuals in the other years were much larger. And the positive residual in 1974 is probably due to posturing or to forces other than skill; it is difficult to believe that Nixon's positions on roll call votes exerted much influence in the year Congress forced him to resign. On average, Nixon won about 5 percent less often than predicted in the Senate. His success rate in the House, however, was much better than expected for his entire first term. Indeed, his success rate relative to the base line in the House is better than any other president's in the study, including Johnson's and Reagan's. During his first term, Nixon won an average of about 16 percent more often than expected. The residuals turned negative in 1973, presumably due to the revelations of the Watergate scandal. Thus Nixon's reputation as unskilled may have decreased his success rate in the Senate, but the supposed lack of skill does not appear to have hurt his success in the House.

Carter got off to a bad start in both chambers and tended to improve over the course of his term, results consistent with conventional wisdom. His success rates in 1977 were far below the predicted level (-13.9 percent in the House, -16.7 percent in the Senate). After the first year, Carter's success rate began to improve. Although the residuals in the House were all negative, by 1980 his success rate was only slightly less than predicted. In the Senate, his success rates for the last three years of his term were about as predicted or slightly better. In general, Carter did worse than he should have in the House (four-year average $= -7.75$ percent), but about as should be expected in the Senate (average $= -1.25$ percent).

Other Presidents

Kennedy is generally viewed as less skilled than Johnson, yet Kennedy's success rate was very close to the predicted level and increased slightly in both chambers over the three years he served. Comparing his relative success to Johnson's for the comparable three years reveals that Johnson began his term above the base line, but his residuals declined and turned negative after the midterm election losses. Kennedy started relatively lower than Johnson, but his residuals increased and remained positive even after midterm.

Eisenhower began his presidency with success rates better than predicted in both chambers. Residuals in the Senate were positive for every year of his two terms except 1959, although several were very small. Residuals in the House behaved more erratically. After a good first year, his success rate fell precipitously to well below the base line. And the decline began in 1954, before the midterm change in party control. The residuals remained strongly negative until 1958, when they began to fluctuate around the baseline.

Honeymoons

A frequently mentioned aspect of presidential-congressional relations is the notion of a "honeymoon" period for the president. The honeymoon refers to the early part of a president's term, when his popularity with the public is usually at its highest and the Washington press corps and members of Congress are predisposed to give him the benefit of the doubt.[10] The length of the honeymoon is not defined precisely, but one year seems to be the maximum. This period is widely viewed as the most propitious time for presidential initiatives. But paradoxically, the first year is also a period of learning and adjustment for the president, so there is no guarantee that he will be able to exploit the potential benefits of the honeymoon.

Washingtonians' expectations are high (perhaps unreasonably so) during a president's first year in office. Even though our base line model includes variables to account for greater expected success early in the president's term (i.e., the president's popularity and the number of years of service), some presidents seem to have benefited from a honeymoon over and above what should normally be expected. Others seem to have had no honeymoon at all. Eisenhower, Johnson, and Reagan won more often than expected in both chambers during their first year in office. The remaining presidents in our study had less impressive first-year success rates. Kennedy and Nixon did about as well as or slightly better than should be expected in one chamber and slightly worse in the other. Ford and Carter did considerably worse than predicted in both chambers.

Note that the two presidents perceived as most skilled, Johnson and Reagan, had first-year success rates above the base line in both chambers. This unusual success may have been sufficient to surpass the high expectations of the Washington community and seal their reputations against tarnish from poorer performances later in the term. The two presidents perceived as least skilled had first-year success rates below the base line in one or both chambers. Although Nixon's success rate was near what should be expected and

10. The author of a popular American government textbook hints at the possible origin of the analogy. The "honeymoon" is the period "during which, presumably, the president's love affair with the people and the Congress can be consummated" (Wilson 1983, 327).

Table 8.2 Presidential Success on Important Votes in the House and Senate

PRESIDENT AND CONGRESS	HOUSE		SENATE	
	%	(N)	%	(N)
Majority Presidents				
LBJ				
88th	83	(12)	69	(13)
89th	82	(27)	71	(46)
90th	57	(21)	71	(24)
Total	73	(60)	71	(83)
RWR				
97th	—	—	74	(39)
98th	—	—	82	(33)
Total	—	—	78	(72)
DDE				
83rd	79	(14)	70	(10)
JFK				
87th	65	(26)	70	(20)
88th	85	(13)	67	(6)
Total	72	(39)	69	(26)
JEC				
95th	75	(28)	65	(17)
96th	73	(33)	68	(34)
Total	74	(61)	67	(51)
Minority Presidents				
RWR				
97th	70	(30)	—	—
98th	57	(49)	—	—
Total	62	(79)	—	—
GRF				
93rd	50	(4)	67	(3)
94th	48	(27)	63	(19)
Total	48	(31)	64	(22)
DDE				
84th	40	(15)	47	(17)
85th	56	(18)	79	(14)
86th	82	(17)	57	(21)
Total	42	(50)	60	(52)

Table 8.2 (*Continued*)

PRESIDENT AND CONGRESS	HOUSE		SENATE	
	%	(N)	%	(N)
RMN				
91st	77	(17)	58	(19)
92nd	69	(13)	46	(26)
93rd	42	(24)	71	(24)
Total	59	(54)	58	(69)

Carter's performance improved in later years, their initial success rates failed to live up to expectations and their poor reputations persisted.

Thus it appears that an unusually successful honeymoon is important to developing a reputation as skilled; anything less leads to a reputation as unskilled. Kennedy's reputation is consistent with this generalization. He did worse than the base line in the Senate and about as predicted in the House. This performance failed to exceed expectations, leading to a reputation as unskilled. Ford is viewed as skilled despite success rates below the base line in both chambers. But Ford's first year was not a typical honeymoon because he was not elected and assumed office in the midterm election year. Eisenhower seems to be the only exception. He had success rates above the base line in both chambers during his honeymoon year, yet he never developed a reputation as highly skilled.

Important Votes

Some might object to this analysis of presidential skills based on all conflictual votes, arguing that the impact of skills will be observable only on important votes. The relatively small number of important votes in some years prevents us from estimating the base line model. We can, however, examine presidential success on important votes, exploring whether skilled presidents are more successful than unskilled presidents on this subset of votes. To control for the advantages of majority status, we separate majority and minority presidents. Table 8.2 reports success rates on important votes, with presidents listed in order of their reputation as skilled or unskilled.

This analysis of important votes provides little support for the proposition that skilled presidents are more successful than unskilled presidents. While the rankings in the Senate are consistent with the skills argument, most of the differences are small. Among majority presidents, the two presidents with reputations as highly skilled have the highest success rates—Reagan won 78 percent and Johnson won 71 percent. Carter, who is reputed to be the least skilled, has the lowest success rate (67 percent). Note, however, that the difference between Johnson's success rate and the success rates of the less skilled Eisenhower and Kennedy is only one or two points. The ranking of minority presidents in the Senate is also consistent with the skills argument, but again the differences are modest. The highly skilled Ford won 64 percent of important roll calls compared to 60 percent for Eisenhower and 58 percent for Nixon.

The pattern in the House is less consistent with the skills theory. Among majority presidents, Johnson's overall success rate was lower than Eisenhower's and Carter's and only one point higher than Kennedy's. Although Johnson won more than 80 percent of important votes in the 88th and 89th Congresses, his success rate of 57 percent in the 90th was the lowest of any majority president. Furthermore, Johnson's highest success rates were lower than Kennedy's success rate in the first session of the 88th Congress and only three to four points higher than Eisenhower's when Republicans controlled the 83rd Congress. The differences among minority party presidents are small. While highly skilled Ford was the most successful minority president in the Senate, he was the least successful in the House. Nixon, the least skilled president, was only three points less successful than Reagan. And notice that Nixon's success rate during his first term was 73 percent—eleven points higher than Reagan's first term success rate.

Thus evidence from the analysis of important votes fails to provide convincing support for the skills theory. Although some patterns are consistent with what one would expect if skills influence success, the differences are small and are present in only one chamber.

The limited power of the president's legislative skills to overcome the disadvantages of minority status can be clearly seen by highlighting President Reagan's experiences over his two terms in office. Although our data measure presidential success only through 1984, we can analyze Congressional Quarterly's key votes to examine Reagan's experiences with the 100th Congress following the loss of Republican control of the Senate in the 1986 elections. During the 100th Congress, Reagan won only 24 percent of the House key votes and 43 percent of the Senate key votes.

Among the 31 key votes on which Reagan took a position, the October 1987 Senate vote on the confirmation of Judge Robert Bork to the United States Supreme Court is a particularly important case that highlights the limited effectiveness of presidential persuasion. Congressional Quarterly noted that Reagan "had made Bork's confirmation one of his highest priorities and had put his personal prestige into an extensive . . . lobbying effort" (*Congressional Quarterly Almanac* 1987, 8c). Indeed, one could argue that this vote rivals the 1981 budget cut votes in importance, because getting Bork confirmed to a lifetime appointment on the Court would mean that Reagan's conservative agenda could endure long after he left office.

The Democrats regained control of the Senate in the 1986 elections, but the president hoped to get a majority to confirm Bork with solid Republican support and votes from conservative (cross-pressured) southern Democrats—the same type of coalition that gave him victories on the 1981 budget cuts in the Democrat-controlled House. But the president's best efforts, which included calling undecided senators, failed miserably. Six Republicans and sixteen of eighteen southern Democrats joined a highly unified Democratic party base to defeat the Bork nomination by a humiliating 58–42 margin.

Close Votes

As a final test of the skills theory, we analyze success on close votes. This analysis focuses on situations in which skilled presidential leadership has the potential to influence the small number of votes necessary to turn a defeat into a victory. If skills matter, then skilled presidents should win more close calls than unskilled presidents.

Because there were several years with small numbers of close votes, we calculated success rates by Congress.[11] As was the case with important votes, the small number of close votes precludes estimating our base line model with all three variables. To control for the advantages of majority status, however, we again analyze majority and minority presidents separately. Moreover, limiting the analysis to close votes controls for the effects of other forces. Although political conditions other than majority or minority status may affect how frequently close votes occur, once such forces have caused the division to be close (however often that happens), if skills are important their effects should be evident in more wins on the close calls.

Table 8.3 reports success rates on votes decided by a margin of 10 percent or less. This analysis also provides only limited support for the skills explanation. The success rates of majority presidents on close House votes differ by very little. Johnson's 74 percent average, however, lags behind Carter (76 percent), Kennedy (79 percent), and Eisenhower in the 83rd Congress (78 percent). Among majority presidents in the Senate, Reagan was most successful on close votes, winning an average of 80 percent. Johnson's 69 percent average, however, again lags behind Kennedy's 73 percent and is only slightly ahead of Carter's (64 percent). Eisenhower's 52 percent success rate in the 83rd Congress is the lowest for majority presidents.

---

11. Aggregating by Congress yielded a sufficient number of close votes, although there is one with less than ten (the 83rd, with nine close votes). The 93rd Congress also continues to present a problem for analysis because only six close votes occurred after Ford assumed the presidency in 1974.

Table 8.3 Presidential Success on Close Votes in the House and Senate

PRESIDENT AND CONGRESS	HOUSE		SENATE	
	%	(N)	%	(N)
Majority Presidents				
LBJ				
88th	72	(25)	74	(27)
89th	74	(34)	61	(36)
90th	75	(44)	71	(58)
Total	74	(103)	69	(121)
RWR				
97th	—	—	74	(42)
98th	—	—	88	(33)
Total	—	—	80	(75)
DDE				
83rd	78	(9)	52	(23)
JFK				
87th	79	(24)	76	(45)
88th	79	(14)	67	(15)
Total	79	(38)	73	(60)
JEC				
95th	68	(47)	48	(27)
96th	82	(60)	72	(47)
Total	76	(107)	64	(74)
Minority Presidents				
RWR				
97th	73	(26)	—	—
98th	56	(41)	—	—
Total	63	(67)	—	—
GRF				
93rd	50	(6)	67	(12)
94th	39	(28)	65	(17)
Total	41	(34)	66	(29)
DDE				
84th	35	(17)	43	(28)
85th	38	(21)	64	(22)
86th	53	(17)	41	(32)
Total	60	(45)	49	(82)

Table 8.3 (*Continued*)

PRESIDENT AND CONGRESS	HOUSE		SENATE	
	%	(N)	%	(N)
RMN				
91st	75	(12)	54	(24)
92nd	67	(24)	42	(31)
93rd	37	(30)	64	(36)
Total	55	(66)	54	(91)

Among minority presidents in the House, Reagan won the most close votes (63 percent). But Nixon, one of the least skilled leaders, had the second highest rate (55 percent). And as was the case in the analysis of important votes, Nixon's first-term success rate on close votes was higher than Reagan's. In the Senate, unskilled Nixon won an average of 54 percent of close votes compared to the 49 percent rate for the more highly skilled Eisenhower. Although Ford had the lowest success rate among minority presidents in the House (41 percent), his 66 percent average in the Senate ranks him as the most successful minority president in the upper chamber.

The Senate's vote in April 1987 to override the president's veto of a bill reauthorizing $88 billion dollars for highways and mass transit demonstrates that even the most intense and skilled personal lobbying by the president is sometimes incapable of adding even a single vote to turn a defeat into a victory. Following an easy override of the president's veto in the House, Senate Majority Leader Robert Byrd (D–West Virginia) brought the issue to the Senate floor. On April 1, the attempt to override the veto failed by a single vote. Thirteen Republicans had voted with all but one Democrat—Terry Sanford of North Carolina—to pass the bill over the president's objections. Following some parliamentary maneuvering to permit a reconsideration of the vote, the Democrats were set to try again on the following day. Over the next several hours Senator Sanford was the target of intense lobbying from his Democratic colleagues in the House and Senate and phone calls from prominent Democrats in North Carolina urging him to change his vote. Just four hours after the first vote, Sanford announced he would vote to override. If the president were to win, he had to persuade at least one of the thirteen Republicans to change his vote.

On the morning of the vote, the president made a rare personal visit to Capitol Hill to use his widely acclaimed charm and persuasive skills in face-to-face meetings with the thirteen Republican Senators who had voted against him the previous day. President Reagan, along with Vice-President Bush, White House Chief of Staff and former Senate Majority Leader Howard Baker, and Transportation Secretary Elizabeth Dole, met twice with the thirteen Republicans. According to published reports, the president promised all kinds of political benefits in return for a switch in an individual's vote. In the end, however, he failed to change a single vote. Despite the president's putting his personal prestige on the line in a gallant public attempt to influence the votes of his own partisans, each of the thirteen voted to override his veto a second time. When Democratic Senator Terry Sanford switched his position from no to yes, the president's veto was overridden (Starobin 1987, 604–6).

CONCLUSIONS

In sum, the evidence presented in this chapter provides little support for the theory that the president's perceived leadership skills are associated with success on roll call votes in Congress. Presidents reputed as highly skilled do not win consistently more often than should be expected given the effects of the partisan balance in Congress, the president's popularity, and the cycle of decreasing influence over the course of his term. Presidents reputed as unskilled do not win consistently less often relative to this base line. Moreover, skilled presidents do not win significantly more often than unskilled presidents on either important votes or on close votes, in which skills have the greatest potential to affect the outcome.

Because of the difficult task of establishing a definitive test of the skills theory, some may argue that it is premature to reject this explanation of presidential success based on the tests reported in this chapter. It might be argued that these findings by themselves do not deny that leadership skill is an important component of presidential-congressional relations. Failure to find systematic effects in general does not necessarily refute the anecdotes and case studies demonstrating the importance of skills.

We acknowledge that this analysis of skills, based on quantitative differences in success across presidential administrations, is a limited test because it cannot take into account the difficulty of winning on certain types of issues. Although we did not observe the expected differences in the overall success rates, it may be the case that skilled presidents are better able to get Congress to pass controversial and difficult policies, while the wins of unskilled presidents are more mundane. In addition, we recognize that ranking presidents on a legislative skill dimension is a crude measure. And perceptions of presidents' leadership change over time, as the revisionist interpretations of Eisenhower demonstrate. Ideally, we would like to have a more precise and reliable measure of presidential leadership skill.

Since the necessary measures and data are not available, we have been forced to try to devise a better test based on the available information. In this chapter, we have attempted to provide a systematic analysis of presidential success across presidents whose reputations as legislative leaders are quite different. We believe this analysis is a reasonable attempt that improves on the case study approach and on quantitative analyses that do not use a common base line.

Although our analysis cannot definitively refute the skills theory, if it is to be believed, the burden of providing systematic evidence must rest with the theory's proponents. Given the problems that plague the interpretation of the case study material, we must note how little hard evidence for the skills theory there is, especially when the importance of other variables is much clearer. In the absence of such hard evidence, we agree with those who argue that the skill with which the president pursues and exercises power operates at the margins (Edwards 1986a, 1980, chap. 7; Rockman 1984, 214; King 1983, 254). We are quite certain, however, that, given the lack of a definitive test, the debate over the importance of presidential leadership skills has not been resolved.

CHAPTER 9

CONCLUSIONS

> There aren't any great men. There are just great challenges that ordinary men like you and me are forced by circumstances to meet.
>
> Admiral Halsey

The challenges facing the president are indeed great.[1] The public looks to the president to solve a host of increasingly complex social, economic, and political problems. Solving these problems would be difficult even if the president had unilateral power to formulate policy. But the American system of divided powers magnifies the challenges confronting the president. The difficulties which the president faces are compounded further by a selection process which demands that presidential candidates encourage the public's perception that if elected they will be able to solve the nation's problems successfully. But as Lowi (1985) notes, presidential successes always seem to lag behind public expectations. The result is often the perception of a failed presidency.

Along these lines, much has been written about the failed presidencies of Johnson, Nixon/Ford, and Carter. The verdict is still out on Ronald Reagan. Reagan succeeded where his immediate predecessors could not and won a second term. And his popularity remained remarkably high through most of his administration, almost as if the nation were longing for a success after the string of failures. But as Rockman (1984) observes, public approval is only one of several indicators of a successful presidency. More important than public approval is the president's success in solving the nation's problems. In the American system, success in solving problems depends in large part on success in the legislative arena. Although Reagan began his term with a dazzling performance in the legislative arena, the image of that impressive start faded

---

1. The words in the epigraph are attributed to Admiral William F. Halsey but unverified. They were spoken by James Cagney in his portrayal of Admiral Halsey in the United Artists film version of Halsey's life, *The Gallant Hours*.

rapidly. By the time Reagan completed his second term, his presidency began to look more and more typical—cabinet members and presidential advisors subject to criminal investigations and indictments; the Iran-Contra scandal that sapped his popularity and raised questions about his competence; presidential vetoes overridden; a Supreme Court nominee rejected by the largest margin ever; key presidential initiatives defeated despite intense lobbying by the president personally; and the largest budget and trade deficits in history.

Given the legacy of failed presidencies, a number of analysts have questioned whether it is possible for the modern president to meet the great demands placed on the office while operating under a constitutional structure based on the premise of separate institutions sharing power. Phrasing the question in such a way ignores the fact that presidents are never total failures. Every president has experienced both success and failure. Nonetheless, it is also true that some presidents are more successful than others. Theories of presidential-congressional relations need to account for such differences both across presidents and over time within a single administration. It is against this background that we analyzed presidential success on the floor of Congress, focusing particularly on the conditions and agents that facilitate a linkage between president and Congress.

AN OVERVIEW OF THE STUDY AND ITS FINDINGS

A rich body of research on presidential-congressional relations has identified four agents that can reduce the conflict between the president and the Congress. These are political party, political ideology, presidential popularity, and presidential leadership skill. Although these explanations of presidential success are not mutually exclusive, they offer competing perspectives. Most analysts recognize that each explanation illuminates part of the drama of the president in the legislative arena, but they disagree about which should be placed at center stage.

The four explanations cluster into two general perspectives. The prevailing perspective in much of the literature emphasizes what might be called a presidential explanation of success: whether the president succeeds or fails is mainly a function of his leadership and persuasive skills (Neustadt 1960; Kellerman 1984) and his ability to rally public support (Neustadt 1960; Edwards 1980, 1983; Kernell 1986). The other perspective emphasizes a congressional explanation: whether the president succeeds or fails is mainly a function of the partisan and ideological make-up of Congress.

The basis of the presidency-centered explanation rests with Neustadt's (1960, 33) observation that "what the constitution separates our parties do not combine." Without a strong party system to fall back on, Neustadt argues, the president's success depends on his ability to use available resources to persuade other actors to do what they otherwise might not have done. This explanation emphasizes the president's reputation among Washingtonians as being skilled at using the vantage points of the office and the president's ability to reach beyond the Washington community and mobilize public support. Success, therefore, is a function of what the president does or does not do. While the partisan and ideological composition of Congress may set broad limits, a skilled and popular minority president can overcome the lack of a partisan majority and persuade Congress to support his preferences. Similarly, an unskilled or unpopular majority president can squander the advantages of party control.

While presidency-centered explanations have dominated much of the literature, our reading of the available evidence led us to focus on an alternative explanation of presidential success. We argued in chapter 2 that, although none of the linkage agents are exceptionally strong, the evidence is clear that party and ideology affect congressional behavior in systematic and predictable ways. In contrast, evidence that presidential variables (i.e., popularity and skills) affect presidential success is ambiguous. Our theoretical framework emphasizes party and ideology as the prime determinants of presidential support from members of Congress and shifts the presidency-centered variables to the margin. According to this thesis, congressional support for the president is mainly a function of members' partisan and ideological predispositions operating within constraints imposed by the institutional structure of Congress (i.e., party leadership and congressional committees). Between elections, the basic parameters of presidential-congressional relations set by these institutional forces in Congress are relatively fixed. Although the president's leadership skill and his popularity with the public may influence success at the margins, there is little the president can do to move members of Congress very far from their basic political predispositions. Over the longer term, however, perceptions of the president's leadership skill and his public standing may influence presidential-congressional relations by altering the political composition of Congress through the electoral process.

The results of our analysis of presidential success on roll call votes from 1953 to 1984 tend to support the Congress-centered thesis rather than the one emphasizing presidential variables. In interpreting these results, we are fully aware that floor votes are only one element of presidential-congressional relations. There are numerous instances of the president and Congress in conflict or cooperation that are hidden from public scrutiny because they never reach the floor for a roll call vote. Despite the multiple arenas of presidential-congressional interaction, however, presidential success or failure on roll call votes is one important point in the process. Indeed, from the standpoint of understanding the operation of popular government, success on the floor of Congress may be the most important element of executive-legislative relations. Because floor votes are the point in the process most susceptible to public scrutiny, presidential success on roll call votes is the primary criterion used by the public, the media, the Congress, and even the occupants of the White House to judge how the president is doing. As we argued in chapter 1, roll call votes are a basic commodity of presidential-congressional relations.

Neustadt is correct that weak political parties in American politics do not bridge the gap created by the constitutional separation of powers. We would add: neither does skilled presidential leadership or popularity with the public. In fact, the forces that Neustadt stressed as the antidote for weak parties are even less successful in linking the president and Congress than are weak parties.

Our findings indicate that members of Congress provide levels of support for the president that are generally consistent with their partisan and ideological predispositions. Because party and ideology are relatively stable, facing a Congress made up of more members predisposed to support the president does increase the likelihood of success on the floor. There is, however, considerable variation in the behavior of the party factions. As expected, cross-pressured members are typically divided, and when they unify, they unify against about as often as they unify for the president. Even members of the party bases who have reinforcing partisan and ideological predispositions frequently fail to unify for or against the president's position.

Our analysis of party and committee leaders in Congress reveals that support from congressional leaders is associated with unity of the party factions. The party bases are likely to unify only if the party and committee leader of a party take the same position. But party and committee leaders within each party take opposing stands on a significant proportion of presidential roll calls. Because members of the party factions and their leaders frequently fail to unify around a party position, there is considerable uncertainty surrounding the outcome of presidential roll calls.

Presidency-centered variables, however, provide an even weaker explanation of presidential success. We found little support for the thesis that the weakness of legislative parties increases the importance of presidential skill or popularity for determining presidential success on roll call votes. Our analysis reveals that presidents reputed to be highly skilled do not win consistently more often than should be expected given the conditions they faced. Similarly, presidents reputed to be unskilled do not win significantly less often than expected. The analysis of presidential popularity reveals that the president's standing in the polls has only a marginal impact on the probability of success or failure.

A Multivariate Test of Congress-Centered and Presidency-Centered Variables

The analysis in the previous chapters, however, explored the impact of each of the linkage agents without fully controlling for competing explanations. In order to explore the relative impact of the various linkage agents, we constructed a multivariate probit model that analyzes presidential success or failure on roll calls as a function of Congress-centered and presidency-centered variables. The independent variables are:

> Number of members from the president's base voting on vote i
>
> Number of members from the opposition base voting on vote i
>
> Position of the president's party leader on vote i—majority presidents
>
> Position of the president's party leader on vote i—minority presidents
>
> Position of the opposition party leader on vote i—majority presidents
>
> Position of the opposition party leader on vote i—minority presidents
>
> Position of the president's committee leader on vote i—majority presidents
>
> Position of the president's committee leader on vote i—minority presidents
>
> Position of the opposition committee leader on vote i—majority presidents
>
> Position of the opposition committee leader on vote i—minority presidents
>
> Whether the president was reputed to have high skills
>
> Whether the president was reputed to have low skills
>
> Presidential popularity at the time of vote i—president high skills
>
> Presidential popularity at the time of vote i—president medium skills
>
> Presidential popularity at the time of vote i—president low skills
>
> Foreign policy votes—Republican presidents
>
> Foreign policy votes—Democratic presidents

This specification captures most of the relevant factors discussed in earlier chapters. We can examine the effects of support from various party leaders separately for majority and minority presidents. We can also estimate the impact of presidential skills on success. Furthermore, this model permits us to determine whether the effects of presidential popularity differ by presidential skill level. Finally, given the results in chapter 6, the model allows for the effects of foreign policy content to differ for Democratic and Republican presidents. The probit estimates for the House and Senate are presented in table 9.1.

The results of this analysis support the conclusions reached in previous chapters. Only the Congress-centered variables have strong, statistically significant effects in both chambers. The effects of presidency-centered variables are much weaker and are not statistically significant in one or both chambers.[2]

The coefficients of the two party base variables are relatively strong and statistically significant in both the House and Senate. Furthermore, the effects of support from the party and committee leaders confirm prior expectations. The opposition party committee leader under majority party presidents (i.e., the ranking minority member) in the Senate equation and minority presidents' committee leader (i.e., the ranking minority member) in the House equation are the only leader variables that do not have a significant impact.

Most important, presidency-centered variables collectively contribute much less to our ability to explain presidential success than do Congress-centered variables.[3] The skills variables do not exert a significant impact on presidential success in either chamber. Indeed, the coefficient for high skills is negative in the House model. Presidential popularity has a statistically significant effect only in interaction with high skills. While this finding suggests that highly skilled presidents may be better able than less skilled leaders to exploit the benefits of public approval, the impact on the probability of success is quite limited when compared to the effects of the partisan and leader variables. Finally, the signs of the two foreign policy variables are in the predicted direction, but they are not statistically significant. Recall, however, that part of the effect of the foreign policy context uncovered in chapter 6 worked through the positions taken by the party and committee leaders. Democratic leaders are more supportive of Republican presidents on foreign policy votes, and leaders' positions have been controlled for in these models.

Effects of Congress-Centered and Presidency-Centered Variables on the Probability of Success

In order to see the differential impact of the Congress-centered and presidency-centered variables, we used the coefficients from the probit models to estimate probabilities of success under different conditions. We assumed the following conditions to make the estimates: (1) the size of the majority party base was equal to 200 in the House and 44 in the Senate (i.e., the averages under majority party presidents); (2) the size of the minority party base was

---

2. As we noted above, statistical significance is not the same thing as substantive significance. Given the large number of cases, significance tests are most useful as a basis to reject weak variables. If a variable fails to achieve normally expected levels of statistical significance, then we can confidently reject it as unimportant. Variables that are statistically significant must be evaluated in light of their substantive effects on the probability of success.

3. Note that adding presidency—centered variables to the probit model does not improve the percentage correctly predicted over the model in chapter 5 that included only leaders' positions and majority/minority status (see table 5.7).

Table 9.1 Probit Estimates of the Effects of Congress-Centered and Presidency-Centered Variables on Presidential Success

	HOUSE		SENATE	
	b	(s.e.)	b	(s.e.)
Congress-centered variables				
Size of president's base	.004	(.002)	.026	(.006)
Size of opposition base	−.004	(.002)	−.024	(.007)
President's party leader—majority	1.220	(.181)	1.259	(.109)
President's party leader—minority	.758	(.159)	.719	(.144)
Opposition party leader—majority	.827	(.161)	.674	(.112)
Opposition party leader—minority	1.264	(.131)	1.114	(.130)
President's committee leader—majority	.767	(.162)	.809	(.102)
President's committee leader—minority	.110	(.145)	.298	(.138)
Opposition committee leader—majority	.292	(.142)	.157	(.107)
Opposition committee leader—minority	.737	(.134)	.909	(.119)
Presidency-centered variables				
President high skills	−1.586	(.971)	.428	(.703)
President low skills	−.110	(.950)	.894	(.699)
Presidential popularity—high skills	.026	(.007)	.009	(.005)
Presidential popularity—medium skills	−.004	(.014)	.010	(.010)
Presidential popularity—low skills	−.002	(.006)	−.004	(.005)
Policy context				
Foreign policy vote—Republican president	.178	(.129)	.143	(.102)

Table 9.1 (*Continued*)

	HOUSE		SENATE	
	b	(s.e.)	b	(s.e.)
Foreign policy vote—				
Democratic president	−.255	(.144)	−.208	(.128)
Intercept	−1.138	(1.031)	−2.116	(.697)
% correctly predicted	80		83	
Null prediction	64		67	

Note: Entries are probit coefficients. Standard error of the estimate in parentheses.

equal to 150 in the House and 31 in the Senate (the averages under minority party presidents); (3) the president received the support from his party's two leaders, but not from the opposition party leaders. To observe the impact of presidential skill and presidential popularity, we generated probabilities for high-, medium-, and low-skilled presidents at 50 percent and 60 percent approval. The predicted probabilities are in table 9.2.

We see that the greatest change in the probability of success is associated with changing the president's party base from a majority to a minority. Across different levels of skill and popularity, the probabilities of success for majority presidents average around .80, while the probabilities for minority presidents average less than .30. Empirically, minority party presidents win a greater percentage of votes than predicted by these assumed votes. The explanation for this discrepancy is that on some meaningful percentage of votes, minority presidents take positions that attract the support of either the opposition party leader, the opposition committee leader, or both. Adding the support from one or more of the majority party's congressional leaders improves their odds of victory. For example, support from the committee chair increases the probability of winning for minority party presidents to averages of .55 in the House and .60 in the Senate. But even with the support of the committee chairman, the probability of success for minority party presidents remains smaller than for majority party presidents.

We can also see the effects of presidency-centered variables—skills and popularity—on the probability of success. The interpretation of the effects of skill, however, must be cautious because of the small number of presidents in each category. For example, Johnson is the only high-skilled majority president in the House model; Ford is the only high-skilled minority president in

Table 9.2 Estimated Probabilities of Presidential Victory under Various Conditions of Presidential Skill and Popularity

	HOUSE		SENATE	
	$\hat{z}$	$\hat{p}$	$\hat{z}$	$\hat{p}$
Majority Presidents				
High skill—popularity 50%	.76	.78	1.23	.89
High skill—popularity 60%	1.02	.85	1.32	.91
Medium skill—popularity 50%	.85	.80	.85	.80
Medium skill—popularity 60%	.81	.79	.95	.83
Low skill—popularity 50%	.79	.79	1.05	.85
Low skill—popularity 60%	.75	.77	1.01	.84
Minority Presidents				
High skill—popularity 50%	−.50	.31	−.47	.32
High skill—popularity 60%	−.24	.41	−.38	.35
Medium skill—popularity 50%	−.67	.25	−.85	.20
Medium skill—popularity 60%	−.71	.24	−.75	.24
Low skill—popularity 50%	−.73	.23	−.66	.24
Low skill—popularity 60%	−.76	.22	−.70	.24
Committee chair (average)		.55		.60

Note: Z-scores estimated from probit equations. The estimated $\hat{p}$ is the probability that the president's position wins under the specified condition given average base sizes for majority and minority presidents and support from the president's party and committee leaders in Congress.

the Senate model. With this caveat in mind, we see that the differences in the probabilities across presidents with different reputations are small and do not vary as expected.

For majority party presidents, the level of skill has little effect on the chances of victory. Given the values assumed above for base size and leaders' support, and if public approval is at 60 percent, high-skilled presidents are more likely to win than are presidents with reputations as less skilled. The increase in probability under these conditions, however, is less than .10 in both chambers. If popularity is at 50 percent, the changes in probabilities for different skill levels are even smaller, and in the House the probability of victory for high-skilled presidents is actually less than for medium- and low-skilled presidents.

Skills have a somewhat greater effect for minority party presidents, but the impact remains limited in general. The largest difference occurs in the

House for popular presidents. At 60 percent public approval, a high-skilled president is .19 more likely to win a conflictual roll call than a low-skilled president. At 50 percent approval, the changes across skill levels are less than half as great (.06 to .08). In the Senate, a high-skilled minority president is .12 more likely to win than are medium-skilled presidents. But the probabilities do not change consistently across the three skill levels—low-skilled presidents are more likely to win than are medium-skilled presidents.

The effects of public approval are also weak and inconsistent. Popularity has a small impact in the House, but only for high-skilled presidents. If public approval increases from 50 percent to 60 percent, the probability of victory increases .07 for a high-skilled majority president and .10 for a high-skilled minority president. At other skill levels, popularity has no effect. Indeed, the probabilities of victory are slightly lower at 60 percent approval. In the Senate, increases in public approval have little or no effect on the probability of success regardless of the president's reputed skill.

These results support our argument that presidential popularity and leadership skills have a limited and inconsistent impact on success; certainly much less effect than Congress-centered variables. While the interaction of high skills and high popularity tends to improve the odds of victory, especially for minority presidents in the House, gaining the support of the committee chair increases the probability more.

DOES IT MATTER WHO IS CHOSEN PRESIDENT?

These findings might lead one to ask: If presidential success in Congress is mainly a function of variables beyond his control, does it matter who is elected to the presidency? While the president's leadership skill and his popularity with the public may have less effect on legislative success than the composition of the Congress and what congressional leaders do, there are other reasons why it matters who is elected president.

Importance of Differences in Policy Preferences
In analyzing whether the choices made by the electorate matter, we will first consider the significance of differences in the policy positions advocated by presidential candidates. Generally speaking, Democrats running for office take policy positions that differ from Republicans'. Analysis of party platforms reveals that party positions differ and that the president, once elected, attempts to fulfill promises in the platform (Fishel 1985). Our own analysis of the ideological positions taken by each of the presidents from Eisenhower through Reagan indicates substantial differences between Democratic and Republican presidents (see table 6.5). The issue, however, is not whether presidential candidates differ, but whether such differences matter.

Who the president is, as defined by the policies he advocates, has a major impact on the president's relationship with Congress. The president's greatest influence over policy comes from the agenda he pursues and the way it is packaged. There can be no doubt that some presidents altered the direction of American government. Franklin Roosevelt's New Deal agenda expanded the range of policies and programs considered in Congress. Ronald Reagan's agenda to reduce, or at least slow down, the growth of government combined with massive budget deficits limited the scope of what Congress can do. The nature of presidential-congressional relations would have been fundamentally different if the voters had reelected Herbert Hoover in 1932 or Jimmy Carter in 1980. In his analysis of Congress during the 1960s, Huntington (1973, 28) argued that the president controlled the congressional agenda. He quoted Senator Abraham Ribicoff to support his point:

> Congress has surrendered its rightful place in the leadership in the law-making process to the White House. No longer is Congress the source of major legislation. It now merely filters legislative proposals from the President, straining out some and reluctantly letting others pass through. These days no one expects Congress to devise the important bills.

Other analysts have challenged the view that the president controls the congressional agenda (Moe and Teel 1970; Orfield 1975). But even these revisionists do not deny that the president plays a major role in influencing the congressional agenda. A more recent analysis by Paul Light (1983) concludes that while the president's impact on the agenda can be quite significant, he is not in a unilateral position to define the agenda. Instead, the president must compete with other actors for influence over the agenda.

Our thesis is that even if the president exerts significant influence over what issues Congress will legislate, he cannot control, or even greatly influence, the outcome of such deliberations. Once a given part of the agenda reaches the floor of Congress, the president's bargaining and popularity are insufficient to change the outcome, except in relatively rare cases. This thesis, however, is not meant to minimize the importance of agenda-setting powers.

Furthermore, our explanation of presidential success on floor votes centers on the shared preferences between a president and the Congress defined by the partisan-ideological predispositions of the members. The election of a president advocating policies that run against congressional predispositions generates substantial conflict. While unified party control is no guarantee of success on any given vote, the probability of defeat increases significantly when the branches are controlled by different parties. From this perspective, the selection of one bundle of policy preferences over a competing set of policies has a major impact on presidential-congressional relations.

The Importance of Presidential Leadership

The evidence presented in this book provides little support for the theory that the president's leadership skills and his popularity with the public are strongly associated with success on roll call votes in Congress. These findings do not deny that presidential leadership and popularity are important components of presidential-congressional relations. Failure to find systematic effects in general does not necessarily refute the anecdotes and case studies demonstrating the importance of the president. Although we have raised questions about the evidence in some of the literature, certainly there are occasions when the president's standing with the public and what he does (or fails to do) changes the outcome of a vote. Our analysis does suggest, however, that such cases are not representative of presidential-congressional relations: in general, presidential variables have a very limited influence on the probability of success on the floor of Congress.

Yet saying that presidential variables matter in a few cases does not, and cannot, resolve the debate over the importance of presidential leadership skill. Can we reconcile the prevailing emphasis on presidential leadership in the literature with the empirical evidence to the contrary? If presidential variables do not systematically affect vote success, is there some other general effect?

As we discuss presidential leadership, it is important to keep in mind that we are not analyzing a representative sample of politicians. Within the population of all politicians, the range in political skills is probably great. But occupants of the Oval Office are not average Americans or even average politicians. The very fact that they occupy the Oval Office indicates that they are unusual. The American dream that any boy or girl can grow up to be president turns out to be largely illusion. The "political race [for the presidency] as elsewhere has usually been won by those who had the advantage of starting from a favorable position" (Pessen 1984, 171). Even with a favorable start, it is a rare politician who has the drive and qualities necessary to survive the grueling race to win a major party nomination and presidential election. In fact, it may be intense drive and ambition that distinguishes presidents from other politicians (Hess 1988, 114).

Scholars have observed that the skills necessary to win the presidency are not the same skills necessary to govern (Cronin 1980, 19–22, 169; Polsby 1983). While this observation is true, national campaigns are nonetheless a major testing ground where politicians demonstrate to the American people that they are presidential timber. The political skills required to win the presidency are surely related (albeit imperfectly) to the skills necessary to bargain with politicians in Congress. Even Ford, who ascended to the presidency without first being tested in the crucible of a national campaign, had distinguished himself among national politicians by being selected minority leader of the House.

In short, presidents are not randomly selected from the population. They invariably come from the upper tail of the distribution. Hence, when we think about presidential leadership, we should remember that the variation across presidents is probably truncated. While the difference between the political skills of a small-town mayor and a president is probably great enough to make a systematic difference in success, the variation from the most to the least skilled president is not. For example, the difference between the skills of Jimmy Carter and Ronald Reagan is comparatively small and not likely to make much difference, except in the perceptions of Washingtonians.

Perceptions, of course, are important, and it is here we can observe the general effects of leadership. Indeed, in politics perceptions are usually more important than objective reality. We began this chapter by noting that greatness is something that is thrust upon ordinary people when they are forced to respond to great challenges. But successfully meeting a challenge is not enough; the great leader is one whose successes are *perceived* as great. In the words of Ralph Waldo Emerson (1903, 105), "Not he is great who can alter matter, but he who can alter my state of mind."

Perceptions of presidential leadership affect how members of Congress and other participants in the process feel about the president. Unskilled and unpopular presidents are perceived as failures even if their success rate is fairly typical. Such a president may score some significant victories, but his style so alienates the other players that even his supporters do not feel good about the victory. And when such a president suffers the inevitable defeat, the failure tends to be remembered because that is what participants' perceptions led them to expect.

President Carter illustrates the point well. He made several mistakes and suffered some important defeats early in his term, resulting in a poor reputation and strained relations with Congress. By 1978 Carter's performance improved. One of his most significant achievements was winning ratification of the Panama Canal treaties in 1978. The two-thirds coalition was patched together at the last minute after the longest Senate floor debate in more than fifty years. Without Carter's skilled lobbying and efforts to build public support, the treaties almost certainly would have been defeated. Yet despite a presidential performance that was the model of skilled persuasion, the victory actually diminished Carter's power and reputation (Moffett 1985, 10–11).

Skilled, popular presidents, in contrast, are perceived as successes even if they do not win more often than should be expected given the political capital and conditions they inherited. But their style makes their supporters feel good about supporting them and being associated with their programs, even though the president probably would have received their support anyway. When a skilled president loses an important vote, the perceived reputation causes the president's excuses to be accepted. If the reputation begins to tarnish, it can be restored by winning another "big one." President Reagan appears to have successfully pursued this strategy, maintaining the so-called Teflon presidency well into his second term.

But despite Reagan's style and popularity, the constitutional separation of powers eventually worked as intended. Lyndon Johnson's observation quoted in chapter 1 that there was never a "Congress that didn't eventually take the measure of the president it was dealing with" applies equally to Reagan. In the last years of his term, Reagan put his personal prestige on the line to persuade the Senate to sustain his veto of the highway bill and to confirm Robert Bork to the Supreme Court. He failed in both cases. In the end, "Reagan added luster but little clout to [the] office" (Rapp 1989, 3).

In addition, perceptions of leadership skill affect the president's electoral fortunes. Because the public makes retrospective judgements, the perception of a failed presidency can lead to the defeat of an incumbent administration (Key 1966; Fiorina 1981). One of the themes of Reagan's presidential campaign in 1980 was President Carter's lack of leadership. Carter's reputation as an inept leader was transmitted to the American people through the media over the course of his term. Reagan's campaign was able to exploit this perception and make it an issue. As president, Reagan developed a reputation as a skilled leader which worked to his advantage when he ran for reelection in 1984.

Third, perceptions of leadership skill affect a president's standing in history. Presidents certainly worry about how history will judge them. But how history judges a president is important for more than personal vanity. Because the number of presidents is small and the power of the office is great, the way each president exercises those powers greatly influences future occupants of the office. Skilled leadership may expand the prerogatives of future leaders and set the benchmark against which they are judged. Mistakes or abuse of power may limit the power of future presidents and make leadership more difficult.

Finally, the president's professional reputation affects the leeway he has to pursue his policy goals. Presidents who are viewed as unskilled are continually on the defensive. Their explanations of problems tend to become excuses; compromises become "waffling." Skilled presidents have more room to maneuver. When they suffer a loss, as every president does, they still have leeway to pursue other items on their agenda or to try again to turn the defeat into a victory. Reagan's efforts to secure aid for the Contras in Nicaragua during the 99th Congress (1985–86) illustrate the point. After losing several important votes by close margins on the House floor, the President eventually got a bill through the House giving him most of what he wanted, again by a thin margin. It is hard to believe that Carter would have been able to prevail after so many setbacks. However, even Reagan was swamped by the political context. Reagan's request in the 100th Congress (1987–88) for additional aid for the Contras was defeated in the House by a narrow margin despite intense lobbying and appeals to the public.

Thus the president matters, but how much and in what way is determined mostly by the outcome of the last election. We can use a theatrical metaphor to describe the politics of the president in the legislative arena. Separation of power creates two arenas in which the president must perform—an executive arena and a legislative arena. In the executive arena, the president performs the constitutional roles of chief executive, commander in chief, and so forth. When the president performs in the executive arena, he exercises substantial control over all facets of the show: he writes the script; he hires the actors; he chooses the props; he sets the stage; he decides when the curtain rises.

When the president enters the legislative arena, he has less control. He may write some important scenes in the script, but other scenes have already been written by legislative actors. Moreover, the stage has already been set; the actors have already been cast. He must perform with the props on the set, on a timetable set by congressional leaders and committees. Regardless of how skilled his performance or how much the audience likes him, he cannot alter the basic set. At this point in the production, the president is one actor among many competing for influence. And the modern president must perform in the legislative arena to a much greater degree than earlier presidents.

A system in which the president and Congress are weakly linked has profound consequences for governing. We turn to this issue in the following section.

CONSEQUENCES FOR GOVERNING

To some observers of the American political scene, the weakness of the president as a legislative actor greatly hampers the development of national policy that is responsive to the needs and interests of the public. Some analysts argue that the problems associated with formulating policy have become so severe that the nation is undergoing a crisis of governance. There is a growing perception among many politicians and academics that the system is in need of reform (Hardin 1974; Sundquist 1986; Goldwin and Kaufman 1986).

In the decade of the 1980s, no single issue demonstrates the inability of the national government to deal effectively with complex problems than the government's failure to make significant reductions in the federal budget deficit. In spite of a vast amount of rhetoric from politicians about how important it is to reduce the deficit, the government has for the most part failed to solve the problem. Undoubtedly, there is no single, simple explanation for the failure to solve a problem so complex as the deficit. Quite often, however, blame for the crisis of governance focuses on the structure of government. For example, Lloyd Cutler (1986, 1–2), former counsel to President Carter, argues:

> A particular shortcoming in need of a remedy is the structural inability
> of our government to propose, legislate, and administer a balanced pro-
> gram for governing. In parliamentary terms one might say that under
> the U.S. Constitution it is not now feasible to "form a government."
> The separation of powers between the legislative and executive
> branches, whatever its merits in 1793, has become a structure that
> almost guarantees stalemate today.

A system of separate institutions sharing power leads to stalemate because there is no guarantee that the president and a majority in both houses of Congress will share a common conception of "good public policy." The lack of consensus on what constitutes good public policy can be traced to several factors. First, the president and members of Congress represent different interests. Textbook descriptions of the president typically point out that the president is the only elected official whose constituency is the entire nation. This means that the president must piece together a national electoral coalition drawn from the diverse interests present in American society. It does not mean, however, that the president will respond to all of the diverse interests that comprise a highly pluralistic nation. There will always be some interests who are not well represented by the current occupant of the White House.

Members of Congress also must put together electoral coalitions, but their coalitions are constructed from less diverse populations comprising fewer interests. A typical member of Congress therefore represents a more homogeneous set of interests than does the president. But, paradoxically, Congress acting collectively must consider the preferences of a wider set of interests than does the president, because each of the smaller constituencies has an active advocate in Congress. Irrespective of which party controls Congress, almost every group in American society will have some member who will try to protect and promote the group's interest. For example, even if the Democrats control a majority of the seats, groups aligned with the Republican party are represented by some members who will use the rules and institutional arrangements in Congress to protect their interests. Furthermore, given the weakness of congressional parties, there is a reasonable chance that congressional policy will reflect the preferences of these groups. In contrast, there is little likelihood that typical Democratic constituencies would gain much of a hearing in the policy deliberations of a Republican administration.

The lack of agreement over policy also flows from differences in political ideology. For much of the past four decades, split party control of the federal government has resulted in a conservative Republican president interacting with a predominantly liberal Congress. Liberal Democrats, unable to win the presidency with any regularity, have used their dominance of the legislature to pursue their policy aims. Samuel Huntington (1981) argues that during the 1960s and 1970s "Congress became the institutional channel through which liberal forces attempted to promote changes in American government, American society, and most noticeably, American foreign policy" (207). As liberals have pursued their agenda for America in the halls of Congress, they have been opposed by Republican presidents pursuing an alternative agenda.

Furthermore, the president's ability to persuade Congress to support his policy preferences by appealing to a member's own self-interest has been made much more difficult because members of Congress have managed to insulate themselves from the public's evaluation of the president and of the institution in which they serve. A president must have the support of Congress to succeed, but individual members of Congress have no great need of the president. As Anthony King (1983, 251) notes, from the congressional perspective, dependency between the president and Congress is largely a one-way street:

> The president thus cannot help you to secure reelection, and it is most
> unlikely that he will be able, to any significant degree, to raise or lower
> your standing on Capitol Hill. He lives in his political house at one end
> of Pennsylvania Avenue; you live in your political house at the other
> end. He needs you, but on the face of it you have no great need of him.

The public evaluates the president in terms of the success or failure of his program. The same is not true of members of Congress—the public does not hold them individually accountable for collective policy outcomes. The weakening of party as an electoral force and the increasing localization of congressional elections has resulted in an electoral uncoupling of Congress and the president. In his analysis of the contemporary electoral system, Fiorina (1987, 431) notes that "each individual member emphasizes his or her personal qualities and record, each is expected to work for the interests of the district or state; electoral success is largely dependent on meeting these expectations." While there is some evidence that the reelection rate of congressional incumbents continues to be tied to the state of the economy and to citizen evaluations of the president (Jacobson and Kernell 1981), the strength of presidential coattails has declined significantly (Calvert and Ferejohn 1983). Representatives and senators are reelected largely on their personal qualities, not on the performance of the Congress or the government in general. Even during a bad year for their party, most congressional incumbents, especially House incumbents, are not really challenged. Furthermore, the separation of congressional and presidential elections has led to a sharp increase in split ticket voting resulting in divided partisan control of the branches of government.

Since the key to reelection is keeping the folks back home satisfied, members of Congress accentuate parochialism in policymaking. When confronted with a choice between voting the district or voting with the president, members of Congress are likely to choose the district. Critics complain that an electoral system which separates presidential and congressional elections, along with a policymaking process based on a set of rules that provides individual members with powers to protect local interests, leads to policies that do not serve the nation as a whole. Furthermore, because members of Congress can avoid being held personally responsible for the failure to enact policies that are in the national interest, this process ultimately leads to the demise of accountable government (Cain, Ferejohn, and Fiorina 1987, 198).

According to this argument, because the president represents a national constituency and is held accountable for government's failures, the president is the key to establishing a policymaking process that will favor national interests over parochial interests. The dilemma is that the president is held accountable for the success of his efforts, but he lacks the power to control the fate of his legislative program. For example, Cutler (1986, 3) argues that under the current system "we cannot fairly hold the president accountable for the success or failure of his program because he lacks the constitutional power to put that program into effect." The legacy of failed presidencies, therefore, can be traced directly to the electoral system that allows representatives and senators to win reelection even though they are unresponsive to presidential leadership. Indeed, many are reelected *because* they opposed the president.

Individual members of Congress reelected in a candidate-oriented system based heavily on the advantages of incumbency are not made to answer for the condition of the nation and therefore have less personal stake in the state of the nation. Given the nature of the contemporary electoral system, there is little chance that the president will be able to convince members of Congress that their fates are intertwined with his, regardless of how skilled or how popular the president is. According to one critic of this system, the problems of recent decades will continue "until members of Congress believe that their personal fate coincides with that of the president, and that both depend on doing well by the country" (Fiorina 1987, 431).

Dissatisfaction with the way in which the electoral system links the president and the Congress has led several analysts to propose various reforms, each of which is aimed at strengthening the electoral linkage between the president and Congress (Hardin 1974; Sundquist 1986; Goldwin and Kaufman 1986). Some reformers propose that we amend the Constitution to create a parliamentary system of government. Others accept the principle of separation of powers, but argue that we should amend the Constitution to establish several reforms that would more closely link the branches of government. Some argue that we do not have to change the Constitution but should take legislative steps to strengthen the control of political parties over the electoral machinery.

Implicit in each of these proposals is the belief that if the president were stronger, the system would be better able to formulate policies in response to popular preferences. Furthermore, lines of accountability would be strengthened because the public would know whom to blame (i.e., the president and his party in Congress) if they were dissatisfied with public policy. Between elections, the president would have a great deal of latitude to formulate policy. Those segments of the public who disagreed with the president's proposals would have little recourse other than to oppose the administration at the next election. Certainly, the prospects of stalemate would be reduced, because those who disagreed with the president would have little power to prevent the president from formulating national policy.

The view that American politics is in need of a strong president who can act decisively and be held accountable by the public is compatible with a view of democracy articulated by Joseph Schumpeter (1942). According to this view, democracy works best when the masses limit their participation to voting and do nothing to interfere with the policymaking actions of a more able elite. On election day the public can vote to keep the same set of elites in power or to replace them with another set. While the exact nature of policymaking by the elite is not well spelled out, a likely model is a responsible party system, because it greatly simplifies the voter's task of evaluating the current set of elites.

We must recognize, however, that what some have called policy stalemate results from the difficulty of working out compromises among diverse interests in a highly pluralistic society. Giving increased power to the president to formulate solutions to complex problems does not guarantee that his solutions would be wise or benevolent, or would necessarily even work. The price of increasing presidential power and maximizing accountability would be the weakening of representation of diverse interests in government decision making. Yet there is no guarantee that trading representation for accountability would result in policies more satisfactory than stalemate. For example, in 1964 Congress passed the Gulf of Tonkin Resolution authorizing the president to respond to a perceived international threat. In 1969 and 1970 Congress passed legislation authorizing the president to institute wage and price controls to curb inflation. In each case, the president used the authority to act decisively, but in hindsight many have questioned the wisdom and effectiveness of these actions.

Since there is no guarantee that the president's policies will be wise and effective, making it easier for the public to fix blame and to "kick the rascals out" in the next election may not be a satisfactory solution to the dilemma. Some policy mistakes are not easily corrected. If a policy mistake does permanent or long-term damage, being able to fix blame is small consolation. And even if policy mistakes are correctable by replacing policymakers in the presidency and Congress, such a system might waste tremendous resources if control of government frequently alternates between regimes pursuing widely different ideological agendas. Although abandoning harmful and ineffective programs is desirable, identifying bad programs is not an objective exercise. In many cases a new regime would abandon old programs and start new ones solely for ideological reasons. Society would have to bear not only the start-up costs of new programs, but also the costs of shutting down old ones.

Given the trade-off, it is not at all clear that the public would choose accountability if by necessity it had to be coupled with unchecked power. For example, two polls conducted in 1984 showed that a majority of the electorate believed that the country would be worse off if voters gave President Reagan a Republican-controlled Congress that would pass nearly everything he wanted (Sundquist 1986, 87). This reluctance to give the president such power occurred during an election in which the public reelected the president by a decisive margin. But, as one study noted, "If voters fully understood the larger consequences of getting what they want in the small, they might find it less attractive" (Cain et al., 211).

Under the current arrangement, elections determine the cast of actors who have the responsibility for governing. Presidential elections grant constrained power to an individual to develop national policy and propose that policy to the legislature. Congressional elections decide which individuals, who have an ideological viewpoint that reflects a particular set of constituency interests, will represent the district in Washington. Whether these separate decisions select a president and Congress that share similar policy perspectives has the greatest effect on how successful the president is likely to be when dealing with the Congress. But even when the electoral process produces unified party control, the weakness of political parties means that a close link between these actors does not necessarily result. Between elections, it is difficult for any president to alter the course of congressional deliberations. Rather, congressional policies reflect the workings of a highly pluralistic institution that works out solutions to social problems by trying to accommodate different interests. This situation creates a great deal of frustration among politicians and academics who seem to desire a more rational system of strong presidential leadership.

For those who fear the concentration of power in the hands of any political

DEFINING AND MEASURING PARTY
FACTIONS

Separating members of Congress into the four party factions is tedious but straightforward. The first step is to identify a set of roll calls that involve ideological issues. Two frequently used indicators of general ideology are indexes calculated by Americans for Democratic Action (ADA), a liberal group, and Americans for Constitutional Action (ACA), a conservative group. The positions taken by these two groups reflect an underlying liberal/conservative dimension that is relatively stable for the time period of this study (Poole 1981).

We chose ADA/ACA votes because these groups identify votes and establish the liberal (or conservative) position based on some a priori criteria. CQ's "Conservative Coalition" scores are another generally valid and reliable indicator of ideology. This measure of ideology, however, is defined exclusively by the behavior of the members (a majority of Republicans and southern Democrats voting against a majority of northern Democrats) rather than an a priori definition of the conservative position before the vote occurs. We preferred to use a measure that defined ideology based on substantive judgments rather than informal voting patterns.

ADA and ACA publish indexes indicating how often each member voted in agreement with the liberal (ADA) or conservative (ACA) position. Using these indexes in an analysis of presidential-congressional relations, however, is problematical because some of the votes used to measure members' ideology are also presidential roll calls used to measure members' support for the president. To avoid this tautology, we purged votes on which the president expressed a position from the lists of votes selected by ADA and ACA and reconstructed liberalism scores for members of Congress from 1953 to 1984. The liberal position on a roll call is defined as a vote that agrees with ADA's position or disagrees with ACA's position.[1] Our liberalism scores indicate the percentage of liberal votes out of all ADA/ACA roll calls on which the member voted (i.e., the scores are not affected by absences).

We used roll calls selected by both ADA and ACA in order to have enough votes to calculate an index (we wanted a minimum of ten). Although each

---

1. The measure of liberalism has face validity. Both groups expressed positions on the same vote 297 times between 1957 (the first year ACA published ratings) and 1984. On these votes, they took opposing positions on all but ten votes. The rare votes on which ACA and ADA agreed were not used because the "liberal" position was not clear.

group typically selected between ten and twenty votes per year in each chamber, eliminating roll calls on which the president expressed a position reduced the number of usable votes. Using votes selected by both groups and calculating scores for the two years of each Congress produced more than ten votes for all but three cases (the 87th House and Senate and the 88th House). In these cases, we had no choice but to add other votes to the usable ADA/ACA votes in order to have enough votes to calculate a meaningful liberalism score. We chose CQ's "Conservative Coalition" votes in these cases because they are a more consistent indicator of underlying ideology than indexes calculated by other groups—for example, the National Farmers' Union or the AFL-CIO (Poole 1981).

To define the party factions operationally, we use the mean liberalism score for each party to determine the party mainstreams in each Congress. Using the mean party liberalism in each Congress permits the measure to reflect any changes in the ideological positions of the parties over the three decades covered in this study. Cross-pressured members are defined as those who have liberalism scores closer to the mean of the opposition party than to the mean of their party. Members of the political bases are those who have liberalism scores closer to the mean of their party than to the opposition party mean.

Once the members of the four party factions were identified for each Congress, levels of support for the president's position from the four factions were coded as variables on each roll call ($n = 1,856$ in the House and $2,604$ in the Senate). Thus, for each roll call, we can determine how many votes the president received from each party faction.

INTERPRETING RESULTS FROM PROBIT ANALYSIS

Probit analysis produces Maximum Likelihood Estimates (MLEs) similar to regression coefficients. MLEs describe the impact of each independent variable on the probability of an event's occurrence. As is the case for regression coefficients, the sign of the coefficient indicates whether a variable increases or decreases the probability, and the size of the coefficient relative to its standard error indicates the level of statistical significance. Unlike regression coefficients, however, MLEs do not directly indicate the marginal impact of an independent variable on the dependent variable. Instead, probit coefficients are estimates of change on the cumulative normal distribution associated with a one-unit change in an independent variable with all other independent variables in the model held constant.

Although probit coefficients are not probabilities, the relationships they estimate can be converted into probabilities. To determine the marginal impact of an independent variable, one must use the probit equations to estimate predicted values under different combinations of values of the independent variables. These predicted values are estimates of points on the cumulative normal distribution (i.e., z-scores) that can be converted into probability estimates using a table of the cumulative normal distribution.

Specifically, the predicted z-scores are derived by substituting selected values of the independent variables into the equation, multiplying each value by its probit coefficient, and summing across all elements of the equation. Each predicted z-score corresponds to a given probability in a table of the cumulative normal distribution. For example, a predicted z-score of zero corresponds to a probability of .50; a z-score of -1.00 corresponds to a probability of .16; a z-score of $+1.00$ corresponds to a probability of .84; and so on. These probabilities may be interpreted as the probability that the dependent variable is 1—the president's position prevails, in our case—given the particular combination of values of the dependent variables. Comparing the predicted probabilities under different conditions indicates the marginal impact of a variable on presidential success.[1]

---

1. An excellent description of how to interpret probit coefficients may be found in Arnold (1979, 78–80, 111–12).

REFERENCES

Abramowitz, Alan I., and Jeffrey A. Segal. 1986. Determinants of the outcomes of Senate elections. *Journal of Politics* 48 (May): 433–39.

Adler, Bill, ed. 1966. *Presidential wit from Washington to Johnson*. New York: Trident Press.

Alston, Chuck. 1988. Reagan's support index up—but not much. *Congressional Quarterly Weekly Report*, 19 November, 3323–30.

Arnold, R. Douglas. 1979. *Congress and the bureaucracy: A theory of influence*. New Haven: Yale University Press.

Asher, Herbert. 1980. *Presidential elections and American politics*. Rev. ed. Homewood, Ill.: Dorsey.

Benton, Wilbourn E., ed. 1986a. *1787: Drafting the U.S. Constitution*. Vol. 1. College Station: Texas A&M University Press.

Benton, Wilbourn E., ed. 1986b. *1787: Drafting the U.S. Constitution*. Vol. 2. College Station: Texas A&M University Press.

Bolling, Richard. 1965. *House out of order*. New York: E. P. Dutton.

Bond, Jon R., Cary Covington, and Richard Fleisher. 1985. Explaining challenger quality in congressional elections. *Journal of Politics* 47 (May): 510–29.

Bond, Jon R., and Richard Fleisher. 1980. The limits of presidential popularity as a source of influence in the U.S. House. *Legislative Studies Quarterly* 5 (February): 69–78.

Bond, Jon R., and Richard Fleisher. 1984. Presidential popularity and congressional voting: A reexamination of public opinion as a source of influence in Congress. *Western Political Quarterly* 37 (June): 291–306.

Bond, Jon R., Richard Fleisher, and Michael Northrup. 1988. Public opinion and presidential support. *Annals* 499 (September): 47–63.

Brady, David W., and Phillip Althoff. 1974. Party voting in the U.S. House of Representatives, 1890–1910: Elements of a responsible party system. *Journal of Politics* 36 (August): 753–75.

Brady, David W., and Charles S. Bullock III. 1980. Is there a conservative coalition in the House? *Journal of Politics* 42 (May): 549–59.

Bryce, James. 1888. *The American commonwealth*. New York: Macmillan.

Burns, James MacGregor. 1956. *Roosevelt: The lion and the fox*. New York: Harcourt, Brace and World.

Burns, James MacGregor. 1963. *The deadlock of democracy: Four-party politics in America*. Englewood Cliffs: Prentice-Hall.

Cain, Bruce, John Ferejohn, and Morris Fiorina. 1987. *The personal vote: Constituency service and electoral independence*. Cambridge: Harvard University Press.

Califano, Joseph A., Jr. 1975. *A presidential nation*. New York: W. W. Norton.

Campbell, Angus, et al. 1960. *The American voter.* New York: John Wiley.

Christenson, Reo M. 1982. Presidential leadership of Congress. In *Rethinking the presidency,* ed. Thomas E. Cronin, 255–70. Boston: Little, Brown.

Clausen, Aage R. 1973. *How congressmen decide: A policy focus.* New York: St. Martin's.

Cohen, Richard E., and William Schneider. 1987. Moving to the center. *National Journal,* 3 March, 672–701.

Collie, Melissa P., and David W. Brady. 1985. The decline of partisan voting coalitions in the House of Representatives. In *Congress reconsidered,* ed. Lawrence C. Dodd and Bruce I. Oppenheimer, 272–87. 3d ed. Washington, D.C.: CQ Press.

Congressional Quarterly Almanac. Annually, 1953–87. Washington, D.C.: Congressional Quarterly, Inc.

Congressional Quarterly, Inc. 1965. *Congress and the nation: 1945–1964.* Vol. 1. Washington, D.C.: Congressional Quarterly, Inc.

Congressional Quarterly, Inc. 1969. *Congress and the nation: 1965–1968.* Vol. 2. Washington, D.C.: Congressional Quarterly, Inc.

Congressional Quarterly, Inc. 1976. *Guide to Congress.* 2d ed. Washington, D.C.: Congressional Quarterly, Inc.

Congressional Quarterly, Inc. 1982a. Presidential support. *Congressional Quarterly Weekly Report,* 2 January, 19.

Congressional Quarterly, Inc. 1982b. Ground rules for CQ support-opposition. *Congressional Quarterly Weekly Report,* 20 January, 20.

Congressional Quarterly, Inc. 1983. Democrats showed renewed strength in '83. *Congressional Quarterly Weekly Report,* 31 December, 2782–83.

Cooper, Joseph, and David W. Brady. 1981. Institutional context and leadership style: The House from Cannon to Rayburn. *American Political Science Review* 75 (June): 411–25.

Corwin, Edward S. 1973. *The Constitution and what it means today.* 13th ed. Rev. and ed. by Harold W. Chase and Craig R. Ducat. Princeton: Princeton University Press.

Covington, Cary R. 1985. Presidential coalition building among cross-pressured members of Congress: The effects of visibility. Presented at the annual meeting of the Midwest Political Science Association, Chicago, 18–20 April.

Covington, Cary R. 1986. Congressional support for the president: The view from the Kennedy/Johnson White House. *Journal of Politics* 48 (August): 717–28.

Covington, Cary R. 1987a. Mobilizing congressional support for the president: Insights from the 1960s. *Legislative Studies Quarterly* 12 (February): 77–95.

Covington, Cary R. 1987b. Presidential-congressional exchanges: Discerning patterns and principles in the distribution of presidential favors. Presented at the annual meeting of the Midwest Political Science Association, Chicago, 9–11 April.

Covington, Cary R. 1988. Guess who's coming to dinner. *American Politics Quarterly* 16 (July): 243–65.

Cox, D. R. 1970. *The analysis of binary data.* London: Methuen.

Cronin, Thomas E. 1980. *The state of the presidency.* 2d ed. Boston: Little, Brown.

Cronin, Thomas E., 1982. Presidents and political parties. In *Rethinking the presidency,* ed. Thomas E. Cronin, 287–302. Boston: Little, Brown.

Crotty, William. 1984. *American parties in decline*. 2nd ed. Boston: Little, Brown.

Crotty, William J., and Gary C. Jacobson. 1980. *American parties in decline*. Boston: Little, Brown.

Cutler, Lloyd N. 1986. To form a government. In *Separation of powers—does it still work?* ed. Robert A. Goldwin and Art Kaufman, 1–17. Washington, D.C.: American Enterprise Institute.

Davidson, Roger H. 1969. *The role of the congressman*. Indianapolis: Pegasus.

Davidson, Roger H. 1984. The presidency and Congress. In *The presidency and the political system*, ed. Michael Nelson, 363–91. Washington, D.C.: CQ Press.

Davidson, Roger H. 1985. Senate leaders: Janitors for an untidy chamber? In *Congress reconsidered*, ed. Lawrence C. Dodd and Bruce I. Oppenheimer, 225–52. 3d ed. Washington, D.C.: CQ Press.

Davidson, Roger H., and Walter J. Oleszek. 1985. *Congress and its members*. 2d ed. Washington, D.C.: CQ Press.

Davis, Eric. 1979. Legislative liaison in the Carter administration. *Political Science Quarterly* 94 (Summer): 285–94.

Davis, Eric. 1983. Congressional liaison: The people and the institutions. In *Both Ends of the Avenue*, ed. Anthony King, 59–95. Washington, D.C.: American Enterprise Institute.

DeClercq, Eugene, Thomas L. Hurley, and Norman R. Luttbeg. 1975. Voting in American presidential elections. *American Politics Quarterly* 3 (July): 222–46.

Deering, Christopher J., and Steven S. Smith. 1985. Subcommittees in Congress. In *Congress reconsidered*, ed. Lawrence C. Dodd and Bruce I. Oppenheimer, 189–210. 3d ed. Washington, D.C.: CQ Press.

Denison, Ray. 1985. *The people's lobby: AFL-CIO report on the 98th Congress*. Washington, D.C.: AFL-CIO Department of Legislation.

Dyson, James W., and John W. Soule. 1970. Congressional committee behavior on roll call votes: The U.S. House of Representatives, 1955–1964. *Midwest Journal of Political Science* 14 (November): 626–47.

Edwards, George C. III. 1980. *Presidential influence in Congress*. San Francisco: W. H. Freeman.

Edwards, George C. III. 1983. *The public presidency: The pursuit of popular support*. New York: St. Martin's Press.

Edwards, George C. III. 1984. Presidential party leadership in Congress. In *Presidents and their parties: leadership or neglect?* ed. Robert Harmel, 179–214. New York: Praeger.

Edwards, George C. III. 1985. Measuring presidential success in Congress: Alternative approaches. *Journal of Politics* 47 (May): 667–85.

Edwards, George C. III. 1986a. Presidential legislative skills: At the core or at the margin? Paper presented at the 1986 annual meeting of the Midwest Political Science Association, Chicago, 10–12 April.

Edwards, George C. III. 1986b. The two presidencies: A reevaluation. *American Politics Quarterly* 14 (July): 247–63.

Edwards, George C. III. 1989. *At the margins: Presidential leadership of Congress*. New Haven: Yale University Press.

Emerson, Ralph Waldo. 1903. The American scholar. In *Nature, addresses, and lec-*

tures, 79–115. Boston: Houghton, Mifflin. Originally an oration delivered before the Phi Beta Kappa Society, Cambridge, Mass., 31 August, 1837.

Evans, Rowland, Jr., and Robert D. Novak. 1971. *Nixon in the White House: The frustration of power.* New York: Random House.

Felton, John. 1986. Hill overrides veto of South Africa sanctions. *Congressional Quarterly Weekly Report,* 4 October, 2338–42.

Fenno, Richard F., Jr. 1973. *Congressmen in committees.* Boston: Little, Brown.

Fenno, Richard F., Jr. 1978. *Home style: House members in their districts.* Boston: Little, Brown.

Ferejohn, John A. 1974. *Porkbarrel politics: Rivers and harbors legislation, 1947–1968.* Stanford: Stanford University Press.

Ferejohn, John A., and Randall L. Calvert. 1984. Presidential coattails in historical perspective. *American Journal of Political Science* 28 (February): 127–46.

Fiorina, Morris P. 1981. *Retrospective voting in American national elections.* New Haven: Yale University Press.

Fiorina, Morris P. 1984. The presidency and the contemporary electoral system. In *The presidency and the political system,* ed. Michael Nelson, 204–26. Washington: D.C.: CQ Press.

Fiorina, Morris P. 1987. The presidency and Congress: An electoral connection? In *The presidency and the political system,* ed. Michael Nelson, 411–34. 2d ed. Washington, D.C.: CQ Press.

Fishel, Jeff. 1985. *Presidents and promises: From campaign pledge to presidential performance.* Washington, D.C.: CQ Press.

Fleisher, Richard, and Jon R. Bond. 1983a. Beyond committee control: Committee and party leader influence on floor amendments in Congress. *American Politics Quarterly* 11 (April): 131–61.

Fleisher, Richard, and Jon R. Bond. 1983b. Assessing presidential support in the House: Lessons from Reagan and Carter. *Journal of Politics* 45 (May): 745–58.

Fleisher, Richard, and Jon R. Bond. 1986. Presidential-congressional relations on economic votes, 1957–1980. *Polity* 18 (Spring): 498–513.

Frazier, Martin. 1988. Chapman, Atkins get appropriations. *Roll Call,* 18 December, 8.

Froman, Lewis A., Jr. 1963. *Congressmen and their constituencies.* Chicago: Rand McNally.

Gallup, George, 1953–84. *The Gallup opinion index* [various months]. Princeton: American Institute of Public Opinion.

Goldwin, Robert A., and Art Kaufman. 1986. *Separation of powers—does it still work?* Washington, D.C.: American Enterprise Institute.

Greenstein, Fred I. 1982. *The hidden-hand presidency: Eisenhower as leader.* New York: Basic Books.

Hall, Richard L. 1987. Participation and purpose in committee decision making. *American Political Science Review* 81 (March): 105–28.

Hamilton, Alexander. [1788] 1961a. Federalist 73. In *The Federalist papers,* ed. Clinton Rossiter, 441–47. New York: New American Library.

Hamilton, Alexander. [1788] 1961b. Federalist 75. In *The Federalist papers,* ed. Clinton Rossiter, 449–54. New York: New American Library.

Hamilton, Alexander. [1788] 1961c. Federalist 77. In *The Federalist papers*, ed. Clinton Rossiter, 459–64. New York: New American Library.

Hardin, Charles M. 1974. *Presidential power and accountability: Toward a new constitution*. Chicago: University of Chicago Press.

Harmel, Robert, and Kenneth Janda. 1982. *Parties and their environments*. New York: Longman.

Hess, Stephen. 1988. *The presidential campaign*. Washington, D.C.: Brookings Institution.

Hill, David B., and Norman R. Luttbeg. 1983. *Trends in American electoral behavior*. 2d ed.: Itasca, Ill.: F. E. Peacock.

Hinckley, Barbara. 1981a. *Coalitions and politics*. New York: Harcourt Brace Jovanovich.

Hinckley, Barbara. 1981b. *Congressional elections*. Washington, D.C.: CQ Press.

Holley, Joe. 1987. Mr. Sam's legacy. *The Texas Observer*, 31 July, 18–19.

Holsti, Ole R., and James N. Rosenau. 1984. *American leadership in world affairs: Vietnam and the breakdown of consensus*. Boston: Allen and Unwin.

Huntington, Samuel P. 1973. Congressional response to the twentieth century. In *The Congress and america's future*, ed. David B. Truman, 6–38. 2d ed. Englewood Cliffs: Prentice-Hall.

Huntington, Samuel P. 1981. *American politics: The promise of disharmony*. Cambridge: Harvard University Press.

Jackson, John E. 1974. *Constituencies and leaders in Congress*. Cambridge: Harvard University Press.

Jacobson, Gary C. 1987. *The politics of congressional elections*. 2d ed. Boston: Little, Brown.

Jacobson, Gary C., and Samuel Kernell. 1983. *Strategy and choice in congressional elections*. 2d ed. New Haven: Yale University Press.

Janda, Kenneth. 1980. *Political parties: A cross-national survey*. New York: Free Press.

Jewell, Malcolm E. 1973. Linkages between legislative parties and external parties. In *Legislatures in comparative perspective*, ed. Allan Kornberg, 203–34. New York: David McKay.

Johannes, John R., and John C. McAdams. 1981. The congressional incumbency effect: Is it casework, policy compatibility, or something else? An examination of the 1978 election. *American Journal of Political Science* 25 (August): 512–42.

Jones, Charles O. 1970. *The minority party in Congress*. Boston: Little, Brown.

Jones, Charles O. 1981. Congress and the presidency. In *The new Congress*, ed. Thomas B. Mann and Norman J. Ornstein, 223–49. Washington, D.C.: American Enterprise Institute.

Jones, Charles O. 1983. Presidential negotiation with Congress. In *Both ends of the avenue*, ed. Anthony King. Washington, D.C.: American Enterprise Institute.

Jones, Charles O. 1988. *The trusteeship presidency: Jimmy Carter and the United States Congress*. Baton Rouge: Louisiana State University Press.

Kearns, Doris. 1976. *Lyndon Johnson and the American dream*. New York: Harper and Row.

Kellerman, Barbara. 1984. *The political presidency: Practice of leadership from Kennedy through Reagan.* New York: Oxford University Press.

Kernell, Samuel. 1977. Presidential popularity and negative voting: An alternative explanation of the midterm congressional decline of the president's party. *American Political Science Review* 71 (March): 44–66.

Kernell, Samuel. 1978. Explaining presidential popularity. *American Political Science Review* 72 (June): 506–22.

Kernell, Samuel. 1986. *Going public: New strategies of presidential leadership.* Washington, D.C.: CQ Press.

Kessel, John. 1984. *Presidential parties.* Homewood, Ill.: Dorsey.

Key, V. O., Jr. 1964. *Politics, parties, and pressure groups,* 5th ed.: New York: Thomas Crowell Company.

Key, V. O., Jr. 1966. *The responsible electorate.* Cambridge: Harvard University Press.

Kiewiet, D. Roderick, and Mathew D. McCubbins. 1988. Presidential influence on congressional appropriations. *American Journal of Political Science* 32 (August): 713–36.

King, Anthony. 1983. A mile and a half is a long way. In *Both ends of the avenue,* ed. Anthony King, 246–73. Washington, D.C.: American Enterprise Institute.

Kingdon, John W. 1968. *Candidates for office: Beliefs and strategies.* New York: Random House.

Kingdon, John W. 1981. *Congressmen's voting decisions.* 2d ed. New York: Harper and Row.

Koenig, Louis W. 1981. *The chief executive.* 4th ed. New York: Harcourt Brace Jovanovich.

LeLoup, Lance T., and Steven A. Shull. 1979. Congress versus the executive: The "two presidencies" reconsidered. *Social Science Quarterly* 59 (March): 704–19.

Leuchtenburg, William E. 1983. *In the shadow of FDR: From Harry Truman to Ronald Reagan.* Ithaca: Cornell University Press.

Light, Paul C. 1981–82. Passing nonincremental policy: Presidential influence in Congress, Kennedy to Carter. *Congress and the Presidency* 9 (Winter): 61–82.

Light, Paul C. 1983. *The president's agenda: Domestic policy choice from Kennedy to Carter (with notes on Ronald Reagan).* Baltimore: Johns Hopkins University Press.

Lowi, Theodore J. 1985. *The personal president: Power invested, promise unfulfilled.* Ithaca: Cornell University Press.

MacNeil, Neil. 1963. *Forge of democracy: The House of Representatives.* New York: David McKay Company.

Madison, James. [1788] 1961a. Federalist 47. In *The Federalist papers,* ed. Clinton Rossiter, 300–308. New York: New American Library.

Madison, James. [1788] 1961b. Federalist 48. In *The Federalist papers,* ed. Clinton Rossiter, 308–13. New York: New American Library.

Malbin, Michael, 1983. Rhetoric and leadership: A look backward at the Carter energy plan. In *Both ends of the avenue,* ed. Anthony King, 212–45. Washington, D.C.: American Enterprise Institute.

Manley, John F. 1970. *The politics of finance: The House Committee on Ways and Means*. Boston: Little, Brown.

Manley, John F. 1973. The conservative coalition in Congress. *American Behavioral Scientist* 17 (November/December): 223–47.

Mann, Thomas E., and Raymond E. Wolfinger. 1980. Candidates and parties in congressional elections. *American Political Science Review* 74 (September): 617–32.

Matthews, Donald R., and James A. Stimson. 1975. *Yeas and nays: Normal decision making in the U.S. House of Representatives*. New York: John Wiley.

Mayhew, David. 1974. *Congress: The electoral connection*. New Haven: Yale University Press.

Milkis, Sidney M. 1984. Presidents and party purges: With special emphasis on the lessons of 1938. In *Presidents and their parties: leadership or neglect?* ed. Robert Harmel, 151–75. New York: Praeger.

Moe, Ronald C., and Steven C. Teel. 1970. Congress as policy-maker: A necessary reappraisal. *Political Science Quarterly* 85 (September): 443–70.

Moffett, George D. III. 1985. *The limits of victory: The ratification of the Panama Canal treaties*. Ithaca: Cornell University Press.

Mueller, John. 1970. Presidential popularity from Truman to Johnson. *American Political Science Review* 64 (March): 18–34.

Naylor, A. F. 1964. Comparisons of regression constants fitted by maximum likelihood to four common transformations of binomial data. *Annals of Human Genetics* 27 (March): 241–46.

Neustadt, Richard E. 1960. *Presidential power: The politics of leadership*. New York: John Wiley.

Neustadt, Richard E. 1980. *Presidential power: The politics of leadership from FDR to Carter*. New York: John Wiley.

Nie, Norman, Sidney Verba, and John Petrocik. 1979. *The changing American voter*. Enlarged ed. Cambridge: Harvard University Press.

Oleszek, Walter J. 1984. *Congressional procedures and the policy process*. 2d ed. Washington, D.C.: CQ Press.

Orfield, Gary. 1975. *Congressional power and social change*. New York: Harcourt Brace Jovanovich.

Ornstein, Norman J. 1983. The open Congress meets the president. In *Both ends of the avenue*, ed. Anthony King, 185–211. Washington, D.C.: American Enterprise Institute.

Ornstein, Norman J., et al. 1984. *Vital statistics on Congress, 1984–1985 edition*. Washington, D.C.: American Enterprise Institute.

Ornstein, Norman J., Robert L. Peabody, and David W. Rohde. 1985. The Senate through the 1980s: Cycles of change. In *Congress reconsidered*, ed. Lawrence C. Dodd and Bruce I. Oppenheimer, 113–33. 3d ed. Washington, D.C.: CQ Press.

Ostrom, Charles W., and Dennis M. Simon. 1985. Promise and performance: A dynamic model of presidential popularity. *American Political Science Review* 79 (June): 334–58.

Peabody, Robert L. 1981. Senate party leadership: From the 1950s to the 1980s. In

Understanding Congressional Leadership, ed. Frank H. Mackaman, 51–115. Washington, D.C.: CQ Press.

Peppers, Donald A. 1975. The "two presidencies" eight years later. In *Perspectives on the presidency,* ed. Aaron Wildavsky, 462–71. Boston: Little, Brown.

Pessen, Edward. 1984. *The log cabin myth.* New Haven: Yale University Press.

Peterson, Mark. 1986. Congressional responses to presidential proposals: Impact, effort, and politics. Presented at the annual meeting of the Midwest Political Science Association, Chicago, 9–12 April.

Polsby, Nelson W. 1983. *Consequences of party reform.* New York: Oxford University Press.

Polsby, Nelson, W. 1986. *Congress and the presidency.* 4th ed. Englewood Cliffs: Prentice-Hall.

Polsby, Nelson W., Miriam Gallaher, and Barry S. Rundquist. 1969. The growth of the seniority system in the U.S. House of Representatives. *Amerian Political Science Review* 63 (September): 787–807.

Poole, Keith T. 1981. Dimensions of interest group evaluation of the U.S. Senate, 1969–1978. *American Journal of Political Science* 25 (February): 49–67.

Poole, Keith T., and Howard Rosenthal. 1984. On the political economy of roll call voting. Presented at the annual meeting of the American Political Science Association, Washington, D.C. 30 August–2 September.

Rapp, David. 1989. Reagan added luster but little clout to office. *Congressional Quarterly Weekly Report,* 7 January, 3–15.

Reilly, John E. 1988. America's state of mind: Trends in public attitudes toward foreign policy. In *The domestic sources of American foreign policy,* ed. Charles W. Kegley, Jr., and Eugene R. Wittkopf, 45–56. New York: St. Martin's Press.

Riker, William H. 1959. A method for determining the significance of roll calls in voting bodies. In *Legislative behavior: A reader in theory and research,* ed. John C. Wahlke and Heinz Eulau, 377–84. Glencoe: Ill: Free Press.

Riker, William H. 1962. *The theory of political coalitions.* New Haven: Yale University Press.

Ripley, Randall B. 1969. *Majority party leadership in Congress.* Boston: Little, Brown.

Ripley, Randall B. 1983. *Congress: Process and policy.* 3d ed. New York: W. W. Norton.

Rivers, Douglas, and Nancy Rose. 1985. Passing the president's program: Public opinion and presidential influence in Congress. *American Journal of Political Science* 29 (May): 183–96.

Rockman, Bert A. 1984. *The leadership question: The presidency and the American system.* New York: Praeger.

Schlesinger, Arthur M., Jr. 1978. *Robert Kennedy and his times.* New York: Ballantine.

Schneider, Jerrold E. 1979. *Ideological coalitions in Congress.* Westport, Conn.: Greenwood.

Schneider, Jerrold E. 1984. Congressional coalitions: Recent findings and the future of ideological coalitions. Presented at the annual meeting of the American Political Science Association, Washington, D.C. 30 August–2 September.

Schumpeter, Joseph A. 1942. *Capitalism, socialism and democracy.* New York: Harper and Brothers.

Shelley, Mack C. II. 1983. *The permanent majority: The conservative coalition in the United States Congress.* University, Ala.: University of Alabama Press.

Sigelman, Lee. 1979. A reassessment of the two presidencies thesis. *Journal of Politics* 41 (November): 1195–1205.

Sinclair, Barbara. 1981. Coping with uncertainty: Building coalitions in the House and the Senate. In *The new Congress,* ed. Thomas E. Mann and Norman J. Ornstein, 178–220. Washington, D.C.: American Enterprise Institute.

Sinclair, Barbara. 1983. *Majority leadership in the U.S. House.* Baltimore: Johns Hopkins University Press.

Smith, Hedrick. 1982. The president as coalition builder: Reagan's first year. In *Rethinking the presidency,* ed. Thomas E. Cronin, 271–86. Boston: Little, Brown.

Smith, Steven S., and Christopher J. Deering. 1984. *Committees in Congress.* Washington, D.C.: CQ Press.

Souraf, Frank. 1983. *Party politics in America.* 5th ed.: Boston: Little, Brown.

Starobin, Paul. 1987. Highway bill veto overrideen after close call in the Senate. *Congressional Quarterly Weekly Report,* 4 April, 604–5.

Stimson, James. 1976. Public support for American presidents. *Public Opinion Quarterly* 40 (Spring): 1–21.

Sullivan, Terry. 1988. Headcounts, expectations, and presidential coalitions in Congress. *American Journal of Political Science* 32 (August): 567–89.

Sundquist, James. 1981. *The decline and resurgence of Congress.* Washington, D.C.: Brookings Institution.

Sundquist, James. 1986. *Constitutional reform.* Washington, D.C.: Brookings Institution.

Thomas, Martin. 1985. Election proximity and senatorial roll call voting. *American Journal of Political Science* 29 (February): 96–111.

Tufte, Edward R. 1975. Determinants of the outcomes of midterm congressional elections. *American Political Science Review* 69 (September): 812–26.

Udall, Morris K. 1988. *Too funny to be president.* New York: Henry Holt.

Valenti, Jack. 1975. *A very human president.* New York: W. W. Norton.

Wayne, Stephen J. 1978. *The legislative presidency.* New York: Harper and Row.

Wehr, Elizabeth. 1987. Wright finds a vote to pass reconciliation bill. *Congressional Quarterly Weekly Report,* 31 October, 2653–55.

Wildavsky, Aaron. 1966. The two presidencies. *Trans-Action* 4 (December): 7–14.

Wilson, James Q. 1983. *American government: Institutions and policies.* 2d ed. Lexington, Mass.: D. C. Heath.

Wright, Gerald C. 1976. Linear models for evaluating conditional relationships. *American Journal of Political Science* 20 (May): 349–73.